# BENCHMARKING and THRESHOLD STANDARDS in HIGHER EDUCATION

# BENCHMARKING and THRESHOLD STANDARDS in HIGHER EDUCATION

Helen Smith, Michael Armstrong and Sally Brown

Published in association with the Staff and Educational Development Association

First published in 1999



Kogan Page Limited
120 Pentonville Road
London N1 9JN



---

**British Library Cataloguing in Publication Data**

A CIP record for this book is available from the British Library.

ISBN 0 7494 3033 8

---

Typeset by Kogan Page
Printed and bound by Biddles Ltd, Guildford and King's Lynn

# Contents

# The Contributors

**Alex Appleby** is Senior Lecturer at Newcastle Business School, University of Northumbria. He is Route Leader for the Masters in Total Quality Management and Senior Research Associate for the UNN's Regional Competitiveness Project. Current research activities include Quality Management, improving operations and staff motivation.

**Michael Armstrong** is Head of Academic Programme Administration at the University of Northumbria at Newcastle. He was formerly the coordinator of the CATS scheme and one of the designers of the unitized curriculum that was adopted by the university in 1994. He has recently been involved with a major project within the Northern Universities Consortium for Credit Accumulation and Transfer (NUCCAT) that compared the regulatory frameworks of some 29 northern universities from the perspective of standards and diversity. His other research interests include the application of Total Quality Management (TQM) in the context of higher education.

**John Bell** is Professor of Public and Comparative Law at the University of Leeds and a former Pro-vice-chancellor for Teaching and Learning. He has been a leading member of the Law Subject Benchmarking Group and has prepared drafts for it. He has previously coordinated the DfEE-funded Law Discipline Network and the HEQC project on Graduate Standards in Law

**Dr Stuart Billingham** is Programme Director for the combined honours degree at the University of Northumbria's Carlisle Campus, where he also directs the strategic development of the undergraduate curriculum. His main research interest is in equal opportunities, particularly in the higher education curriculum. He has published on this theme, contributed to national and international conferences, and is currently working on the relationship between equal opportunities and quality assurance in higher education.

**Sally Brown** is a director of the Institute for Learning and Teaching and Visiting Professor for the Robert Gordon University. She was formerly Head of Quality Enhancement at the University of Northumbria at Newcastle. She is Events Coordinator for the Staff and Educational Development Association (SEDA) and series editor of the Kogan Page–SEDA book series. In addition, Sally is a consultant to the Oxford Centre for Staff and Learning Development. She writes extensively and undertakes workshops and consultancy on teaching, learning and, particularly, assessment. She has written, co-written, edited or co-edited more than 20 books for Kogan Page and other publishers.

**T Dary Erwin** is Director of Assessment of the Centre for Assessment and Research Studies and Professor of Psychology at James Madison University (USA). He recently instituted a doctoral program in assessment and is a frequent contributor to the assessment literature, writing on assessment practice and public policy.

**Sinclair Goodlad** is Director of the Humanities Programme and Professor of Sociology of Higher Education at the Imperial College of Science, Technology & Medicine. He studied at Cambridge and at the London School of Economics, and has lectured at Delhi University and at the Massachusetts Institute of Technology. For periods in 1983 and 1986, he was Visiting Associate at the Center for Studies in Higher Education at the University of California, Berkeley. From 1985 to 1987, he was on secondment from ICSTM as Secretary of the Voluntary Sector Consultative Council, representing the interests of 18 colleges to the (then) Department of Education and Science and to the National Advisory Body for Public-sector Higher Education. He has written and edited books on theories and methods of higher education, including *The Quest for Quality: Sixteen forms of heresy in higher education*, and was for seven years Editor of the international journal *Studies in Higher Education*. He is a Fellow of the Society for Research into Higher Education, the publications committee of which he chairs.

**Sally Gosling** is head of learning and development at the Chartered Society of Physiotherapy (CSP). She coordinates the CSP's strategic work on continuing professional development (CPD)/lifelong learning and advises universities on developing CPD programmes for the profession. She has written articles on Masters-level learning within physiotherapy and co-authored an article on physiotherapy and specialization in the European Union.

**Ian Haines** is Dean of the Faculty of Science, Computing and Engineering at the University of North London and is also Chair of the UK Deans of Science Group and Secretary of the European Association of Deans of Science. He was a quality assessor for chemistry in 1992–93 in the first round of subject quality assessments, and is a member of the Chemistry Benchmarking

Group set up by the Quality Assurance Agency (QAA). He is also involved as an Academic Reviewer in Chemistry in the first testing of the benchmarking statement. He recently completed five years as Chair of the Accreditation Panel of The Royal Society of Chemistry and will be Chair of its Education and Qualifications Board from 1999 to 2003. He is also a member of the Management Advisory Committee at the Science, Technology and Mathematics Council and a member of a QAA group working on a code of practice for external examiners.

**Dr Stephen Jackson** is Assistant Provost (Learning) at Liverpool John Moores University, having taught population geography and acted as subject leader for geography within social sciences. His particular interest is historical urban geography. The present post has a brief for the development of teaching and learning initiatives and responsibilities for learning and information services within the University, together with chairing the Academic Quality and Standards Committee. He also acts as an auditor for the Quality Assurance Agency.

**Dr Rebecca Johnson** is Project Officer for the Assessment and the *Expanded* Text project, funded by the Higher Education Funding Council: England (HEFCE) fund for the development of teaching and learning. Based at the University of Northumbria, she coordinates the work of a consortium of departments of English universities. Prior to the project she worked as a university lecturer in English and as an assistant librarian responsible for archival literary materials.

**Linda Leach** is a senior lecturer in the Educational Development Department at Wellington Polytechnic, New Zealand. Her key teaching and research interests lie in adult education and include self-directed learning, assessment and tertiary teacher education.

**Dr James Philip Margham** is Assistant Provost (Capability) at Liverpool John Moores University, having taught higher organism genetics and acted as programme leader for an undergraduate programme in biology. The present post involves responsibility for regulatory structures within the University's modular scheme, new curricular developments (especially self-managed learning) and learner support, including careers. His particular interests centre on issues around credit and, until November 1998, he chaired the Northern Universities Consortium for Credit Accumulation and Transfer (NUCCAT), a consortium of 38 universities involved in regional and national initiatives on credit and modularity.

**Jenny Moon** currently works in learning support at the University of Wales Cardiff. Much of the knowledge on which the chapter in this book is based, however, was gained when she worked in the Higher Education Credit Initiative Wales project on credit developments in Wales. In particular, she developed guidelines for writing learning outcomes and on level descriptors. She continues these interests as a member of the QAA's National Advisory Group on Standards in Multidisciplinary Education. Other than these standards issues, Jenny is interested in the role of reflection in learning and professional education, and her book on this subject is also being published by Kogan Page in 1999. Indeed, reflection was the subject matter for her PhD. Her current application of this interest is on learning journals and related assessment issues in higher and professional education.

**Guyon Neutze** is a senior lecturer in the Educational Development Department of Wellington Polytechnic, New Zealand. He teaches on the Master of Education in Philosophy course, focusing on assessment, and is involved in an extensive programme to deliver the Bachelor of Education qualification to Maori educators. Other interests are poetry and philosophy. He has written books in both these subject areas.

**Helen Smith** is a senior lecturer in the faculty of Health, Social Work and Education at the University of Northumbria at Newcastle. She is based in the faculty's Academic Development Unit where the main focus of her work is quality assurance and enhancement. In addition to her work in quality assurance, she retains a keen interest and teaching role in her professional area of physiotherapy. Her other research interests in the field of quality are staff motivation, the effectiveness of institutional annual review and mentoring.

**Digby Warren** currently holds a post at senior lecturer level in the Academic Development Programme at the University of Cape Town. He has been working in the field of higher education development since 1992, mainly in the areas of course and curriculum design and concomitant staff development, particularly in the humanities and social sciences. Previously, he was a lecturer in history at UCT for five years, building on prior experience as a high school teacher.

**Dr David Woodhouse** is Director of the New Zealand Universities Academic Audit Unit, which is responsible for auditing the academic quality assurance and control procedures of New Zealand's universities. He is active internationally in quality assurance, providing advice and training on educational quality assurance in a number of countries. Currently, he is President of the International Network of Quality Assurance Agencies in Higher Education; edits the Network's newsletter; is on the Board of the Global Alliance for Transnational Education (an international organization dealing with the quality of education offered across national boundaries) and is an executive editor of the international journal *Quality in Higher Education*. Before working in New Zealand, David Woodhouse was Deputy Director of the Hong Kong Council for Academic Accreditation, with responsibility for the quality of degree courses in Hong Kong. Before that, he was a faculty member in mathematics, computer science and computer education in universities in several countries, and was at various times head of a department and dean of a faculty. His leisure interests include multisport, drama and flying light aircraft.

**Harvey Woolf** is Head of Collaborative Academic Developments at the University of Wolverhampton. His interest in comparative assessment issues dates from his days as the course leader of a multisubject modular scheme. This interest has been extended by acting as an external examiner and moderator for a range of programmes and institutions and by membership of the Student Assessment and Classification Working Group. He has written on the role of external examiners and has contributed to volumes on modularity in the United Kingdom. His main teaching interest is in European resistance and collaboration in the Second World War.

**David Yarrow** is a Principal Lecturer in Newcastle Business School, a faculty of the University of Northumbria at Newcastle. His current role is Project Manager – Benchmarking, managing a team of researchers and facilitators whose activities include coordination of a regional benchmarking scheme and operation of the University's Best Practice Club and Benchmarking Network.

**Nick Zepke** is Head of the Educational Development Department at Wellington Polytechnic. His research and teaching interests include the politics and history of post-school education, futures studies, assessment and curriculum design of online distributed education.

# Foreword

While the application of benchmarking methods in higher education might appear to be a recent phenomenon, the principles that underpin our desire to collaborate in order to learn about, evaluate and improve our own practice have been applied for a long time. What is new is the attempt to attach new meanings, develop new processes and reinterpret what has gone before in terms of two different notions of benchmarking, namely:

- developmental benchmarking – promoting best practice;
- regulatory benchmarking – assuring quality and standards.

Much of the conflict and confusion in discussions about the pros and cons of benchmarking for higher education relates to the inbuilt tension between these two different purposes.

In some respects, benchmarking is a metaphor for professional life. When we begin our careers as higher education teachers, we search for, and hopefully find, good role models to emulate. We strive to improve ourselves by observing and learning from others and compare what we have achieved against the objectives we and others have set. My professional interest in benchmarking (although I did not know it at the time) began in 1990 when I joined Her Majesty's Inspectorate. As the inspector for geoscience education in the polytechnics and colleges I was privileged to witness the teaching styles of colleagues and be able to discuss with them, in an open and constructive way, how they promoted and assessed learning. My overarching impression was one of committed and caring people wanting to do a good job and provide the best possible educational experience for their students. The experience of trying to evaluate the quality of the educational process and the standards of the students' achievements revealed to me the meaning of diversity (of context, of process, of outcome). From my privileged position I was able to appreciate that the expectations of teaching teams were different and that these resulted in different demands in the assessment process and different outcomes – as revealed in the products of assessment.

With the benefit of hindsight, I realize that I was acting as a type of analysed and synthesized the information, provided feedback to departments and individuals on their own practices or outcomes, and suggested ways in which their practices might be improved based on what I had experienced elsewhere. This process revealed that, while there were no absolute best practices, there were plenty of examples of what most higher education teachers and departments would consider were better than their own. I like to think that the report I produced – 'Geology and Earth Science in the Polytechnics' – provided information that departments could use to compare and improve their own practice. What was missing from this process of course, was the bringing together of participants to share, compare, evaluate their practice and learn from each other more directly.

I finally discovered process benchmarking while working on the Graduate Standards Programme for the Higher Education Quality Council. Motivated by the need to identify new ways of evaluating and assuring academic standards in a multipurpose mass higher education system, our conception of benchmarking was driven by the idea of creating more opportunities for the people who created the standards to develop a better shared understanding of the meaning of those standards. We explored this via a series of action research projects – Pilot Studies in Benchmarking Assessment Practice (Quality Assurance Agency (QAA), 1998). The recommendation made in the final report of the Graduate Standards Programme – for benchmarking to be promoted via self-selected groups of institutions and departments – reflected the insights we gained in the course of this development work. Simultaneously, we supported a number of subject associations to undertake their own benchmarking surveys. These studies demonstrated that, with relatively little support, a subject community could map its own territory and provide much useful information on course structures, curricula content, assessment practice and the qualities, skills and capabilities expected of a graduate in that subject.

The strategic steer for the regulatory benchmarking of standards in UK higher education came via the recommendations of the National Committee of Inquiry in Higher Education (the Dearing Report). The Committee was aware of the work of the Graduate Standards Programme, but another important influence was the work undertaken by the Academic Standards Panels established by the Australian Vice-chancellors' Committee. These panels conducted a rolling programme of subject reviews based on institutional visits and the evaluation of extensive statistical and documentary information relating to provision and student outcomes. The published reports contained a wealth of quantitative and qualitative contextualized information on such matters as admissions criteria; student enrolments, progression and outcomes; graduate destinations; common and distinctive course objectives; curricula content and structures; delivery modes and assessment; options and specialisms. It is also worth noting that information was included on particular skills and qualities developed in students as a result of studying their subjects. Issues that affected teaching, learning and outcome standards were discussed and guidance to help improve practice was provided. These included examples of good practice in the use of supervisors' reports, assignment assessment sheets, thesis examination reports and examination essay marking schemes.

It is important for readers to be aware that policy on QAA subject benchmarking (based on the Dearing conception of expert panels) is a matter of public debate and practical evaluation. This volume makes a positive contribution to that debate by raising issues and questions that must be addressed in the development process. Contributors offer a range of views and personal insights on benchmarking and proposals for the benchmarking of academic standards. Some of these are sceptical of the methodology and or the value of undertaking the journey we have embarked on. Others adopt a more pragmatic view, such as 'the issues that underlie the need for regulatory benchmarking cannot be ignored'. Such views provide a measure of the challenges that subject benchmarking will need to overcome in the development process. Unfortunately, the idea that benchmarking is a useful research and development tool for higher education tends to be submerged in the debate on policy-related issues, and the contributions that highlight the benefits for learning and self-improvement help redress this imbalance. The full benefits of subject benchmarking will perhaps only be realized as a result of an approach that combines the dimensions of self-regulation with self-improvement. Finally, we can learn much from the perspectives of colleagues in other higher education systems. Their contributions remind us that there are different approaches to regulatory benchmarking, but that the solutions for one context are not necessarily appropriate for another.

Norman Jackson
Assistant Director, Quality Assurance Agency
Senior Research Fellow, University of Surrey

# Introduction

The specification of standards in higher education has long been the subject of academic debate in countries around the world. A means by which all stakeholders in higher education – be they the students, their parents, potential employers, academics and those who fund higher education provision, privately or publicly – can be informed reliably, explicitly and in ways that are readily understood exactly what is being provided by those who develop and deliver the curriculum is a goal that has proved elusive.

This book aims to explore the underpinning issues that need to be taken into account if this goal is to be achieved, as well as questioning whether or not the exercise is ultimately achievable or, indeed, worth while. Focusing primarily on the UK experience, but providing as a counterbalance reviews of international activity in this area, we aim to expose many of the uncertainties inherent within attempts to define and describe what students following higher education courses should be achieving if their learning is to be accredited in meaningful ways, while at the same time embracing the potential of the process as a powerful developmental tool when it is used appropriately.

In the UK, following publication of the reports of the National Inquiry into Higher Education (the Dearing and Garrick Reports), the Quality Assurance Agency (QAA), in its consultative response, proposed that there should be a clearer articulation of higher education standards at the level of the subject, as a guide to those both within and outside the sector. This articulation of standards is being undertaken by 'expert teams' that include representatives of the academic community and the QAA. The teams will be known as subject benchmarking groups. It is clear that subject benchmarking will make a strong contribution to the UK's future quality assurance framework, providing explicit statements of outcomes and offering clearer expression of the quality of academic provision measured against nationally used descriptions.

Benchmarking information will help the new cadres of academic reviewers to make informed judgements in the setting of standards. These will enable categorization, it is suggested, of UK departments into three categories: below minimum thresholds, exceeding minimum thresholds and achieving standards appropriate for the 'typical' student.

Much is still to be determined in this area but this book is designed to help unravel some of the interwound threads that form this rich tapestry.

The first part of the book – A Rationale for Benchmarking and Threshold Standards – explores the key issues associated with benchmarking in higher education at the current time, which sets the context for the whole book. In the first chapter, Historical and Contextual Perspectives on Benchmarking in Higher Education, Michael Armstrong, outlines the key influences on the debate in the UK and brings together some of the major elements of the development of the benchmarking process. He traces the origins of benchmarking in the UK through the work of the Graduate Standards Programme and subsequent developments led by the QAA and poses some key questions about its viability and practicality.

In the second chapter, Sally Brown asks 'How can threshold standards assure and enhance quality?' Having reviewed some of the problematic issues thrown up by the sometimes mechanistic approach that benchmarking can prompt, she takes a pragmatic approach by exploring how enhancement and continuous improvement can be linked to the assurance of standards by means of the establishment of threshold standards on which to build.

Benchmarking Theory – A Framework for the Business World as a Context for its Application in Higher Education is the next chapter, written by Alex Appleby. He tracks the development of benchmarking in commercial and professional contexts, referring to the theories on which the work being undertaken in higher education is based. The case against benchmarking in higher education is offered in the chapter that follows by Sinclair Goodlad. He robustly challenges the assumption that the business model is readily transferable to the higher education context.

Part II – Operational Issues for Benchmarking and Threshold Standards in Higher Education – investigates issues around the implementation of benchmarking, drawing on relevant experience across the sector. In Chapter 5 – Describing Higher Education – Some Conflicts and Conclusions – Jenny Moon explores issues related to level descriptors, learning outcomes and benchmark standards. She provides an overview of the current debate, drawing on her own experiences in a Department for Education and Employment (DfEE)-funded project in Wales on credit development. She provides a creative solution to the problem of modal or threshold standards. For individual modules, learning descriptors can provide a clear threshold, while level descriptors can provide modal standards from the perspective of the course.

Next, Harvey Woolf looks at institutional comparisons – reality or illusion? This chapter warns against a simplistic reading of crude institutional-level data and calls for a more comprehensive and reasoned approach to any published comparisons. Discussion of issues related to benchmarking across subjects in an institution is provided next by J P Margham and S Jackson. They provide detailed analysis of student results across the different schools of Liverpool's John Moores University and discuss the possible influences of marking practice, student entry profile and professional body associations to explain the results

In the final chapter in Part II – The Business Approach to Benchmarking – An Exploration of the Issues as a Background for its Use in Higher Education – David Yarrow draws on the experience of a major diagnostic benchmarking project in the North East of England involving 700 business organizations to suggest some clear pointers for higher education if benchmarking is to be a fruitful exercise.

Part III provides UK perspectives in the development and use of benchmarks and threshold standards. It reviews current UK experience in piloting the QAA methodology in law and chemistry, as well as looking at the experiences of subjects with professional body involvement in benchmarking and threshold standards.

Chapter 9 – UK Experiences in the Development of Benchmarking and Threshold Standards – is by Ian Haines. He was a member of the QAA Chemistry Benchmarking Group and describes the outcomes of this pilot group. Next follows Benchmarking in Law by John Bell, who chaired the QAA Law Benchmarking Group. In this chapter, he provides a description of the context and process through which the group worked, together with an evaluation of the group's work.

Sally Gosling explores collaborative accreditation – benchmarking in a professional and academic partnership to recognize programmes of continuing professional development – by means of a case study. She describes a collaborative approach to the accreditation of professional development of physiotherapists, which, while not part of the QAA pilot exercise, throws some interesting light on the process as it might be applied nationally.

The next chapter is Benchmarking, Assessment and the Multidisciplinary Curriculum by Rebecca Johnson. It is based on her work looking at English and the expanded text as part of a Fund for the Development of Teaching and Learning (FDTL)-funded project. Her strong focus on assessment provides a timely reminder of its importance in the curriculum design and development debate. The final chapter of Part III is by Stuart Billingham and in it he develops this theme further, taking a critical view of attempts to use a benchmarking approach to cross- and multidisciplinary degrees.

Moving away from a UK focus, Part IV – International Perspectives in the Development and Use of Benchmarks and Threshold Standards – explores the practices of benchmarking and assessment internationally, examining experiences and looking for areas of commonality and best practice. In Chapter 14 – International Benchmarking – Fact or Fantasy? – Helen Smith reviews international approaches to benchmarking, both in those countries where it is already being implemented and in those where the influence of these approaches is starting to have an impact on the perception of standards. The chapters that follow explore views and experiences from the USA, New Zealand and South Africa.

The first of these is Dary Erwin's chapter – The United States' Perspective on, and Experiences of, Performance Indicators and Threshold Standards – How is Quality Determined? – that provides a valuable review of the way performance indicators of all kinds, including financial ones, impact on the educational process and the extent to which institutional autonomy is challenged.

This is followed by two chapters on New Zealand's experience of benchmarking. The first, by David Woodhouse, is on assuring standards in New Zealand's universities. The second, on assuring standards across and within subjects, describing experiences in New Zealand's polytechnics is by Nick Zepke, Guyon Neutze and Linda Leach, entitled Benchmarks and Threshold Standards – A New Zealand Polytechnic's Perspective on the Approach. The two systems in New Zealand provide valuable comparisons for the UK due to the divergence in approaches taken between the two sectors in higher education there.

The last chapter of Part IV is by Digby Warren and describes the South African experiences of benchmarking. At the cutting edge of development, South African universities can, and must, take radical approaches to quality assurance in the quest for high standards and equality of experience for students. The book concludes in Chapter 19 with a series of questions that remain unanswered but which need to be addressed if we are to engage fully in the effective process of benchmarking. Some ideas for future development are also suggested. These questions are adapted from a range of issues that were debated in the Staff and Educational Development Association (SEDA) one-day conference on benchmarking held in Manchester in December 1998 and provide a useful series of prompts for action for those responsible for taking the debate further.

The process of editing this book has made us aware that there is a need for considerable further work in the area before we feel it would be possible to articulate and apply meaningful benchmark standards within, across and between subjects and institutions, let alone nations. However, we feel that there is value in continuing to work towards these goals and hope that the issues raised and discussed in these pages will help take us forward in this process.

Helen Smith
Michael Armstrong
Sally Brown

# Part I

## A Rationale for Benchmarking and Threshold Standards

1

# Historical and Contextual Perspectives on Benchmarking in Higher Education

*Michael Armstrong*

This chapter seeks to provide an historical background to the present situation of subject benchmarking and, in so doing, identify the key current issues. The nature of recent changes in the higher education sector, the work of the Higher Education Quality Council, chaired by Sir Ron Dearing, (HEQC), and the report of the National Committee of Inquiry into Higher Education (NCIHE) are considered in some detail. The importance of the role of external examiners is discussed and the conclusions of the Graduate Standards Programme (GSP) are contrasted with the Dearing Report's recommendations. The framework for quality assurance produced by the Quality Assurance Agency for Higher Education (QAAHE) is also discussed, particularly in relation to other (business-originated) concepts of benchmarking. Finally, several problematical issues are highlighted in relation to subject benchmarking, including the need for clear guidance from qualification frameworks with respect to unit/module failure and the underlying concepts of learning outcomes and level descriptors.

## RADICAL TRANSFORMATION

Higher education in the UK has undergone an extraordinary transformation in recent years. In 1963 there were 26 UK universities and 250,000 students, representing around 6 per cent of the 18–21 age group. The majority of students were male, had two or more GCE A levels (or three Scottish Highers) and were from a relatively homogenous and élite educational background.

The situation today is radically different with respect to:

- the number of institutions that have their own degree-awarding powers;
- the size of the student population;
- a huge increase in the number of mature and part-time students;
- significant growth in collaborative provision with further education establishments;
- the entry profile of students;
- the range and nature of higher education courses (many new types of professional/vocational programmes; credit accumulation and transfer and accreditation of prior learning is now widely used; the vast majority of higher education provision is now modularized or unitized in some form; the traditional single-discipline boundaries of honours degrees are increasingly being eroded);
- a major expansion of postgraduate student numbers, especially part-time students.

Detailed information regarding this fundamental change in higher education can be found, for example, in the excellent 'background essay' in Volume 2 of the Graduate Standards Programme Final Report (HEQC, 1997); in the Harris Report (HEFCE, 1996); and in the good contextual introduction in Green (1994).

## INCREASING GOVERNMENT INFLUENCE AND DIRECTION

Changes in the political and financial context of higher education have been equally dramatic. The small and élite higher education system of the 1960s was highly autonomous and funded to a very generous level by almost unquestioning governments, whatever their political persuasion. However, the rapid expansion of higher education via the new red-brick universities and polytechnics placed increasing pressure on this comfortable arrangement. Fast growth (to achieve the target of having 30 per cent of 18–21-year-olds in higher education by the year 2000 – which was met by the mid 1990s) was a government objective because of a perceived need to improve the competitiveness of British industry and commerce by increasing the level of training/skills/education of the workforce in order to take advantage of new technologies and opportunities.

A key element of the government-led transformation of higher education was the need to guarantee value for money and provide public accountability. The concept of market forces was introduced to higher education in very much the same way as it was applied to many other areas of the public sector. It was clear that the government wanted 'more for less' – the resources available for higher education had to grow at a slower rate than the participation rate and so higher education institutions therefore had to demonstrate the same efficiency gains as other public-sector institutions. The style of management of higher education institutions had to change as a result, 'managerialism' becoming the dominant motif (Trow, 1993).

Of course, stemming from this approach and practical application of market-driven philosophy, there arises the unavoidable question of quality. Does 'more for less' mean that the 'more' will be of a lower quality than before? This has been the key question for higher education over the past decade.

## SPECIFIC DEVELOPMENTS IN RELATION TO QUALITY

With the elimination in 1992 of the binary divide between universities and polytechnics, a single new system of accountability with regard to quality was imposed on two very different traditions and histories. The former polytechnics had been used to the overview of the Council for National Academic Awards (CNAA), the activities of HM Inspectorate and the control of ownership by local education authorities. However, the old universities, apart from teacher training, had never been exposed to such systematic external scrutiny. The autonomy of universities was long-held and jealously protected. In 1990, the Committee of Vice-chancellors and Principals (CVCP) set up the Academic Audit Unit (AAU) in response to growing demands for accountability, but this body was not about setting specific standards or promoting uniform systems. Rather, its object was simply to ensure that the universities' own stated means of quality assurance, whatever they were, were actually being applied.

This clearly did not fully satisfy government requirements with respect to accountability and so the unified sector of 1992 was suddenly exposed to the quality assessment functions of the new Higher Education Funding Councils (the HEFCs). Provision in all subject/discipline areas was to be periodically assessed by the HEFCs and the results, graded on a set scale, made public. Exceptionally poor or good results would have an effect on government funding. With respect to research activity, a similar principle was applied via the 1992 and 1996 Research Assessment Exercises (RAEs) that graded all departments' research activities and allocated funding accordingly.

In response, the sector itself extended the activity of the AAU by the creation of the new Higher Education Quality Council, which also took on the access and quality enhancement functions of the CNAA. The HEQC periodically audited the quality assurance arrangements of higher education institutions and produced a comprehensive public report. A new single agency incorporating both functions (audit and assessment) began operation in 1998 – the Quality Assurance Agency for Higher Education (QAAHE). It cannot be overstated that this body is not an agency of higher education itself, as the HEQC was.

A point of note is that the clear government concern with 'quality' in higher education did not result in the promotion of the practice and philosophy of Total Quality Management (TQM) as such, unlike government efforts in the manufacturing sector and elsewhere (for example, the publication by the DTI of a series of booklets comprising the 'Management in the 90s' programme, with titles such as 'Total Quality Management', 'The Quality Gurus', 'TQM and Effective Leadership', 'The Case for Costing Quality', 'Best Practice Benchmarking' and so on). The key concern of government appears to have been a need to push the sector into of more basic considerations, such as competition, marketing, value for money and public accountability.

## STANDARDS ON THE GOVERNMENT'S AGENDA

Government concern over quality in a 'more for less' environment of rapidly expanding higher education focused in 1994 on the question of comparability of academic standards. The question asked was very basic and simple: how can we be assured that higher education institutions are delivering the same quality in their 'production' of degrees? What is it that is the essence of 'graduateness' in the higher education sector?

The then Secretary of State for Education asked this question of higher education collectively in 1994. In the summer of 1994, the CVCP and the Standing Conference of Principals (SCOP) asked the HEQC to consider the development of threshold standards for undergraduate degrees. The HEQC responded with a three-fold strategy, which was to:

- focus on academic standards in the audit process (as outlined above);
- investigate and consult on strengthening external examining ('Strengthening External Examining' 1996b);
- investigate and consult on the desirability and feasibility of developing threshold standards for first degrees, the Graduate Standards Programme (GSP final report was published 1997).

The definition of academic standards adopted by the HEQC in 1994, after consultation with member institutions, was:

> explicit levels of academic attainment which are used to describe and measure academic requirements and achievements of individual students or groups of students
>
> (HEQC, 1997)

From October 1994, due to pressure from government and elsewhere, the HEQC specifically included in its audit process the question of academic standards. Institutions were asked questions designed to establish how they defined and determined their standards, what comparators they used to ensure that their standards were broadly in line with those of their institutions, and how they ensured that their standards were in fact being maintained.

## THE GRADUATE STANDARDS PROGRAMME (GSP)

In a small, élite, higher education system, standards could be implicit. Implicit standards were held in a community of practice and belief that was small enough to actually work (although probably only ever within disciplines and not across the sector as such). However, with a mass higher education system, the shared understandings of an academic élite are simply not a sufficient basis for standards. Brennan (1996) points out that the standards debate and comparability does matter because we must not devalue the currency of degrees obtained from the less fashionable institutions. Also that if higher education fails to answer questions about standards and comparability with evidence, they will be answered with prejudice and snobbery (a problem some would say is exemplified in the popular league tables).

Middlehurst (1996) points to four key themes in the standards debate.

- *Compatibility*: given the recent changes in the higher education sector, can 'broad compatibility' of degrees across subjects and higher education institutions still exist?
- *Security and reliability*: degrees must be reliable in terms of a tradable value as a currency within the higher education and employment markets and the internal systems, and values that ensure that the currency is relatively fixed (rather than floating) must be secure.
- *Nature and purpose*: expectations of what a degree is will vary over time, and it seems unreasonable to think that they shouldn't. After all, why should standards be the same in 1939 as 1999?
- *Ownership and control of standards*: the debate about degree standards is one of the ways in which higher education is being called to account by a variety of interest groups for its place and contribution to the wellbeing of society in the next century.

> When subject knowledge is a primary focus of degree-level education and academics are subject experts, ownership and control of standards by academics is unlikely to be seriously disputed. However, when students want more choice and 'relevance' in their education, and when they are paying for it, when employers are becoming more demanding in their specific requirements, and when taxpayers (with government as

> proxy) want to determine value for public money, the question of ownership and control of standards becomes disputed territory.
>
> (Middlehurst, 1996)

Middlehurst recognizes that five areas will need to be addressed if academic standards in the wide sense are to be assured:

- the conduct of academic staff (which is both input and process);
- the educational background, ability, motivation and learning approaches of students (both input and process);
- curriculum design and content, learning activities and support for learning, and the assessment regime (process);
- the granting of an award and recording of student attainment (output);
- the institutional context that provides a framework for articulation, assurance, maintenance and enhancement of standards (input, process and output).

By contrast, the GSP was concerned only with degree standards in the specific sense of output standards. Arriving at a 'standard' for a degree should involve, as the first stage, the specification and articulation of the characteristics and level of performance required. However, this first stage is the weakest in current practice, and is often altogether missing or only inserted at the end rather than the beginning by norm-referencing.

> The rationale behind the ascribing of marks and gradings is often missing, or at least is not always apparent or public. This provides a fundamental difficulty where students, employers and taxpayers are seeking information about the nature, level and reliability of degree standards; it also makes it potentially more difficult for academics, as teachers and examiners, to achieve reliability, consistency and comparability in relation to standards.
>
> (Middlehurst, 1996)

The Interim Report of the GSP (HEQC, 1995) was clear in its findings.

- The notion of comparability of standards, as hitherto understood, no longer commands general respect and the concept of comparability needs to be redefined in the context of a large and more diverse sector.
- Academic standards are generally implicit rather than explicit.
- There is confusion and ambiguity in the titles of awards.
- Threshold standards do not match easily with the honours degree, and the notion of 'satisfactory' performance is usually pitched somewhere in the second class honours category.

- It is worth exploring the qualities expected of graduates ('graduateness'), including generic attributes and skills, as a possible basis for threshold standards.
- There is, across higher education, a desire to find ways of articulating the basis, standards and criteria for judgement associated with programmes of study in explicit and publicly accessible terms.

These issues are discussed further in the next chapter.

These interim findings were confirmed by the audit reports from September 1994 to July 1995 (49 in total were analysed). The conclusion from these audit findings with respect to standards was that:

> The analysis of audit material shows that institutions have in place a significant number of systems and procedures which are intended to assure academic standards [publication of regulations; validation procedures which approve aims, objectives and assessment criteria and involvement of peer review in that and in course review; standardized criteria for classification; external examiners and examination boards; monitoring of pattern of degree results; professional body involvement; and operation of course monitoring systems]. However, with a small number of exceptions, these were not achieving their aim, principally because of a lack of explicit criteria relating to standards. Institutions put a great deal of emphasis on the external examiner system, but there were few yardsticks by which to judge comparability of standards. Modularization increased student numbers and collaborative partnerships and particularly overseas links, compounding the difficulties because academic staff can no longer rely on common understandings with networks of peers to support and verify standards.
>
> (HEQC, 1996a)

## EXTERNAL EXAMINERS IN HIGHER EDUCATION

The point concerning external examiners is critical and reflects the radical changes occurring in the higher education context.

> The response to auditors' questions were remarkably uniform, in that almost total reliance appeared to be being placed on the external examiner system as the guarantor of standards. It was believed to provide the necessary safeguards and security of standards, despite the lack of clarity about what was being safeguarded.
>
> (HEQC, 1996a)

However, the work of the HEQC in this area shows this sort of reliance to be a very high-risk strategy indeed. It was found necessary urgently to strengthen external examining because of the rapidly changing/expanding context of higher education, hence the publication in 1996 of a major report, 'Strengthening External Examining' (HEQC, 1996b).

Summary findings include that:

- in many cases, the external examiner system no longer operates on the basis of ensuring fairness at the level of the individual student;
- the external examiner system has become fragmented due to the focus of appointment often being on 'peer' institutions;
- external examiners by themselves can no longer ensure comparability of standards without greater agreement on explicit definitions of academic standards and the parameters of comparability that are encompassed by the system (HEQC, 1996b). The report clarifies the principles, purposes and application of a national framework for external examining, but the stress is very much on seeing the external examiner system as:

  > *one* [emphasis added] element of a comprehensive quality assurance and enhancement framework which is being developed by the higher education sector. ... Together these arrangements are designed to protect the quality and standards of higher education provision in the UK within a now much more widely differentiated system.

Silver and Williams (1996) apply the findings of the earlier 'Silver Report' (Silver, 1995) to the question of national standards. They rehearse the argument that, in the old small, élite higher education system, it was possible to have comparable standards across higher education in subject areas. This was because the institutions were similar enough, with similar enough staff and student intakes, curricula and forms of assessment to enable consensus to be reached on standards via the external examiner system. However, they illustrate clearly how recent radical changes to the sector have all had an effect on the traditional role of the external examiner:

- the increase in student numbers means less sampling by externals of students' work and greater time pressures and workload;
- more diversity means it is increasingly difficult for any one external to have an overview of academic standards in a particular subject discipline;
- new programmes can cover a very wide subject range – for example, business studies – making it very difficult for the expertise of an external to cover the whole range of knowledge;

- modularization and semesterization have brought problems concerning the role for external examiners in two-tier examination boards;
- the move to new/different assessment systems, often based on competences or learning outcomes, raise questions of the preparedness and expertise of external examiners, and so on.

The 'gold standard' is no longer recognizable. Silver and Williams (1996) conclude:

> Because diversity and expansion in the new conditions of mass higher education have had such an impact, the evidence suggests that there is little acceptance of the possibility of 'national' academic standards.

The only means by which this could be achieved, namely some form of national (core) curriculum and external assessment process, is uniformly dismissed. They recognize that a more attainable goal might be to establish minimum acceptable threshold academic standards by subject discipline, but this would need to take account of the diversity of institutional missions and ethos, and also to promote and encourage the achievement of academic standards above the threshold. However, an alternative and more radical approach is favoured:

> to accept that no overall national academic standard is definable at the level of subject (or across subjects). Academic standards, awards and graduates will be different. However, external examiners would remain an important feature of British higher education because they would ensure against academic standards becoming totally unacceptable, working within institutions' declared aims, regulations and procedures. They would therefore act as an external reference point and as an imprimatur for an institution's awards.
>
> (Silver and Williams, 1996)

Under this system, the role of the external examiner would vary depending on the institution and the individual.

> External examiners would operate at the intersection of national academic policies, the academic standards of their subject area, albeit loosely defined, and the academic standards as defined by the receiving institution and the programme of study. That intersection would be negotiated between the external examiner and the internal examiners. That negotiation could be monitored by rigorous quality assurance procedures and confirmed by whatever external quality assurance arrangements are operating.
>
> (Silver and Williams, 1996)

This viewpoint is partially reflected in the final framework suggested by the HEQC (1996b), although the explicit admission of different standards is not so clear.

The National Committee of Inquiry into Higher Education (NCIHE), chaired by Sir Ron Dearing, also recognized clearly the failings of the current external examiner system:

> The external examiner system, through which institutions seek to ensure common standards for their awards, worked well in a small community of institutions. It is inadequate to meet the needs of the much expanded and more diverse system of higher education that we now have.
>
> (HMSO, 1997)

Recommendation 25 of the NCIHE report was therefore that part of the early work of the QAAHE should be to create a UK-wide pool of academic staff recognized by the QAAHE from which institutions must select external examiners.

This recommendation was adopted by the QAAHE in its consultation document of 1998 (QAAHE, March 1998, Part VII). However, the proposals contained therein received little support in the consultation exercise and attracted vociferous criticism, particularly in relation to the proposed reporting relationship of external examiners to the QAAHE. The register of external examiners has been dropped in the final framework, but the importance of training and development opportunities for external examiners and an associated code of practice has been retained (QAAHE, October 1998, Annex 2).

The external examiner remains, then, a key element in the wider context of overall quality assurance, alongside subject benchmarks, programme specifications and qualifications frameworks. The external examiner is one of a number of factors supporting the assurance of standards.

## CONCLUSIONS OF THE GSP – PROGRESS ON STANDARDS AND QUALITY?

The specific focus of the GSP was to explore how broad comparability of standards might be achieved by means of the development of threshold standards and mechanisms for providing assurance of their achievement. The final report of the GSP (HEQC, 1997) states unequivocally that any move towards threshold standards involves the prior attainment of two other objectives:

- the creation of a clear, publicly accessible vocabulary and coherent structures with which to describe and plot the diversity of higher education;

- the establishment of mechanisms to strengthen the exercise of shared academic judgement to provide greater security and comparability of standards within agreed boundaries (Volume 1).

Three general themes are identified in the final report.

- **Comparability** There is no consensus that UK degrees are broadly comparable with one another in terms of an equivalence of output standards. Consequently, what is needed are means by which the level, purposes and standards of programmes and qualifications can be plotted in relation to each other and against agreed benchmarks.
- **Clarity and explicitness** Greater clarity and explicitness are required concerning the purposes of higher education and the aims and standards of programmes of study. However, the judgement of standards in higher education 'are ultimately rooted in the shared (and generally tacit) values of specialist communities' (Volume 1). These values are realized as a result of the practice of the community rather than explicit articulation and, indeed, 'because of the very nature of any process of judgement – there are ultimately likely to be limits to the extent to which standards can be made explicit' (Volume 1). It is recognized, though, that ways of making standards more explicit have to be found. It is claimed that many apparent concerns about standards arise from mismatches between the expectations of graduate employers and the actual attainments of the students. One key reason for this may be the failure of higher education to inform the public of recent changes and innovations in the sector. Greater explicitness would help tackle this.
- **Assessment and the strengthening of academic judgement** Obviously, standards cannot be rigorous unless the work of students is assessed by valid and reliable methods. Those involved in assessing students, both administrative and academic staff, should be as well prepared as possible in two senses: by having a clear appreciation of the technical aspects of assessment; and by being part of a shared assessment culture. Recent developments with respect to modularization and resultant examination board practices give rise for concern. What is needed are new opportunities for staff to discuss and compare students' work, and these should be linked to the consideration of assessment issues in programme design, validation and review. The role of external examiners is important and should be strengthened and clarified along the lines suggested by the HEQC in its earlier publication 'Strengthening External Examining' (HEQC, 1996b).

Five specific issues emerged from the work of the GSP:

- threshold standards;
- the meaning of levels and credit;
- the need for a national awards framework;
- the general attributes expected of graduates;
- the relationship between graduate standards and key skills.

It is worth while looking in some detail at the conclusions with regard to threshold standards.

The findings of the GSP suggest that threshold standards are not (yet) generally feasible. Three main reasons were given for this:

- the legacy of higher education practice in not making standards explicit, which means there is simply no generally agreed vocabulary with which to define threshold standards or to locate them within the context of particular programmes of study;
- the belief that it is not yet possible to assess threshold standards with consistency and accuracy;
- the idea of a positive threshold standard is not generally accepted – that is, the standard 'satisfactory' performance appears to be at the second-class level rather than at the bottom of the third class, and the latter is therefore expressed largely in negative terms.

> The inescapable conclusion is that it is not possible to move immediately to the development of a general threshold for all degrees in a particular broad subject area, still less for degrees irrespective of subject.
>
> (HEQC, 1997, Volume 1)

Progress can be made with respect to an environment in which such threshold definitions might be feasible by first making progress in the other related areas mentioned above, by attaining greater explicitness with regard to programme outcomes, by the development of a vocabulary to plot similarities and differences between programmes, by the development of an awards framework, and by strengthening the cultural basis of peer judgements on standards. This is the only practical way forward seen by the GSP. As we shall see, this advice was not heeded.

The recommendations of the GSP were to do with enhancing self-regulation. This was made clear in the consultation paper preceding the final report:

> The aim is not to define academic standards *per se*, but to strengthen the means by which standards are established, compared and assured. The recommendations are designed to protect individual institutional

> autonomy and to maintain collective responsibility for standards within the academic community. National curricula or national examinations are not proposed.
>
> (GSP Consultation Paper, December 1996, N/96/222(a))

The final report:

> envisages that both the articulation of standards and their assurance would be founded on a triangle of responsibility, between higher education institutions, subject and professional groups and the QAAHE, with contributions from students and employers where appropriate. This suggests strongly that the focus of external quality assurance must be on the effectiveness with which institutions determine *their* standards, and monitor and ascribe *their* achievement. [emphasis added]
>
> (HEQC, 1997, Volume 1)

The GSP strongly recommended that progress with respect to standards should be made by the continuing creation and enhancement of a national framework for the sector that would encompass the wide range of areas outlined above. The approach is very much bottom-up and is an evolutionary process leading to greater explicitness, confidence and the dissemination of good practice. Codes of practice rather than dictat and regulation are envisaged. Although the beginning of the GSP was very much outcome-focused, the conclusion of the study has reinforced the importance of process considerations at all stages of higher education. In the final report, the HEQC rejected explicitly:

- the development of national curricula or national assessment arrangements;
- the separation of teaching from summative assessment;
- the exploration of the use of external tests as an approach to threshold standards.

## THE REPORT OF THE NATIONAL COMMITTEE OF INQUIRY INTO HIGHER EDUCATION (THE DEARING REPORT)

The report of the NCIHE paid great attention to the issue of quality assurance of higher education provision. The underlying themes are clear:

- demonstrating value for money to all customers;
- clearer articulation of what will be delivered and how it is verified;

- ensuring that more (students) do not mean less (quality);
- continuous improvement.

> no public service can automatically expect increasing public expenditure to support it. Higher education needs to demonstrate that it represents a good investment for individuals and society.
>
> (HMSO, 1997)

> Expansion in student numbers must not be at the cost of lowering the standards required for awards. Nor should it result in lowering the quality of provision or in increasing numbers of drop-outs or failures.
>
> (HMSO, 1997)

> In return for additional contributions from graduates, institutions must make much clearer what they are offering to students. They must work continually to improve the quality of teaching and they must approach the mutual assurance of standards with real commitment.
>
> (HMSO, 1997)

The detailed recommendations from Dearing therefore encompassed a wide range of areas including the:

- training of higher education teaching staff (the Institute for Learning and Teaching in Higher Education recommendations 13 and 14);
- review of current programmes of study by higher education institutions to secure a better balance between breadth and depth (recommendation 16);
- development of a progress file for students (recommendation 20);
- development of programme specifications (recommendation 21);
- adoption of the proposed qualifications framework (recommendation 22);
- expansion of the remit of the QAAHE to include quality assurance and public information, standards verification, maintenance of the qualifications framework, and development of a mandatory (for funding) code of practice (recommendation 24);
- early work of the QAAHE to include the development of benchmark information on standards (recommendation 25).

Such recommendations have formed the early agenda of the QAAHE (see below) and represent a significant transition in the overall approach to quality assurance in the following respect. Hitherto the work of the HEQC and the funding agencies in teaching quality assessment have been predicated on the notion of 'fitness *for* purpose', that is, the assurance that self-determined standards are being met. The Dearing Report and subsequent work of the QAAHE have moved the basis for quality assurance of higher education much further towards 'fitness *of* purpose'. The assurance that will be sought in the future is that local standards comply with external criteria (national subject benchmarks, a national qualifications framework, national codes of practice).

It is also important to understand the way in which the Dearing report took forward, or not, the previous work of the GSP of the HEQC. Roger Brown (formerly, Chief Executive of the HEQC) has highlighted the key areas of difference/contention as follows (Brown, 1997).

- A national qualifications framework is at the heart of Dearing's conclusions, and was also, of course, a central proposal of the GSP. However, the GSP saw the awards framework as being essentially descriptive, a tool to help map institutional awards and award categories. For Dearing, it is clear that all award titles will have to conform to the framework and that there will be fewer such titles.
- The development of programme specifications is another key GSP recommendation adopted by Dearing. However, the GSP proposal was for higher education institutions to categorize their programmes within certain broad categories within which they would be left to determine the balance of outcomes. In other words, it was envisaged by the GSP that some programmes would rightly omit some particular category of attributes (such as key skills – see HEQC, 1997, Annex C, Volume 2 of the final report on the GSP). However, Dearing was clear that all programmes should specify outcomes in all categories.
- With regard to threshold standards, Dearing recommended to the QAAHE that, in order to develop these, or minimum, standards of student achievement, the QAAHE should establish small expert teams to provide benchmark information. This has been happening, with three pilot subject benchmarking groups in law, history, and chemistry (this subject is discussed more widely in Chapter 2). However, Dearing seems not to have accepted the serious cautions expressed by the GSP concerning threshold standards (see above). Also, Brown (1997) questions the subject approach of Dearing for the following reasons:
  - many programmes are now multi- or interdisciplinary (see Chapter 9);
  - many programmes, even of the more traditional kind, are not single subject;
  - the idea of a subject is itself contentious in many areas ('design history', clinical biochemistry etc.);
  - how does one take account of the institutional and local dimension, and responsibility?

The thrust of the GSP, according to Brown, was therefore much more towards increasing the opportunities and incentives for those involved in student assessment in order to improve practice and understanding, and this could be done at any level of operation, including at the level of subject, institution or discipline.

Two key omissions in Dearing are noted by Brown: the call to review the honours classification system (which HEQC saw as a major hindrance to threshold standards); and the range of dimensions. The latter are the proposed list of generic attributes that emerged from the HEQC work concerning 'graduateness' (see HQC, 1997, Annex C, Volume 2). The point which Brown makes is that not only is this range of dimensions important in making progress with describing 'graduateness', but it was also the basis of the other core recommendations of the GSP relating to the awards framework and the programme specification. Without such a 'range of dimensions' there is no proper conceptual basis for work on awards, programmes and transcripts.

Finally, Brown makes the point that, with regard to quality assurance, Dearing mentions only external examiners and fails to capture the breadth of the GSP work. The final report made it clear that the appropriateness of standards needed to be tested at numerous other points, such as in relation to the range of awards offered by the institution; links between programmes and awards, or programmes and modules; admission criteria and strategies to fulfil institutional mission; the design, validation and review of programmes; assessment of students; quality of teaching and learning; deployment and development of human and other resources.

A final (non-GSP) criticism of the Dearing Report that needs to be made is the lack of understanding of sophisticated CATS principles within the proposed qualifications framework. The proposal confuses academic level with years of study and does not reflect current CATS thinking (exemplified in the Inter Consortium Credit Agreement project sponsored by the DfEE, HMSO, 1998). We must have both a qualifications framework and a credit framework.

In a major survey of the assessment and regulatory frameworks of some 29 higher education institutions carried out by the Northern Universities Consortium for Credit Accumulation and Transfer (NUCCAT), it was clear that the apparent tension between the module/unit level and the course/award level with respect to assessment practice can only be resolved by the provision of appropriate and interrelating credit and qualifications frameworks (Armstrong, Clarkson and Noble, 1998). The aggregation of student performance and achievement from the module/unit level to the course/award level is a very complex matter, which can involve various and justifiable means of applying compensation for unit/module failure. The credit framework provides guidance at module/unit level; the qualifications framework must embrace this at award/course level – a not insignificant task. It is disappointing to note that the November 1998 QAAHE consultation paper on the postgraduate qualification framework fails to recognize or deal with the distinction between the minimum credit volume to be *studied* and the minimum credit volume to be *achieved* (that is, passed) for the attainment of an award.

The importance of this issue for subject benchmarking is significant. The recent work of the Student Assessment and Classification Working Group (SACWG) with respect to a pilot investigation into benchmarking academic standards has made clear the connection between award regulatory frameworks and the practical implementation of subject benchmarking:

> simple comparisons of achieved performance cannot be made, since marks/grades and degree classifications are not given against fixed criteria which span an individual institution, or a subject discipline – let alone the higher education sector as a whole. ... The amount of variability in the higher education system means that one can only interpret outcome standards with reference to the context from which they emerged.
>
> (Yorke, *et al.*, 1998)

## THE QUALITY ASSURANCE AGENCY FOR HIGHER EDUCATION

Taking up the Dearing baton with respect to benchmarking (which, as we have seen, was a very different concept to that of HEQC) the QAAHE pressed ahead with three pilot studies in history, law and chemistry, while at the same time seeking agreement on an overall quality assurance framework. The final framework created by the QAAHE was clarified, following a consultation process, in October 1998. It is stated clearly that 'programme specifications and subject benchmarks remain as central features of the new model' (QAAHE, October 1998).

The context of this statement is important. It is recognized that views from within the sector were divided, 'with a number of significant reservations being expressed'. The precise nature of responses to the subject benchmarking proposals is later clarified as follows:

> HEIs [higher education institutions] were divided: about 25 per cent expressed support for the principle of benchmarking, many proposed positive suggestions of various kinds; but most were neutral or expressed reservations. A minority were opposed in principle, or highly critical.
>
> (QAAHE, October 1998b)

Nevertheless, because 'there was overwhelming support from employers and students for clear and verifiable information about the outcomes that programmes are intended to achieve' subject benchmarking remains a central feature of the QAAHE framework.

It is explained that one of the key purposes of the new QAAHE approach is to bring about the following:

> There must be independent verification that programmes of study are delivering their intended outcomes; and that student achievement meets the standards required by the institution for its awards, by relevant national subject benchmarks, and by any accrediting professional body.
>
> (QAAHE, October 1998)

However, nowhere is the concept or theory of 'benchmarking' defined.

The concern expressed within the QAAHE framework for external stakeholders sits uncomfortably, but perhaps understandably, with the stress that Jackson (1998a) places on the concept of subject benchmarks as a useful tool for higher education practitioners. He recognizes that the key current use of benchmarking within the QAAHE framework is as an aid to regulation rather than the more universal principle of self-improvement, but goes on to offer a rather more expansive definition:

> Benchmarking is a collaborative learning process to facilitate the systematic comparison and evaluation of practice, process and performance to aid improvement and regulation.
>
> (Jackson, 1998a)

The addition within this definition of the concept of 'improvement' introduces a new dimension in comparison to the official QAAHE position. The published framework reiterates the predictable and rather more limited basis of benchmarking:

> The development of subject benchmark standards was a key recommendation of the Dearing Report, being seen as essential to ensure public and employer confidence that awards, especially at first degree level, were nationally recognized and widely understood. ... Public concern that the transition to mass higher education may have resulted in erosion of degree standards needs to be addressed, and subject benchmarking has the potential to do that.
>
> (QAAHE, October 1998)

This fundamental approach needs to be seen against the context of the growing bureaucracy supporting its application. The ambitions of QAAHE are expansive and potentially extremely costly in the sense of seeking benchmarks in all 42 defined subject areas, which will need to be continually updated in light of experience gained from the review cycles, and expanded to incorporate both modular and non-degree awards. This burgeoning industry of effort, which will probably also stimulate significant effort in the related areas of learning outcomes and level descriptors, has as its prime purpose the achievement of publicly demonstrable confidence in the provision of higher education, rather than the improvement of the core processes that constitute higher education.

It is illuminating to compare this with the current situation in the world of business and commerce. In Chapters 3 by Appleby and 8 by Yarrow, lessons from the theory and practice of business benchmarking are spelled out very clearly. One of the key issues is the benefit that can and should be gained from the process if it is to be worth while and cost-effective. Appleby demonstrates a three-fold typology of metric, diagnostic and process benchmarking. Metric benchmarking is simply the means of comparison with other organizations by the use of metric data (for example, the *Times Higher Education Supplement*'s league tables or TQA scores). The major problem with this approach is that, even if the comparisons made are accurate (which experience in HE shows to be harder in practice than it sounds – the immense complexity necessary to achieve meaningful performance indicators is shown clearly by Cave, *et al.*, 1997), it does not actually lead anywhere. To identify that there is a gap against some metric data (external standard) is quite a different thing from knowing how to close that gap by process improvement!

Diagnostic benchmarking goes one step further and facilitates a comparison, using a predetermined generic model of numerous key attributes/factors, against a wide range of competitor institutions. An organization can therefore receive detailed feedback from this process as regards where it lies in each category against the 'best', the 'norm', and the 'worst'. Particular areas of strength and weakness can be identified, providing some clearer starting point than with simple metric benchmarking. However, the main problem still remains. There is little guidance, other than from the generic model itself, of how to improve.

The current efforts of subject benchmarking lie somewhere between metric and diagnostic benchmarking. The returns, in terms of improvement, will be difficult to realize and coincidental rather than integral. It is only with process benchmarking that the real potential benefit begins to be realized. Process benchmarking involves the direct observation of practice in other institutions. Not only will it identify performance gaps, but, more importantly, it will provide understanding of best practice and therefore lead to real process improvement. The GSP notion of self-selecting subject groupings was much closer to this model than the current QAAHE approach. To put the issue in simple terms, a teaching team in history at University X might be able to learn a great deal more about how to improve their course by undertaking process benchmarking with universities Y and Z than by reading threshold or modal standards produced by a subject benchmarking group.

The point is that a huge amount of effort is going to go into the far inferior metric/diagnostic approach, so why not aim for something much more productive from the outset? A benefit already identified in the pilot benchmark groups has been the experience of the members of the group in taking part in the process of discussion and comparison of practice with colleagues from other institutions. Process benchmarking must surely be worth exploring if we are serious about improving higher education practice.

## PROBLEMS WITH THE BENCHMARKING APPROACH

The QAAHE consultation exercise produced six clear issues, discussed in detail in the final framework document (QAAHE, October 1998). I use this categorization below as the basis for a more comprehensive discussion of the matter.

### The notion of threshold

The three pilot groups in law, chemistry and history have reflected a general concern and confusion regarding the meaning and utility of a threshold standard. As was evident in earlier GSP work, the more meaningful standard to articulate may be that of the typical or 'modal' student achieving a second class honours degree, rather than the absolute threshold of pass–fail at the third class of honours (this is further discussed in Chapter 2).

Part of the reaction to the QAAHE consultation reflects the point made above concerning the potential benefits of benchmarking. There was a strong feeling that to articulate the bare pass–fail achievement was minimalist and of course does not assist in continuous improvement because it is not identifying good/best practice for comparison and aspiration. The QAAHE's response to this concern is to say that it may be more practical for academics to begin with what they know best and define modal standards, but then move to threshold standards. However, is the QAAHE not introducing unnecessary confusion by allowing both a threshold and modal standard to be articulated? Alternatively, should it insist on both being produced at the same time in any subject group?

There is a need to have a more sophisticated view of what student performance at the threshold standard means. I would argue that it actually only makes sense at the unit/module level rather than the course level. There is an assumption being made that students will somehow perform at this borderline level across all units/modules of the programme. In reality, this is not often the case and performance is more likely to range well above and below this level, but resulting in an overall judgement of performance as being at third-class level. This takes us back to the issue of credit and award frameworks. Comprehensive qualifications frameworks, which include clear guidance with respect to the achievement of credit at the unit/module level and the aggregation of this at the award level (which in turn must incorporate clear guidance concerning compensation for failure at unit/module level and condonation of poor performance), need to be produced quickly if real progress is to be made. How can benchmarking of degree output be complete and meaningful without clear guidance with respect to compensation for unit/module failure?

Another assumption evident in some areas of discussion is that a third-class student is typically lazy and not very capable – in other words, a failing or underperforming student. This may be an entirely inappropriate judgement with respect to many students. For example, there could be many who access higher education in less traditional ways for whom a threshold degree performance would be a very positive and significant achievement. This, of course, also raises the issue of whether higher education assessment is and should be criteria- (which implies threshold benchmarking) or norm- (which implies modal benchmarking) referenced.

At a recent SACWG benchmarking conference (Liverpool, 1998) it was apparent that some institutions would want to define a 'harder' threshold than the minimal one that might be articulated by the QAAHE. The implication was that University X might want to say that its students would have to do more than the defined minimum in order to achieve their degree. So what does this mean for the threshold? Surely any threshold, once defined, must apply to all higher education institutions?

By contrast, if continuous improvement was stressed as the basic approach to benchmarking, then would this mean that the threshold level would (must) increase over time? A new saloon car is continually improved during its production lifetime, with more and better accessories and performance being added, even at the entry level. A point made earlier (from Middlehurst's writing) was that we should surely accept that 1930s standards need not necessarily be the same as 1990s standards.

## Outcomes of the benchmarking process

The fear expressed in the consultation responses was with regard to the development of some form of national curriculum. The QAAHE has responded, quite rightly, that it has never steered the benchmarking process towards curricular content, but, rather, towards the appropriate general intellectual outcomes. However, if this is the case, why do we need the huge exercise of 42 subject benchmarks? Surely these general outcomes (a level descriptor for the honours degree, perhaps) can be determined by undertaking something less than the task of benchmarking all 42 subjects. Further, what is the overall relationship of the subject benchmarking 'general' effort to level descriptors?

## Multidisciplinary programmes

The issue here is expressed well by Jackson (1998b):

> credibility in the overall approach will be undermined if benchmark information cannot be developed. While the creation of benchmark information at the level of the award might be a relatively unproblematic exercise in the context of single/major or even joint/minor subject programmes, the process will be more complicated and problematic in multisubject and interdisciplinary programmes where curricula have been integrated to create effectively new subjects for which there is unlikely to be benchmark information.

This problem has been recognized by the QAAHE and it is intended that an appropriate advisory group will be convened to recommend how to proceed with such programmes. However, it should also be noted that Jackson touches on a further problematical area – namely, the way in which new courses are now developed in many universities. The old process of producing a new course from scratch in an holistic fashion is far less common now. By contrast, much of the current development of course curricula is determined by 'churn' at the unit/module level. That is, new courses evolve as units/modules are continually reviewed and improved, and new groupings of units/modules emerge. (Further discussion of this issue is provided by Billingham in Chapter 9).

A further major related limitation of the current approach is that it is purely honours degree-based. There are numerous other qualifications in the subject areas that will need to be benchmarked.

## Stifling creativity and diversity

The fear has been expressed that subject benchmarking might constrain UK higher education to a conventional and outdated approach. Again, the response of the QAAHE is to emphasize the general nature of benchmarking information, the purpose of which is 'to provide agreed reference points in terms of which diversity and innovation may be plotted and understood' (QAAHE, October 1998).

## Timescale

The QAAHE has accepted that the original timescales are optimistic and are now reviewing them. However, if we do not have a comprehensive set of subject benchmarks within the next three years – to include multidisciplinary programmes and other awards – then how can the overall framework hold together?

### Subject areas

There was mixed reaction to the proposed 42 subject areas. The only action at the time of going to press that the QAAHE is therefore undertaking is to review the position of American studies.

As a final comment, it must be noted that the QAAHE has chosen not to link a review of the honours degree to work on threshold standards. This compounds the omission in Dearing, referred to above, and flies in the face of consistent doubts expressed about the honours classifications process, which are more clearly brought into focus when considering a qualifications framework and threshold standards. In the GSP study into academic standards in the approval, review and classification of degrees, it was noted that:

> a substantial number of those who participated in this study recognized a powerful tension between the development of threshold standards and the operation of the classified honours degree, and considered that the classified honours degree system, at least as traditionally operated, may have outlived its usefulness both to the academic community and to other stakeholders.
>
> (HEQC, 1996c)

## THE OVERALL QAAHE FRAMEWORK – PROBLEMS IN INTEGRATION?

The four foundations of the new QAAHE framework are:

1. subject benchmarks;
2. a qualifications framework;
3. programme specifications;
4. codes of practice.

There are strong interrelationships between all four, but in particular the first three must be seen as an integrated set. Subject benchmarks must take into account the qualifications framework (which must, in turn, incorporate a sophisticated CATS framework); programme specifications must incorporate the results of subject benchmarking. All three are critically dependent on the concepts and reality of learning outcomes and level descriptors.

With regard to level descriptors, they must be taken into account by subject benchmarking groups, given the generalist stress that the QAAHE has always sought to impose. Indeed, the work of subject benchmarking can be seen in many ways as the ideal testing ground for the recently improved level descriptors that emerged in the InCCA project. They should also be able to help focus subject groups on that which is actually subject-specific.

With regard to learning outcomes, there is a critical issue raised in Chapter 5 by Jenny Moon that impinges directly on subject benchmarking. Moon describes her personal struggle with the application of threshold standards via learning outcomes and level descriptors. She relates the experience of many in writing learning outcomes, which is that it cannot, in higher education, be a simple extension of the 'mastery' concept of the NVQ. While an NVQ fixes the end-point of learning quite precisely, in higher education it is not intended that learning should be related so precisely to the achievement of learning outcomes at the module/unit level. This is both because such absolute precision is extremely difficult, if not impossible, for higher learning, and that such precision would confine learning, not allowing the learner to extend beyond this or take unexpected paths of development.

The solution to this proposed by Moon is that, by accepting the reality and limitations of learning outcomes, we can most usefully apply this to the threshold, just pass, standard. There should be basic guidance at module/unit level with regard to what must be achieved in order to consider the module/unit passed. By contrast, level descriptors should be a more expansive description of what can be expected of the average (modal) student. Level descriptors are where the achievement of students above the threshold can be seen and recognized.

The point implied for subject benchmarking is clear. If generic level descriptors can fulfil the modal/average requirements for description of learning, and if module/unit learning outcomes are where a threshold/just pass should and can be defined, then the kind of subject-specific learning outcomes being produced should be seen as further explication of the level descriptors and not threshold statements. It is also surely clear that the realm of individual unit/module learning outcomes is not the place where subject benchmarking should be looking.

There is an important point here for programme specifications. Surely programme outcomes cannot be seen simply as descriptions of what will be achieved at threshold level, derived straight from the module learning (threshold) outcomes. The relationship cannot be that clear (particularly given the reality of performance profiles of threshold students – see above). Rather, outcomes articulated at programme level should be the sort of description of learning that is expansive in the sense described above in relation to level descriptors. Otherwise, we greatly limit the programme specification and reduce our programmes to the lowest common expectation. There is a link here also to the need for a qualifications framework(s) that can accommodate more than a crude credit accumulation notion of an award (see above).

## CONCLUSIONS

The above discussion highlights the following:

- benchmarking is a process that has huge potential benefits for higher education, so long as the basic purpose is seen to include improvement and not just measurement;
- the issues are complicated and include:
- the need for clarification with respect to the level of achievement being benchmarked;
- the necessary development of an integrated awards/credit framework that deals with compensation for failure and poor performance within individual units/modules;
- further clarification of the value of subject-specific compared to generic outcomes;
- the wider application of benchmarking to incorporate multidisciplinary programmes and the full range of higher education awards.

The chapters that follow explore these and other issues in more detail.

## REFERENCES

Armstrong, M, Clarkson, P, and Noble, M (1998) 'Modularity and Credit Frameworks: the NUCCAT Survey and 1998 Conference Report', NUCCAT

Brennan, J, *et al.* (1996) 'Changing Conceptions of Academic Standards', Quality Support Centre HE Report No. 4, Open University Press, Buckingham

Brown, R (November 1997) 'National and Institutional Policy: Setting the context', paper to the Warwick conference 'Crossing the Threshold: Responding to the academic standards programme', The School of Independent Studies, Lancaster University

Cave, M, Hanney, S, Henkel, M, and Kogan, M (1997) *The Use of Performance Indicators in Higher Education: The challenge of the quality movement*, 3rd edn, Jessica Kingsley, London

Green, D (ed) (1994) *What is Quality in Higher Education?*, SRHE and Open University Press, Buckingham

HEFCE (1996) 'Review of Postgraduate Education' (Harris Report) HEFCE, Bristol

HEQC (1995) 'Graduate Standards Programme: Interim Report' HEQC, London

HEQC (1996a), 'Learning from Audit 2', HEQC, London
HEQC (1996b) 'Strengthening External Examining', HEQC, London
HEQC (1996c) 'Academic Standards in the Approval, Review and Classification of Degrees', HEQC, London
HEQC (1997) 'Graduate Standards Programme Final Reports (Volumes 1 and 2)', HEQC, London
HMSO (1997) 'Higher Education in the Learning Society', summary report of the National Committee of Inquiry into Higher Education, chaired by Sir Ron Dearing, HMSO, London
HMSO (1998) 'A Common Framework for Learning', report of the DfEE-funded InCCA project, HMSO, London
Jackson, N (1998a) 'Understanding standards-based quality assurance: part 1 – rationale and conceptual basis', *Quality Assurance in Education*, **6** (3)
Jackson, N (1998b) 'Understanding standards-based quality assurance: part 2 – nuts and bolts of the "Dearing" policy framework', *Quality Assurance in Education*, **6** (4)
Middlehurst, R (1996) 'Degree standards and quality assurance: a discussion' in 'Changing Conceptions of Academic Standards', J Brennan, *et al.*, Quality Support Centre HE Report No. 4, Open University Press, Buckingham
QAAHE (March 1998) *Higher Quality*,**1** (3)
QAAHE (October 1998) *Higher Quality*, **1** (4)
QAAHE (November 1998) 'A Consultation Paper on Qualifications Frameworks: Postgraduate Qualifications', *Higher Quality*, **1** (4)
Silver, H, *et al.* (1995) 'The External Examiner System: Possible futures', Quality Support Centre and Open University Press, Buckingham
Silver, H, and Williams R (1996) 'Academic standards and the external examiner system' in 'Changing Conceptions of Academic Standards', J Brennan, *et al*, Quality Support Centre HE Report No. 4, Open University Press, Buckingham
Trow, M (1993) 'Managerialism and the Academic Profession: The case of England', a paper presented to a conference in Milton Keynes in September on 'The Quality Debate', sponsored by *The Times Higher Education Supplement*
Yorke, M, *et al.* (November 1998) 'Benchmarking academic standards: a pilot investigation', draft chapter for forthcoming book published in papers for the fourth SACWAG National Workshop in association with the QAA

## FURTHER READING

Ashworth, A, and Harvey, R (1994) *Assessing Quality in Further and Higher Education*, Jessica Kingsley, London
Barrett R (1996) ' "Quality" and the abolition of standards: Arguments against some American prescriptions for the improvement of Higher Education', *Quality in Higher Education*, **2** (3), pp 201 ff

Chadwick, P (1994) 'A University's TQM Initiative' in *Achieving Quality Learning in Higher Education*, P Nightingale and M O'Neil, Kogan Page, London

Coate, L E (1992) 'Implementing Total Quality Management in a university setting' in *Total Quality Management in Higher Education*, eds L A Sherr and D J Teeter, Jossey-Bass, San Francisco

Colling, C, and Harvey, L (1995) 'Quality control, assurance and assessment – the link to continuous improvement', *Quality Assurance in Education*, **3** (4)

Conway, T, Mackay, S, and Yorke, D (1994) 'Strategic planning in HE: Who are the customers?', *International Journal of Education Management*, **8** (6)

Cuthbert, P F (1996) 'Managing service quality in HE: Is SERVQUAL the answer?', a two-part article in *Managing Service Quality* **6**, (2 and 3)

Deming, W E (1986) *Out of the Crisis*, MIT, Massachusetts

Dill, D (1995) 'Through Deming's eyes: A cross-national analysis of quality assurance policies in higher education', *Quality in Higher Education*, **1** (2)

Ellis, R (ed) (1993), *Quality Assurance in Academic Teaching*, SHRE and Open University Press, Buckingham

Elmuti, D, Kathowala, Y, and Manippallis, M (1996) 'Are Total Quality Management programmes in higher education worth the effort?', *International Journal of Quality and Reliability Management*, **13** (6)

Goodlad, S (1995) *The Quest for Quality*, SRHE and Open University Press, Buckingham

Gummeson, E (1990) 'Nine lessons on service quality' in *Implementing TQM*, ed R L Chase, IFS Publications, London

Harvey L (1995) 'Beyond TQM', *Quality in Higher Education,* **1** (2)

Harvey L (1994) 'Continuous quality improvement: A system-wide view of quality in Higher Education' in 'University-wide change, staff and curriculum development', ed P T Knight, SEDA paper 83, SEDA, Birmingham

HEQC (1994) *Learning from Audit*, HEQC, London

HEQC (1995) Managing for Quality: Stories and strategies, HEQC, London

Hill, F M (1995) 'Managing service quality in Higher Education: The role of the student as primary consumer', *Quality Assurance in Education*, **3** (3)

Ho, S K, and Wearn, K (1995) 'A TQM model for Higher Education and training', *Training for Quality*, **3** (2)

Holmes, G, and McElwee, G (1995) 'Total Quality Management in Higher Education: How to approach human resource management', *The TQM Magazine*, **7** (6)

Lakhe, R R, and Mohanty, R P (1995) 'Understanding TQM in service systems', *International Journal of Quality and Reliability Management*, **12** (9)

Leffel, L G, *et al.* (1992) 'Assessing the leadership culture at Virginia Tech.' in *Total Quality Management in Higher Education*, eds L A Sherr and D J Teeter, Jossey-Bass, San Francisco

Lewis, R G, and Smith, D H (1994) *Total Quality in Higher Education*, St Lucie Press, Florida

Loder, C (ed) (1990) *Quality Assurance and Accountability in Higher Education*, Kogan Page, London

London, M (1995) 'Achieving performance excellence in university administration –Praeger, Westport CT Management', *Quality Assurance in Education*, **2** (3)

Nightingale, P, and O'Neil, M (1994) *Achieving Quality Learning in Higher Education*, Kogan Page, London

Powell, T C (1995) 'Total Quality Management as competitive advantage: A review and empirical study', *Strategic Management Journal*, **16**

Prabhu, V, and Lee, P (summer 1991) 'A training manual for introducing TQM: UNN/EHE service quality', *Sloan Management Review*, pp 29–38

Sherr, L A, and Teeter, D J (eds) (1992) *Total Quality Management in Higher Education* Jossey-Bass, San Francisco

Walton, M (1991) *Deming Management At Work*, Mercury, London

Winter, R S (1992) 'Overçoming barriers to Total Quality Management in colleges and universities' in *Total Quality Management in Higher Education*, eds L A Sherr and D J Teeter, Jossey-Bass, San Francisco

Yorke, M (1994) 'Enhancement-led higher education?', *Quality Assurance in Education*, **2** (3)

2

# How Can Threshold Standards Assure and Enhance Quality?

*Sally Brown*

## THE THRESHOLD STANDARDS DEBATE IN THE UK

In recent years, higher education institutions in the UK have become increasingly interested in a notion that the assurance of standards of educational provision is possible, so long as comparison points are clearly identified within and between organizations. For many years, it was assumed that we all knew what a degree from a British university was worth. While accepting that there was considerable diversity in what such degrees looked like and comprised, there was a confidence that all were broadly equivalent in standing. The previous chapter has provided a historical and contextual framework for the key issues associated with assessing standards by means of benchmarking. This chapter will develop some of these ideas further before questioning the extent to which the definition of benchmarks and threshold standards can promote continuous improvement and enhance quality.

Considerable efforts are being expended in the UK, led by the QAA in a drive to identify both benchmarks and threshold standards that can be used to ensure that judgements on quality are soundly based on evidence rather than assertion.

Positing the means by which academic standards are to be assured, Jackson for the QAA has suggested that:

> Standards-based QA [quality assurance] depends, in the first instance, on institutions and teaching teams making their standards more explicit within certain agreed parameters and then referencing these to a common framework. ... QA processes within such a regime are of two basic types: support structures and mechanisms to help institutions

> and teaching teams to understand and explain their standards and locate them [programmes and awards] on the national framework: [and] checking mechanisms that confirm or question the institutions' own standards.
>
> (Jackson, 1998)

Jackson suggests that standards-based quality assurance will be underpinned by a range of quality assurance processes:

- an institution's own mechanisms for considering/approving/validating and reviewing programmes and academic standards;
- an institution's own external examiners working within the new QAA framework and informed by the products of subject benchmarking groups;
- the provision of information by subject benchmarking groups that would assist subject teaching teams in understanding and formulating their programme outcome standards;
- independent checks on standards by competent peers via new system of independent academic reviewers;
- independent checks by competent peers of the institution's own mechanisms for assuring standards – this process would be aided by a national code of practice framed in terms of what an institution might be expected to demonstrate using its own quality assurance mechanisms (Jackson, 1998)

Every university would lay claim to the assertion that setting and maintaining standards is a key priority, but few to date have moved any great distance in establishing how best to do this. Neither have they proceeded towards tackling the key issue about whether or not there actually is a 'gold standard' for UK university educational provision. A certain coyness is expressed, both at a local and national level, about the linkage between resourcing and output standards, and, indeed, strenuous efforts have been made across the sector explicitly to decouple the two issues. We have all been managing to maintain or even improve standards against steadily declining resources, if we are to believe what our public statements say about us, haven't we? Many would argue that the underlying reason for recent initiatives having been put in place to establish benchmarks and threshold standards is to provide an assurance that more does not necessarily mean worse.

## WHAT IS A BENCHMARK?

Much confusion exists in the sector about what benchmarks actually are. The *Collins* dictionary defines 'benchmarks' in two ways. First, literally a mark on a stone post or other permanent feature, at a point the exact elevation and position of which is known and is used as a reference point in surveying. Second, this term is also used, by analogy, for a criterion by which to measure something – a standard, a reference point.

Peter Milton at a QAA briefing in Manchester on 6 November 1998 indicated that the way the term is being used by the QAA is more as a point of reference than as used in the industrial/commercial world. This approach is well described in Chapters 3 by Appleby and 8 by Yarrow.

One of the problems with using the rhetoric of the organizational management sector and applying it crudely to higher education is the lack of a 'close fit'. Benchmarks of this kind are not really helpful unless you are comparing like with like, and a significant difference between the universities within the UK higher education sector is the extent to which individual universities' mission statements focus on access and widening participation, with allied implications in terms of adding value. It is also important to consider seriously what the purpose of the exercise is; this is more complicated in public services such as education than in organizations that are run to make a profit.

## SOME PROBLEMS AND DIFFICULTIES WITH BENCHMARKING AND THRESHOLD STANDARDS

### Is it possible to define subject benchmarks?

The report of the GSP (discussed in Chapter 1), cast considerable doubt on whether or not this is feasible. It commented that although the principle of direct threshold standards of output for all degrees appears attractive, the specific investigations of the GSP suggest that generally a single threshold is unlikely to be practical or desirable. Furthermore, the HEQC's investigations have suggested that the establishment of a number of multiple thresholds, in the sense of a set of different minima for different clusters of degrees, also raises difficult problems (HEQC, 1997b).

The GSP's final report did, however, indicate direct and indirect methods by which threshold standards might be established, namely:

- direct methods:
- the specification of standards at the level of subjects;
- the specification of common or core curricula, common assessment or external tests;
- the specification of generic attributes;
- indirect methods:
- the achievement of, or movement towards:

- consistency in grade boundaries, including a sharper boundary for progression between 'degrees' and 'degrees with honours';
- consistency in procedures and regulations;
- a strengthening of academic, peer judgement. (HEQC, 1997b).

It argued that generic attributes could usefully be identified as a basis for generalized dimensions but that:

> Standards can only be fixed in relation to specific learning objectives and performance criteria: interpreted through a common culture based on shared practice.
>
> (HEQC, 1997b)

The report also stated:

> It would be neither desirable nor feasible to introduce a national curriculum for UK higher education, nor to introduce universal, common assessment. However, in certain circumstances institutions, parts of institutions, and subject-based and professional bodies may find benefit in sharing curricula and assessment, as is already the case in a few instances. The cost of developing technologically based materials may also lead to shared curricula.
>
> (HEQC, 1997b)

This addresses one of the principal areas of concern that many in higher education fear may be at the heart of the current agenda. However, the Chief Executive of the QAA and the Director of Programme Review regularly refute the suggestion that the QAA has any wish whatever to introduce a national curriculum for higher education in the UK. Worries still remain that veiled hints about what will happen if the sector does not 'sort itself out' on issues of standards and accountability might lead ultimately to yet tighter control, not only of how programmes are specified, but also what they should contain.

The report did, however, identify seven actions to increase comparability and security and strengthen academic judgement. These, it suggested, would work by:

- ensuring that intended standards are given close attention in the design and approval of programmes;
- increasing the training and development opportunities for internal assessors and examiners;
- providing new fora in which examiners may review their practice and calibrate standards;

- strengthening external examining;
- aligning assessment conventions and benchmarking practice;
- developing the use of archives and other data to evaluate standards;
- providing new opportunities for subject associations and PSB's to participate in the identification and review of standards (HEQC, 1997a).

It also suggested five actions to increase clarity and explicitness by:

- promoting and supporting institutional explicitness about standards;
- agreeing to a range of dimensions against which the intended outcomes of degrees should be plotted;
- delineating a descriptive awards framework;
- providing a typology of programmes and means of profiling their interested outcomes;
- agreeing a UK-wide system of student transcripts (HEQC, 1997a).

These suggestions provide an agenda for action that has been built on for development by the working groups that followed.

Following on from the work of the GSP, the Dearing report in England and the Garrick report in Scotland (DfEE, 1998) proposed that standards should be more clearly articulated at subject level across the sector. This work was explicitly designed to build on the work of the GSP and on that of these institutions and subject groupings that had already made progress in working towards the definition of subject standards.

Thinking was also influenced by the work on benchmarks undertaken in Australia. At this stage, thinking in the HEQC focused on benchmarking at the level of departments in self-selected groups with a more developmentally focused agenda. Despite the reservations of the authors of the report, subject benchmarking groups were nevertheless set up to produce statements of standards that could be used to enable the verification and comparison of standards of student attainment across the UK higher education sector.

As indicated in Chapter 1, in the UK, three pilot benchmarking groups in law, chemistry and history were set up in May 1998 to provide benchmarking information to serve a variety of different purposes. Their express aim was:

> to create national reference points in the form of information that will enable institutions to position their standards and to help the sector work towards establishing threshold standards.
>
> (Jackson, 1998)

Such information, it was indicated, would assist:

- when seeking information about higher education institutions in designing and approving programmes and awards;
- external examiners in verifying and comparing standards;
- professional bodies in their accreditation and review of programmes relating to professional competence;
- students' and employers' provision (QAA, 1998).

The task for each subject benchmark group was to:

- produce statements that represent general expectations about standards at the threshold level, for – in the first instance – the award of honours degrees in the subject (to guide institutions and the registered external examiners);
- identify other relevant comparative information that can guide the quality control and assurance processes of programme design, approval, accreditation, examining and review (QAA, 1998).

## Is the work of benchmarking groups, in addressing the threshold standard, working at the right level?

The threshold standard that the pilot groups were asked to concentrate on was the boundary between achievement and non-achievement of an honours degree – that is, looking at what a student has to do, as a minimum, to achieve a third-class honours degree. Benchmarks were to be concerned with 'satisfactory achievement at an agreed level, rather than the highest performance' (QAA, 1998).

This concentration on what many would regard as near failure (as discussed in Chapter 1) led one subject group (law), having initially tried to create a composite set of criteria against which performance could be measured, to look beyond this bare minimum to the achievement of what they termed a typical student:

> *The nature of a threshold statement:* The threshold statement is a set at the bottom of the third-class honours degree. Few law schools will probably be content simply to describe the achievements of their students at this level. Most will prefer to describe the achievement of the *typical* student, rather than the *minimally acceptable* graduate. Such a modal statement would be set at the 2.1/2.2 boundary.
>
> (Extract from the preliminary draft for consultation of benchmark standards for law degrees in England, Wales and Northern Ireland)

Genuine issues arise around the ways in which such boundaries can be set and demarcated, especially as it is recognized that the ways in which academics define the essence of 'graduateness' are so varied. The GSP pointed the way towards rejection of the idea of a national curriculum for higher education, so subject to groups have deliberately shied away from prescribing the content that programmes of learning in the subject areas should include. Subject/content information, therefore, is useful contextualization rather than central to the process.

In concentrating instead on the core intellectual attributes that graduates at threshold level should, as a minimum achieve, it becomes apparent that definitions of these attributes tend to drift towards generalization. Consider, for example, this list of desirable analytical thinking capabilities for achievement by graduates from a very early draft in one of the pilot areas. Such programmes would involve the enhancement of the ability of students to:

- gather, sift, select, organize and synthesize (often on their own initiative) large quantities of evidence – literary, visual, physical, quantitative or oral;
- discriminate between what is relevant and irrelevant, essential and peripheral, for the task in hand;
- appreciate the range of problems involved in the interpretation of this complicated, ambiguous, conflicting and often incomplete material;
- appreciate the limitations of knowledge and the dangers of oversimplistic explanations of cause and effect;
- understand and evaluate the range of conceptual frameworks and theoretical perspectives through which such material is explained and interpreted;
- arrive at and justify their assessment of the validity and merit of contrasting scholarly opinions and theories;
- question received scholarly wisdom and develop and defend their own opinions.

This list, excellent as it is, it could be argued, could equally well apply to any of three pilot groups. In fact, it came from the historians (an early draft of the report of the History at Universities Defence Group working party, point 10). It demonstrates how difficult it is to be specific about the core intellectual attributes associated with a subject area without lapsing into generalization.

Following the advice of the QAA, the group went on to focus on 'modal standards', producing a statement of the key areas of the discipline, in terms of standards that should be sought and achieved by the typical student. The list of learning outcomes they produced is far more useful, I would argue, than the more generic list originally devised:

- command of a substantial body of historical knowledge;
- the ability to develop and sustain historical arguments in a variety of literary forms;
- an ability to read, analyse and reflect critically and contextually on historical texts;
- an appreciation of the complexity of reconstructing the past, the problematical and varied nature of historical evidence;
- an understanding of the various approaches to understanding, constructing and interpreting the past;
- a command of comparative perspectives, which may utilize the ability to compare the histories of different countries, societies or cultures;
- awareness of continuity and change over extended timespans;
- an understanding of the development of history as a discipline and the awareness of different historical methodologies;
- an ability to design, research and present a sustained and independently conceived piece of historical writing;
- the ability to address historical problems in depth, involving the use of contemporary sources and advanced secondary literature;
- clarity and fluency in written expression;
- clarity and fluency in oral expression;
- the ability to participate in group discussion or other forms of collaborative work;
- competence in specialist skills that are necessary for some areas of historical analysis and understanding, as appropriate.

However, the next stage on from the work of identification of key outcomes is working out how to decide whether or not they have been achieved. The group suggested in its report that not all of these outcomes would necessarily be assessed for the purposes of degree classification, which calls into question the links between the learning outcomes identified and assessment because we have no way of knowing whether or not that which is not assessed is within the students' competence. It also provides no indication of level of achievement – exactly how much understanding would a student need to demonstrate and what constitutes competence in each of the areas?

The two other groups took rather different approaches, and their work is discussed in more detail in Chapters 9 by Haines and 10 by Bell. It is safe to say here however that the establishment of threshold standards for different subject areas is an extremely complicated task, based on somewhat questionable assumptions that subject areas share and agree readily definable views of what these standards might comprise. If, however, the work of the pilot subject groups and those that follow them in the coming years is to be of value, it is worth considering how such standards can be used to enhance and assure the quality of students' learning experiences.

## WHAT ABOUT TRANSFERABLE SKILLS?

Many feel that a good way forward in exploring a baseline threshold standard for graduates is via the domain of generic skills. The original list above derived from the historians would provide a starting point for such work. The draft consultation paper produced by the chemistry Benchmarking Group lists eight transferable skills it considered essential for graduate chemists, including:

- communication skills, covering both oral and written communication;
- problem-solving skills relating to qualitative and quantitative information, extending to situations where evaluations have to be made on the basis of limited information;
- numeracy and computational skills, including such aspects as error analysis, order-of-magnitude estimations, correct use of units and data presentation;
- information-retrieval skills in relation to primary and secondary information sources, including information retrieval by means of on-line computer searches;
- information technology skills, such as word processing and spreadsheet use, data-logging and storage, Internet communication and so on;
- interpersonal skills, relating to the ability to deal with other people and engage in team working;
- time-management and organizational skills, as evidenced by the ability to plan and implement efficient and effective modes of working;
- study skills needed for continuing professional development (Chemistry Benchmarking Group, 1998).

This list maps closely on to the kinds of key skills matrices that many universities have been developing, either individually or as part of the Ability-Based Curriculum or other national initiatives, including those funded by the Fund for the Development of Teaching and Learning (FDTL). Of all the elements of the national benchmarking pilot exercises, the move towards identifying and supporting the development of a range of underpinning graduate skills applicable to all higher education degree programmes seems the most promising.

## CAN BENCHMARKING AND THRESHOLD STANDARDS LEAD TO QUALITY ENHANCEMENT?

Once the subject groups in the 42 subject areas that have been identified in the QAA taxonomy are able to agree what constitutes a taxonomy of appropriate competences and a minimum level of achievement in each, the next questions that need to be asked are 'So what?' and 'Where next?'

Benchmarks, the QAA indicated, were to be concerned with outcomes of programmes or subjects, rather than inputs in terms of teaching (QAA, 1998). However the chemistry Benchmarking Group's consultation document (1998) found it impossible to resist the temptation to specify not only a substantial group of chemistry-related cognitive, practical and transferable skills, but also a substantial body of subject knowledge.

Looking on the benchmarking exercise as positively as possible and regarding it as a means of exploring comparability, as well as a means to help subject committees to explore the dimensions of their standards (and values) as a basis for establishing a degree of understanding about desirable comparability, we can return to the original metaphor on which benchmarking is based and suggest that benchmarks can help us to:

- locate ourselves in relation to other points in the landscape;
- help us to understand the level we have reached;
- help us to compare our elevation with that of others higher or lower than us;
- provide information to others about where we stand;
- help us to work out where we started from;
- measure how far we have travelled;
- identify where we need to go next;
- see the base level for all.

Experience across the UK higher education sector in defining student learning for programmes of study in terms of learning outcomes instead of tutor output has, without doubt, had a positive effect, where it has been undertaken positively and uncynically. Departments that have taken seriously preparation for QAA subject reviews in closely scrutinizing their curriculum description documents have frequently achieved a better definition of what it is they are trying to achieve with their students than had existed previously.

By analogy, it also seems possible that a clear definition of threshold standards of achievement in subject areas may help academics, *inter alia*, to:

- clarify for all stakeholders what skills, attributes and capabilities graduates in each discipline need to achieve to meet a minimum level of achievement;
- enable shortcomings in their own programmes to be identified, with priorities identified for remediation;
- recognize the current status of their programmes against a baseline that enables continuous improvement;
- review teaching programmes to ensure fitness for purpose;
- scrutinize assessment strategies and instruments to ensure that they articulate closely with the profile of skills, attributes and capabilities that have been identified;
- compare the achievements of students in their own universities with those of students in other institutions in the UK, with the aim of attaining the highest possible level, while recognizing the respective missions of different kinds of providers;
- recognize the value of UK higher education programmes of study in their subject areas by comparison with those offered in other institutions internationally, with the potential to target the intended marketing of their programmes most appropriately.

## HOW CAN WE BEST MOVE FORWARD IN OUR OWN INSTITUTIONS?

Quality assurance relies on the ability to:

- measure performance against identified standards;
- identify the extent to which targets are set and achieved;
- evaluate accurately how far evidence matches with assertion;
- highlight areas of good practice for congratulation and dissemination and identify poor performance and areas of weakness that need action.

Threshold standards may be used to assure quality as they provide benchmarks that can help academics to:

- evaluate the performance of their students against that of students in other institutions;
- recognize what potential there is to make positive changes;
- set specific, measurable and realistic targets for improvement and devise prioritized action plans for development.

However, it can be hazardous to assume that benchmarks alone can raise standards in higher education. As well as the information that benchmarks can provide, there must be recognition that unequal resource distribution has a powerful impact on different universities' abilities to achieve high standards, because some are historically more favoured than others in terms of resources and all have separate and specific missions that mitigate against uniform goals for achievement. It is important that performance indicators relate directly to the stated aims and objectives and take account of improvement and enhancement, not just raw output scores as these are divorced from contextualization.

It also needs to be seen that management and organizational issues impact on the quality of curriculum delivery in terms of both resources and systems (take, for example, the added value available to institutions where additional premiums for tutorial support in colleges is paid for). Inevitably, tensions exist between a desire to improve access and widen participation and an imperative to continuously improve standards of achievement. Once again, we cannot simply hope for a nil defect model for curriculum delivery as we might in industrial systems, because our admissions do not, and should not, reject at the input stage any imperfect components (or students as we call them). If we want to encourage non-traditional students from entering university, we need to take risks at admission stage, but a corollary of this is the acceptance of some wastage as a result of failure and drop out.

## CONCLUSIONS

Quality enhancement relies on the ability to:

- recognize opportunities to improve performance;
- develop viable strategies to move forward;
- motivate curriculum providers to change practices where these are seen to be below par;
- promote a culture of transformation in which innovation and change are valued;
- explore alternative approaches to doing things, rather than relying exclusively on 'tried and tested' methods;
- undertake critical self-evaluation that recognizes strengths as well as weaknesses;
- provide opportunities for the sharing and dissemination of good practice;
- stimulate and energize those involved.

If threshold standards are to lead to quality enhancement, the community must avoid fostering a culture in which risk and innovation are seen as excessively dangerous, where conformity and compliance are seen as more important than creativity, where blame and culpability cultures interfere with proactive development and where academic freedom is perceived as being eroded by the influence of external agencies.

Academics involved in the pilot groups need to identify and further refine threshold standards and feel that their work is taken seriously. There must be no railroading and no hidden agendas, whereby particular outcomes or expectations are required. The oft-voiced perceived threat that unless the UK higher education academic community 'sorts itself out', a system for standards will be imposed on it from on high, must never be realized. On innumerable occasions, representatives of the QAA have indicated that they have no wish to introduce a national curriculum for higher education, but many academics are concerned that a failure to achieve what might be seen to be acceptable outcomes in benchmarking pilot groups might be followed by an attempt to impose standards centrally.

It should be said that those with the QAA who are leading what is happening on benchmarking and the articulation of threshold standards recognize both the essential complexity of the task and problems associated with the conceptual framework that underpins the exercise. Nevertheless, they would argue that this should not deter the sector from exploring how to apply the principles in different contexts as, they could argue, it provides unparalleled opportunities for us all to reflect on our practice and outcomes in a way that is likely to benefit all stakeholders in the academic community.

In recognizing this opportunity, I would argue for cautious and incremental further development, building on the consensus (such as it is) that exists within subject communities to continue to explore ways in which to move forward. We must, however ensure that we avoid the worst excesses of the National Curriculum as applied to schools in the UK, in which a programme to drive up pupil performance by the identification of levels of achievement for each Key Stage has resulted in what many describe as an ossification of the content of the curriculum, loss of morale among teachers and a diminution of their ability to be innovative and creative.

## ANNEXE 3 OF THE QAA'S BULLETIN 'THE WAY AHEAD', HIGHER QUALITY, 1 (4), OCTOBER 1998

This noted a number of concerns and proposed a revised model.

## Subject benchmarks

The development of subject benchmark standards was a key recommendation of the Dearing Report, being seen as essential to ensure public and employer confidence that awards, especially at first degree level, were nationally recognized and widely understood. Some concerns about benchmarking have emerged from the consultation. Fears were expressed that they might become tantamount to a national curriculum or, alternatively, that they would be so general as to be meaningless. Some felt that the subject-based approach did not cater adequately for interdisciplinary programmes. There was a concern that if thresholds were set at the level of the pass degree this would lead to a reduction in standards. The Agency commends the following points to the benchmarking groups:

- the prime focus should be on the intellectual attributes associated with successful study of a discipline to degree level, so as to avoid the risk of seeming to dictate a curriculum;
- in professionally related fields institutions should make clear whether or not a programme is intended to meet the requirements of a professional body – elements of a benchmark that are included solely to meet a professional requirement should be identified clearly as such;
- in determining the level at which a benchmark should be set, a group should not be bound to adopt the pass–fail borderline – groups might find it more helpful to express a benchmark at a modal level.

The Agency is encouraged by the initial work of the benchmarking groups established so far. It believes the work should be taken forward by:

- evaluating the utility of the initial benchmarks through trialing;
- extending the benchmarking trials so as to widen the range of subjects against which the benchmarking approach can be refined;
- including within the next tranche at least one inherently interdisciplinary subject, such as business studies;
- establishing an advisory group to advise on benchmarking in multidisciplinary and modular programmes generally;
- drawing on the emerging conclusions of the benchmarking groups to inform the development of a level descriptor for the honours degree level of the qualifications framework.

Subject benchmarking groups will also have a role to play in revising the benchmarks in the light of experience. For each standard subject area there will be a subject overview report at the end of each review cycle. This will draw on all of the reports on outcomes achieved by institutions, give a general picture of the health of the subject area and inform any necessary revision of subject benchmark standards. A senior academic in the field, possibly a chairman of a subject benchmarking group, would be commissioned to prepare a report in conjunction with academic reviewers in that field. In the light of this report a benchmarking group would consider whether any amendment to the benchmarks was required.

## SUMMARY OF RESPONSES TO THE QAA'S CONSULTATION EXERCISE IN RELATION TO SUBJECT BENCHMARKING

### QAA bulletin 'The Way Ahead', Higher Quality, 1 (4), October 1998

### General response

The general tenor of the response to these proposals was mixed. Bodies representing students and employers were strongly supportive. Some professional and statutory bodies questioned the need for such activities in fields in which they already prescribed requirements. Higher education institutions were divided – about 25 per cent expressed support for the principle of benchmarking, many proposed positive suggestions of various kinds, but most were neutral or expressed reservations. A minority were opposed in principle, or highly critical.

### Specific issues

Six main issues emerged from the responses:

- notion of threshold;
- outcomes of the benchmarking process;
- multidisciplinary programmes;
- stifling creativity and diversity;
- timescale;
- subject areas.

***Notion of threshold***

Some feared that emphasis on threshold performance would reduce UK higher education to some kind of lowest common denominator. It was argued that it would be better to seek to define the standard of the typical or 'modal' student – which many regarded as that of a second class honours – rather than concentrating attention on the attributes expected of graduates attaining third-class honours honours or pass degrees. These represented, it was said, only a small and untypical proportion of the total graduate population. Several respondents commented that threshold standards would form no basis for differentiation or comparison. They might help to verify minimum standards, but provided neither a basis for comparison nor enhancement. Many thought that, in practice, the benchmark for standards in UK higher education was that represented by the upper second class honours degree, if not the first-class. If this was acknowledged, there seemed to be little point in concentrating attention on threshold standards. It was also pointed out that in normal usage 'benchmarking' was a term used to denote a means for continuous improvement of quality and standards and there was a danger that the proposals, which some regarded as minimalist, would lead to stasis. Attention was also drawn to the need to ensure that subject benchmarking took proper account of distinctive Scottish dimensions, such as the continued importance of the ordinary degree and the Scottish approach to standard-setting in initial teacher education.

***Outcomes of the benchmarking process***

Some feared that the process would lead, albeit unintentionally, to some kind of 'national curriculum'; others, that it would result in statements of such high-level generality that they would be little use in defining and reviewing standards, and would fail to reassure external stakeholders. There were uncertainties as to how best achieve a balance between generality and specificity.

***Multidisciplinary programmes***

There were concerns as to how the process of subject benchmarking might address the question of standards in programmes of study that were not organized around a single discipline or group of disciplines, such as in multidisciplinary programmes, negotiated study and programmes embodying the term 'studies' in their title. There were doubts also as to the relevance of subject benchmarking to vocational and other practice-based learning.

***Stifling creativity and diversity***

Some respondents feared that the process of subject benchmarking might stifle creativity and diversity by constraining UK higher education to a conventional and outdated approach.

***Timescale***

There was a general consensus that the timescale for undertaking subject benchmarking work was too short. Many respondents observed that the process should proceed more slowly to engender ownership of its outcomes by academics. It was suggested that the initial pilots should be completed, their outcomes disseminated and their utility evaluated before the process was further extended to a significant number of additional subjects. Others expressed the opinion that the first three pilot areas were too few and unrepresentative, and should be supplemented by additional subjects to achieve a sample more typical of the wide range of fields to be found in contemporary UK higher education.

***Subject areas***

Comments about the proposed grouping of subject areas were, in general, inconclusive or contradictory. The only consistent comment was that American Studies should constitute a category separate from English.

## The QAA's response and proposals

The Agency acknowledges reservations about establishing benchmark information of standards at the threshold level only. It recognizes that the task of establishing and verifying standards has two distinct but related aspects:

- providing a means to map the comparability of standards – the definition of, say, typical outcomes;
- assuring stakeholders in higher education that all UK degree holders have attained a defined, minimum level of achievement – threshold standards.

Although both are important, it may be that the most effective way of defining threshold standards is to begin by concentrating on some notion of standards more immediately familiar to academics, students and employers – such as typical or 'modal' standards – and then to approach definitions of thresholds from this basis.

It is important to emphasize that the Agency has never intended that the process of benchmarking should be concerned with the question of curricular content. On the contrary, its focus has consistently been on defining the general intellectual outcomes appropriate to a particular subject. This is why, for example, the Agency has proposed highly aggregated subject groupings. Although there is always the danger that such an approach could lead to overgeneralization, the Agency hopes to guard against this by reminding the benchmarking groups that the purpose of their activities is, in the first instance, to provide materials that can be used with profit by external examiners and academic reviewers in the assurance and verification of quality and standards.

The Agency wants to re-emphasize that the process of subject benchmarking is intended to provide general benchmark information on standards that will be flexible and subject to regular review. Its purpose is not to constrain the development of UK higher education but to provide agreed reference points in terms of which diversity and innovation may be plotted and understood, thus providing clearer and fuller public information.

It is recognized that benchmark information constitutes a key element of the 'new compact for higher education' envisaged by the Dearing Report. Its creation will render standards in higher education far more explicit and publicly accessible, and thus satisfy a major precondition for lessening the burden on institutions of external review. This information will have no value unless it commands the support of the academic community and other interested parties, is of practical value and is fully understood by all those involved. In consequence, the process of its generation cannot be rushed. The Agency is, therefore, reconsidering the timetable for this work and its plans for a phased extension to additional subjects. The Agency is also increasingly persuaded that the benchmarking work and its application to external examining and academic review should be carefully evaluated before it is extended on a large scale. For this reason, an external evaluator has been commissioned to report on the work of the first three benchmarking groups and its application to the processes of external examining and academic review. The Agency is also considering the possibility of adding further subjects to the first three benchmarking groups in the near future, to create a sample of subjects more representative of provision within UK higher education as a whole.

Finally, a meeting has taken place between the Agency and representatives of American studies to discuss how that subject might form part of a benchmarking group in the future.

## REFERENCES

Bell, J (1998) 'Benchmark Standards for Law Degrees in England, Wales and Northern Ireland: Preliminary draft and commentary', Leeds

Chemistry Benchmarking Group (1998) 'General Guidelines for the Academic Review of Bachelors Honours Degree Programmes in Chemistry'

DfEE (1998) 'The Learning Age: A Renaissance for a New Britain' (The Dearing/Garrick Report), HMSO, London

HEQC (1997a) 'Graduate Standards Programme Final Report Volume 1: The Report', HEQC, London

HEQC (1997b) 'Graduate Standards Programme Final Report Volume 2: Supplementary Material', HEQC, London

Jackson, N (1998) 'Understanding standards-based quality assurance part II – nuts and bolts of the "Dearing" policy framework', *Quality Assurance in Education*, **6** (4)

Open University (1994) *MBA Programme B889 Performance Measure and Evaluation Block 2*, pp 31–2, Open University Press, Buckingham

QAA (March 1998) ' A Agenda for Quality,' **1** *Higher Quality*, (3), QAA, Gloucester

QAA (October 1998) 'The Way Ahead' *Higher Quality*, **1** (4), QAA, Gloucester

3

# Benchmarking Theory – A Framework for the Business World as a Context for its Application in Higher Education

*Alex Appleby*

'Benchmarking' is a common enough term, used widely in business today, but what is it and how is it used? This chapter looks at benchmarking as a business improvement tool and its growth over the last 20 years or so. There are many different forms of benchmarking. Each will be introduced and discussed and their position on a benchmarking continuum will be established. The links between benchmarking and Total Quality Management (TQM) cannot be ignored, so this connection will be made, along with the key points made by some of the 'quality gurus'.

My own experience in benchmarking has been gained while working in the field of quality management within industry and through research at the Newcastle Business School (University of Northumbria at Newcastle). At the School we have been working with local businesses in benchmarking since the early 1990s. More recently, through our research work, links have been established with all of the major regional support agencies, including the Government Office (North East), Northern Development Company (NDC), Training and Enterprise Councils (TECs), other universities in the region and professional trade associations. This work has allowed us to demonstrate the usefulness of benchmarking to different types of organization, including manufacturers from many sector industries and a wide range of service organizations, among them the public sector, health, education and professional services, utilities and so on.

The aim of this chapter is to unravel some of the confusion and mystique that surrounds benchmarking, but more importantly to go some way to persuading the reader that it is a powerful approach to measurement and continuous improvement – one that should not be overlooked by managers in the higher education sector.

## DEFINITIONS OF BENCHMARKING

What is benchmarking? In its simplest form, benchmarking was developed by the early craftsmen who would mark out their workbenches to give themselves an easy, repeatable way of cutting materials to a given length. In more recent times, reverse engineering has been considered a precursor to benchmarking. Reverse engineering is when organizations strip down and analyse competitors' products to improve the design, cost – of manufacture and functional performance of their own. The focus is primarily on product attributes rather than process performance and best practice (Ziari and Leonard, 1994). In today's highly competitive world, benchmarking goes beyond simply looking at product attributes. It is seen as a tool that allows organizations to measure and compare themselves with the best companies and work towards improving standards of practice and performance. The Department of Trade and Industry (DTI) publication 'Best Practice Benchmarking – Managing in the 90s' makes the point that benchmarking 'is a technique used by successful companies around the world – in all sectors of business, both manufacturing and service – to help them become as good or better than the best in the world' (DTI, 1994).

Benchmarking can seem a daunting prospect to beginners because when they read about the subject it seems overly complicated and often requires resources that seem disproportionate to the claimed benefits. There are many different benchmarking definitions, and this in itself can be the start of misunderstanding and confusion. Here are just a few:

> Benchmarking is the search for best practices, in any company, in any industry, anywhere in the world.
>
> (Evans and Lindsay, 1996)

> Benchmarking is the search for and implementation of best practices.
>
> (Camp, 1995)

> Benchmarking is the continuous process of measuring products, services and processes against the strongest competitors or those renowned in their field.
>
> (Ziari and Leonard, 1994)

> Benchmarking is two things: setting goals by using objective external standards and learning how much and, perhaps more important, learning how.
>
> (Boxwell, 1994)

> A continuous systematic process for evaluating the products, services and work processes of organizations that are recognized as representing

best practices for the purpose of organizational improvement.

(Spendolini, 1992)

On first reading, each definition appears to emphasize different aspects of the benchmarking process. However, closer examination shows that there is actually little difference between them. Indeed, if we combine each of these interpretations, we reveal the key elements of benchmarking to be a continuous, systematic process, involving internal and external measurement of products services and processes, which leads to better practice and improved performance. According to Camp (1995), arguably the founder of today's interest in benchmarking, the process is useful for establishing realistic improvement goals that are not simply an extrapolation of last year's performance. Goals are also more likely to be accepted by employees if they have been demonstrated as achievable by other organizations (Hackman and Wageman, 1995). However, it is not sufficient in itself to simply establish realistic goals – they must also be accompanied with knowledge of 'how' the goals have been reached, not just 'what' has been achieved.

While many authors appear to agree on the key elements of benchmarking, there is still much confusion among practitioners. This is highlighted by a Coopers and Lybrand (1994) survey of benchmarking practitioners who found a lack of consensus about what was meant by the term. The survey looked at *The Times* 1000 companies (larger organizations) and it was found that benchmarking definitions fell into four categories – competitive analysis, performance comparison, best practice and other. The lack of a common definition may be partly explained by its relative newness as a technique and partly because of the many different types of benchmarking postulated by the many different authors. To help overcome the confusion, Camp (1995) suggests that there should be a widely accepted lexicon of benchmarking that is reviewed and maintained by a nationally recognized quality institution.

## THE LINKS WITH TOTAL QUALITY MANAGEMENT

Many would argue that benchmarking is simply a part of the Total Quality Management (TQM) process of continuous improvement. It is therefore worth spending a little time exploring how and where benchmarking fits into TQM.

Looking back through the history of the quality movement, we can see how the focus has shifted from quality control and quality assurance to a philosophy of prevention and continuous improvement. Today, TQM is a holistic approach that provides awareness of the customer–supplier relationship and continuous improvement effort in all departments and functions. There has been much written on the subject of TQM and the philosophy means many things to different people. Some have used an external customer focus, aiming to ensure employee awareness of customer needs and an elimination of faulty goods or service. Others have focused on the tools of quality to encourage problem solving and a 'right first-time' attitude. Many have used teamwork and empowerment in an effort to develop a 'quality' culture, to improve staff motivation and a never-ending cycle of quality improvement. There are as many approaches to TQM as there are consultants selling their own formula for success. Clear messages of the accelerating success of Japanese industry in the 1950s and 1960s forced the industries of the USA and Western Europe to take note of the TQM movement. Suddenly, the quality gurus were in demand by Western industrialists. Table 3.1 highlights some key names in the field of TQM, along with a brief summary of their particular contributions.

**Table 3.1** *The main messages of the quality gurus*

| *Gurus* | *Main messages* |
|---|---|
| W Edwards Deming | Frequently regarded as the father of TQM, he believed that management was responsible for more than 90 per cent of quality problems. He devised a 14-point plan. Quality improvements were achieved by a continuous reduction in process variation using statistical process control and employee involvement. |
| Joseph Juran | He proposed a general management approach and human elements. He believed that less than 20 per cent of quality problems were due to workers. He defines quality as fitness for use. He recommended a project approach to improvements and suggested that an optimum level of quality exists. |
| Kaoru Ishikawa | His approach pays particular attention to statistical methods, using the seven tools of quality problem-solving. He is also recognized for his contributions to the company-wide quality control movement, involving all staff at all levels in Quality Circles. |
| Genichi Taguchi | He developed the 'quality loss function', concerned with the optimization of products and processes prior to manufacture. His methods can be applied off-line in the design phase or on-line during production. |
| Philip B Crosby | His 14-step approach to quality improvement sets out to achieve conformance to requirements by means of prevention not inspection. Crosby believed that quality is free and zero faults should be the target, rejecting statistically acceptable levels of quality. |

At first sight, the focus of the work of each of these authors may appear quite different to one another, but the underlying messages are similar in many ways. TQM continues to grow and evolve and typically carries many different labels. For example, two programmes in which I have been involved in recent years were called 'Customer Service' and 'Quality Through the Looking Glass'. Whatever the programme is called, many of the following features of TQM are usually present:

- senior management-led;
- customer-oriented;
- recognition of internal and external customer–supplier chains;
- a fundamental shift away from quality control to a prevention philosophy
- 'right first time' standard;
- a *kaizen* approach of continuous improvement;
- everybody involved and trained in quality tools and methods as appropriate;
- staff empowered and encouraged to continuously look for ways to improve their own processes;
- measurement of quality costs.

So where does benchmarking align itself to these issues? I see it as a tool of TQM, part of the process methodology of continuous improvement. Earlier in this chapter I said that benchmarking is a continuous process, involving measurement of products, services and processes, leading to better practice and improved performance. By their very nature, the best results are obtained by involving staff, who are process owners. In this way benchmarking develops individuals, broadens their education and knowledge and helps increase motivation. Organizations that have already started TQM will find benchmarking easier and are more likely to achieve successful outcomes. First, because employees will be more receptive to change. Second, they will be more aware of their processes, and understand the key input and output measures. Third, they will probably already be competent in the use of simple problem-solving tools. Finally, communication channels with other staff – internal customers and suppliers – will be open and receptive.

As a result of the efforts of institutions and agencies such as the DTI, the TECs, Quality Foundations and the vast numbers of consultants and academics, benchmarking has become firmly established in Western businesses in the past decade or so. More recently, the emphasis on Quality Awards has further increased awareness of benchmarking. Criteria for the Malcolm

Baldrige Award (USA), the European Quality Award (EFQM) and the British Quality Award (BQF) all require that organizations demonstrate that they are measuring and comparing themselves internally and externally by means of benchmarking.

## THE THEORY–PRACTICE GAP

Research has shown there to be a gap between the practice and theory of benchmarking, especially with newcomers to the process. There are several reasons for this being the case. First, the focus is often on measurement and comparison, rather than on identifying and then exploiting best practices. Second, benchmarking has its roots in, among other things, competitive data-gathering and performance measurement, rather than operational processes. Practitioners may consider that the most valuable element of benchmarking is the identification of performance gaps. So, while performance gaps may be identified, often the understanding of how to close them is missing. Third, there is often poor prioritization of processes selected for study, which often leads to resources being used on projects unlikely to yield the greatest benefits. In reality, benchmarking often falls short of that prescribed in the textbooks. The Coopers and Lybrand (1994) survey noted that the focus of benchmarking effort was 90 per cent on the creation and analysis of metrics and only 10 per cent on change. In its view, the percentages should be reversed, with 90 per cent of effort being put into the search for, and the implementation of, best practices. Any benchmarking programme that does not yield tangible benefits is clearly neither desirable nor sustainable. The conclusions of such efforts would surely be that benchmarking has only limited value and the organization would probably be discouraged from using it in the future.

## THE BENEFITS OF BENCHMARKING

The messages from the theorists and the practitioners are clear: benchmarking, when carried out correctly, offers many benefits. These are listed below, not in any order of priority, but simply as I have come across them as claimed by different authors and practising organizations:

- identification of best practices from any industry, which can then be incorporated into a company's operations;
- it provides realistic targets, which can be shown to have been achieved by other industries;
- reduction in the resistance to change – employees can see that ideas have actually worked in other organizations;

- technical or innovative ideas can be transferred from other industries;
- a broadening of employees' experience and knowledge base;
- used correctly, it can become a tool of continuous improvement and provide employees with the motivation to change;
- it provides better understanding of the competition and any gap that exists;
- a better understanding of customers' needs, leading to fewer complaints and more satisfied customers;
- a systematic framework for objective analysis and evaluation.

Research work is ongoing in many institutions to quantify and validate these claims. However, such is the logic and practical nature of the benchmarking process, that few could argue that benefits must accrue from structured learning of others' good practice.

## TYPES OF BENCHMARKING

Adding to the confusion on the subject of benchmarking is the apparent plethora of benchmarking types. In part, this is due to the many benchmarking practitioners who are keen to tell of their own 'novel' method. Often a 'new approach' is nothing more than another name for a previously documented form of benchmarking. Camp (1989) proposed the first basic taxonomy of benchmarking types and this has been adopted and adapted by many authors following in his footsteps. He identified four basic types of best practice benchmarking:

1. internal;
2. competitive;
3. functional;
4. generic.

A researcher at Newcastle Business School, Friedewald (1998), has unearthed no less than 16 different, 'unique' types of benchmarking reported in the literature (in addition to Camp's four). He concludes that, on closer inspection, most of them do actually fit into Camp's suggested four types. Friedewald's work goes on to develop yet another approach that is worthy of mention – group benchmarking. Each of the above benchmarking types focuses on identifying, observing, measuring and learning from best practice processes. There are a further two that fall short of best practice benchmarking, and they are metric and diagnostic benchmarking.

To clarify, I will consider each of the above-mentioned types of benchmarking under three broad headings:

- metric benchmarking;
- diagnostic benchmarking;
- process benchmarking.

A simple way to consider how they sit together is to view them along a continuum, as shown in Figure 3.1. As can be seen from the diagram, the level of resources required and difficulty increases as we move from metric benchmarking through to full process benchmarking. At the lower end of the scale, metric benchmarking is unlikely to yield any real ideas for change. At best, it will only help define performance gaps. Moving up the scale, diagnostic benchmarking requires a little more effort, but, in return, will identify areas of strength and weakness for the organization. Done correctly, it will also help prioritize exactly which processes should be targeted for improvement activities. At this stage, process benchmarking can then be started in the knowledge that it is being applied in the areas most likely to yield benefits. Process benchmarking requires considerably more resources, effort and time, but those organizations successfully completing the process will be rewarded with the many benefits already discussed.

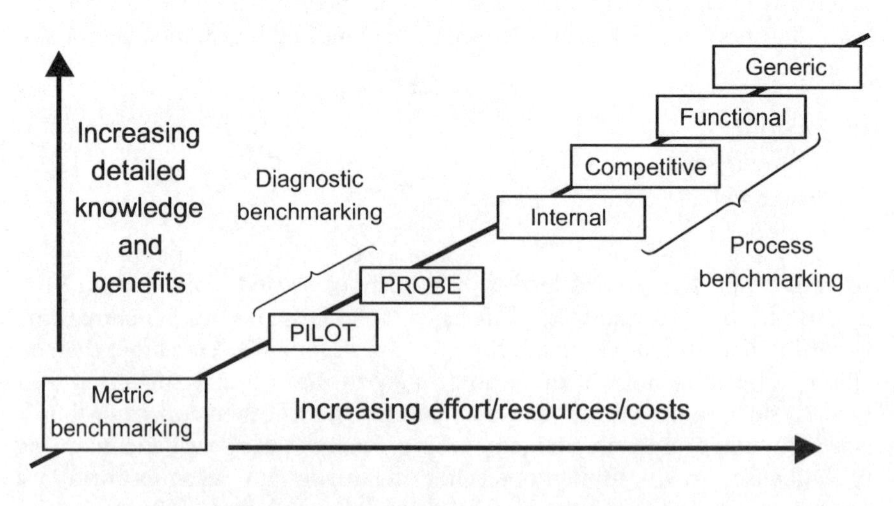


**Figure 3.1** *Positioning of various benchmarking types*

## Metric benchmarking

Many organizations, both manufacturing and service sector-based, use metric benchmarking as a means of direct comparison, both internally and externally, with other organizations. Metrics are performance indicators that are used for comparative measures. Ziari (1998) defines metrics as 'short-term measures which have to be continually calculated and reviewed'. There are many published forms of metric data with which a simple comparison can be drawn. The more obvious examples are in the form of league tables, such as those published by government agencies or public-sector organizations such as the NHS. Another example is the university league tables published by the *Financial Times*. In the manufacturing sector, examples include the publication of 'Manufacturing Winners' by the DTI, *et al.* (1995) or the *Management Today*/Cranfield University's Britain's Best Factories Award.

Internal metric benchmarking is often used by organizations with a number of sites or locations where they use key performance measures as criteria for comparison. Such measures often take the form of costs or manning levels, resources per unit produced, waste or rework levels, inventory turns and so on. They are clearly useful if each site is measured in the same way and then comparisons that are made across the two sites are fair ones. In many cases, however, comparisons are not always like-with-like, especially if they are made externally, with other organizations. Used incorrectly, this form of metric benchmarking can lead to wrong conclusions and if managements' strategic decisions are then based on these outcomes, the results could be detrimental to their businesses. Also, even if the comparisons made are accurate and the results show that a performance gap exists, where does that lead? The next question has to be, 'Well I see the gap, but how do I move forward to close it?' This is the biggest disadvantage of metric benchmarking. It might tell you the 'what' but it does not tell you the 'how'. Camp (1995) makes this point, that gap analysis conducted using such performance measures needs to go further, into a follow-up activity, looking at the processes that produced the results.

## Diagnostic benchmarking

'Made in Europe', a report written by IBM Consultants and the London Business School (Hanson, *et al.*, 1994), paved the way for an approach that measures and compares businesses on world-class scales. The tool used, PROBE (PROmoting Business Excellence), has led the way in what I refer to as diagnostic benchmarking. The hypothesis is that 'the adoption of best practices will result in strong operational performance' (Hanson, *et al.*, 1994). This has been shown to hold true with the high correlation in the results of their survey of over 663 organizations. The tool has been followed by a number of other similar instruments, some of which have been designed for particular industry sectors. One such instrument, developed by researchers at Newcastle Business School, is called PILOT. PILOT is a benchmarking survey tool developed as part of the Regional Competitiveness Project (ref. 196/90/11). It is a three-year project (1996–98), 50 per cent funded by the European Regional Development Fund and led by the Northern Development Company. The tool itself is a questionnaire-based survey instrument based on PROBE that asks around 50 questions on practice and performance measures. On completion of the questionnaire the company is given feedback showing how it compares with all of the other organizations in the database. The feedback, in the form of a scatter plot and quartiles chart, shows its strengths and areas for improvement in a number of key business areas, such as people management, service design, service effectiveness and so on. Best results are obtained when a cross-functional/hierarchical team approach is taken to answer the questions as this ensures an open and honest assessment of the company's performance against the scales. (An example of a PILOT scatterplot is described by David Yarrow in Chapter 8 of this book.)

## Process benchmarking

Here the comparison focuses on key business processes, such as invoicing, order entry, logistics, customer complaints, staff recruitment and so on. The benchmarking process can be carried out in a variety of ways. In its simplest form internal benchmarking promotes in-house comparisons of processes across different departments or functions. Larger organizations with more than one site can make inter-site comparisons. Dale (1994) makes the point that this is a rich source of untapped data for multinational companies. Alternative process benchmarking approaches include:

- competitive benchmarking, which looks to identify practice–performance gaps with direct competitors;
- functional benchmarking, where the comparisons are made with organizations from the same sector, using similar processes;
- generic benchmarking, which looks to identify and transfer innovative 'best practice' from one industry sector to another;
- group benchmarking, where organizations from various sectors come together to benchmark some process of common interest.

The key to process benchmarking is the recognition that most organizations have functions that use similar business processes. Thus, one main advantage of this form of benchmarking is that businesses need not restrict themselves to observing practices in companies that are considered direct competition. They can, and should, widen their benchmarking activities to include partners from different sectors. Any company restricting benchmarking activity to only its own industry may well be 'blinkered', therefore missing an opportunity to observe and learn of innovative new practices from other sectors.

There are, of course, some disadvantages to process benchmarking. First, the nature and complexity of business processes must be clearly understood. This requires careful process mapping and measurement of process metrics. Identifying potential and willing benchmarking partners will also take time, and care is required when observing the processes and activities within partner companies. The nature of the comparison may be complicated and require interpretation and measurement or else performance scales may vary. Finally, a simple transfer of new practices may not always be possible, where there are cultural, demographic or technological barriers.

A structured, systematic approach to process benchmarking will not only identify performance gaps, but will also give understanding of best practices. Many authors recommend the use of a step-by-step process model. Watson (1993) makes the point that many companies starting benchmarking want to create their own 'unique' process. In the research carried out by Friedewald (1998) with Newcastle Business School's Best-Practice-Club we have experienced this same problem. (The Club is run by the School to provide a forum for leading companies in the North East of England to meet with each other in a non-competitive environment, to network and discuss and share best practice.) Many companies at first believe that their problems are unique in nature and therefore must require a unique approach to benchmarking.

There is little doubt that process benchmarking will provide the greatest return of benefits, but it is not without cost. Before benchmarking can take place, the organization must invest time and effort in gaining a detailed understanding of their own processes, otherwise they will learn little in observing others externally. There are many obstacles along the way. Which processes should an organization benchmark?

Often companies have a vast agenda for change. Senior managers and their teams read about examples of best practice or superior performance or they will visit other organizations and come back with a notion that they should try out new ideas in their own workplace. However, care must be taken to ensure that the processes selected for improvement will actually yield the greatest benefits, taking account of costs and timescales for implementation. Organizations often experience problems in simply defining their own processes and need help to process map and identify process measures. Also, they need to identify suitable benchmarking partners willing to share their experiences with them, set up and agree a protocol and carry out the benchmarking study. The masses of new data collected will then need to be analysed and the results understood. Finally, any ideas for change must be communicated and agreed as desirable and workable before implementation can be planned and executed.

***Process classification***

Camp (1995) suggests that there is a need for a standard classification of business processes, just as there are SIC (standard industrial classification) codes for industries. He makes the point that there needs to be some way of quickly getting to a common definition of processes so that benchmarking can begin. According to Camp, the classification system should be process-oriented, take the customer's viewpoint, be simple to use, capable of being explained in everyday language and show all interfaces and relationships. Such a system would provide an effective basis for companies to identify and agree areas of common interest on which they can work together.

***Xerox's approach to process benchmarking***

Probably the most used process model is Xerox's ten-step approach, first reported by Camp (1989). Most other models may have differing numbers of steps, but, essentially, they follow the same Deming cycle of continuous improvement – plan, do, check, act (PDCA). In his book, *Benchmarking for Best Practice*, Ziari (1998) compares no less than 14 different process-based benchmarking methodologies, the majority of which are linked to a continuous improvement (PDCA) or TQM programme. Ziari compares each using a set of seven criteria and concludes that there are many similarities, but that Xerox's method is the more complete approach. The stages in Xerox's model are shown in Figure 3.2.

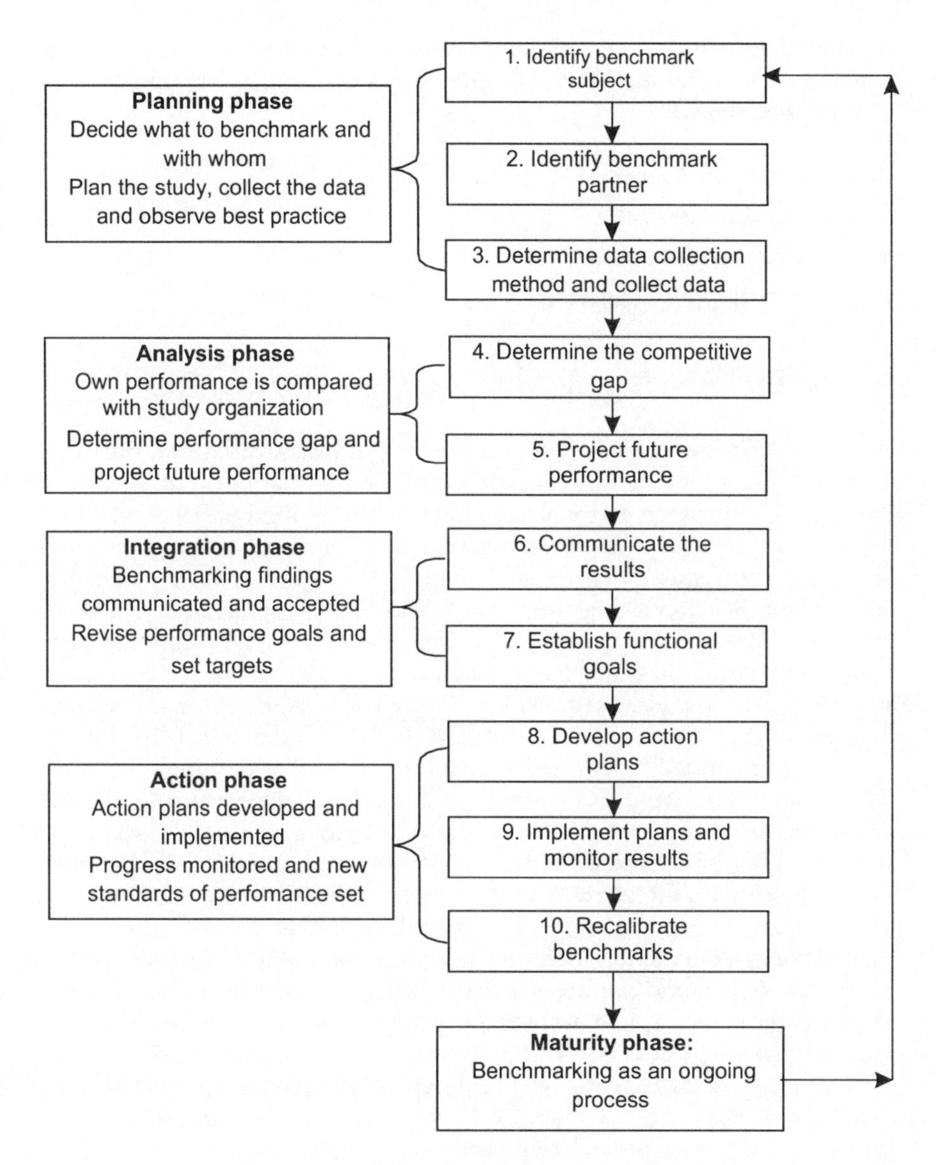


**Figure 3.2** *The formal ten-step benchmarking process (adapted from Camp, 1995)*

Camp (1995) makes the point that there is often a tendency when using a step model to 'jump right in' and determine what to benchmark. Often this can be fatal or, at the very least, cause a lot of backtracking and rework. He recommends that a step zero is used to precede the main activities. He likens it to the quality process of continuous improvement, which comes naturally to organizations that have staff trained in TQM disciplines. This quality process has four steps:

- determine the output;
- identify the customer;
- determine customer requirements;
- develop the specification to meet those requirements.

## MANAGEMENT OF THE BENCHMARKING PROCESS

Most of the benchmarking models focus on the process itself, but the management aspect must not be forgotten. From our experiences at Newcastle Business School, however, we have found that this is often overlooked. Once the decision is made to apply resources to benchmarking activity, it should be closely and regularly reviewed. Camp (1995) makes a clear distinction between the benchmarking process and the role of management, making the point that the 'management process consists of all other activities required to ensure that effective benchmarking investigations are conducted and results are implemented'. There is little point in spending money and time on any investigation if the results are not then used to improve the activity or process initially identified as being capable of benefiting from such action. Camp goes on in his book to outline the management role in some detail, but the main point he makes is that managers should establish a benchmarking programme. He sets out the sequence, saying that they should develop a strategy statement, set expectations, provide management awareness, establish the competences and develop guidelines.

A 'strategy statement' is needed to ensure that employees understand where any benchmarking activity fits in with any existing initiatives. For example, the company may already be working on many other improvement programmes, such as TQM, SPC, self-managed teams, *kaizen* and so on.

Setting expectations is crucial. Employees working on the project must be clear about what they are expected to achieve. Any processes to be benchmarked should be key to the success of the business, and these must be identified and carefully prioritized as target areas. Process performance measures should be established and monitored, with reporting mechanisms to show maintained progress.

Providing management awareness of exactly what benchmarking is and what should be expected is also important. Training should be given so that managers fully understand the resources and the skills required, and to ensure that they give the necessary support.

It is also necessary to establish the competences required. Employees and managers involved in any benchmarking activity require competence in data collection, analysis, library/literature research, quality processes, problem-solving, process mapping, facilitation and project management. It is usually considered vital that the process owner(s) are involved as part of the team because they can provide in-depth knowledge of the process and they are more likely to be willing to take ownership of any improvement activity implementation.

Training in the skills required can be obtained by a variety of means, including short courses, seminars and workshops at universities and colleges. There are also many consultants who offer in-house training, which can then be cascaded down to other employees as the benchmarking becomes a regular activity. Another approach is to become involved in one of the many Best Practice networks that exist these days. Networking and working with other experienced benchmarking practitioners can help newcomers overcome many of the initial problems.The organization needs to develop guidelines to ensure consistency in benchmarking activities. It is usual that such guidelines will cover the protocol required for visits and any legal, ethical or 'sharing-of-information' considerations. Indeed, an agreed protocol on how information can be used or disclosed is an essential requirement, normally one that is insisted on by any company serious about benchmarking. Most benchmarking networks will provide protocol guidelines to new members on acceptance of their application to join.

## CONCLUSION

The aim of this chapter has been to help potential benchmarkers understand some of the theories and practitioner approaches most prevalent today. I hope it has clarified some of the jargon used and goes some way to encouraging you that benchmarking is not something that should be overlooked, another 'flavour of the month' technique. Research carried out by the Newcastle Business School has shown that benchmarking is growing in popularity in all sectors. A survey of 84 prize-winning UK organizations carried out during 1996–97 by Prabhu, Appleby and Riley (1997) has shown that benchmarking for these companies began in 1988, with the greatest interest being shown after 1992. The companies report that today, benchmarking is the most important initiative on their agendas for change in their efforts to achieve best practice. Other research carried out at the Newcastle Business School using the diagnostic benchmarking tool PILOT has developed considerable interest in benchmarking. At the time of writing this chapter, nearly 700 organizations in the North East of England have gone through diagnostic benchmarking as their first step in the process. Early analysis of the research has shown that benchmarking has been recognized as being one of the weakest areas of improvement initiatives in both manufacturing and service organizations, (Appleby and Prabhu, June 1998).

> The single weakest area of practice in the sample overall is the use of benchmarking to seek out and implement the means of improving performance ... the potential for the North East's poor performers to learn from their more advanced neighbours is enormous.
>
> (Prabhu and Yarrow, spring/summer1998)

As a final recommendation, I refer to the report 'Fit for the Future', published by the Confederation of British Industry (CBI), National Manufacturing Council. It states 'The most powerful process any company can adopt, and which delivers immediate, measurable and sustainable productivity improvements, is the transfer of best practice' (CBI, 1997).

## ACKNOWLEDGEMENTS

Friedewald, T (1998; not yet published) Ph.D. research project into the group benchmarking process, University of Northumbria at Newcastle

## REFERENCES

Appleby, A, and Prabhu, V B (June 1998) 'Implementing Best Manufacturing Practice: Are we Winning?', 3rd International Conference on Managing Innovative Manufacturing, University of Nottingham

Boxwell, R (1994) *Benchmarking for Competitive Advantage*, McGraw-Hill, New York

Coopers and Lybrand (1994) *Survey of Benchmarking in the UK: An executive summary*, Coopers and Lybrand, London

Camp, R C (1989) *Benchmarking: The search for industry best practices that lead to superior performance*, ASQC Quality Press, Milwaukee, Wisconsin

Camp, R C (1995) *Benchmarking: Finding and implementing best practices,* ASQC Quality Press, Milwaukee, Wisconsin

CBI (1997) *Fit for the Future: How competitive is British manufacturing?*, CBI, London

Dale, B G (1994) *Managing Quality*, Prentice Hall, Hemel Hempstead

DTI (amended reprint) (1994) *Best Practice Benchmarking: Managing in the 90s*, DTI, London

DTI (1995) *Manufacturing Winners: Creating a World-class manufacturing base in the UK*, DTI, London

Evans, J R, and Lindsay, W M (1996) *The Management and Control of Quality*, 3rd edn, South Western Publishing Company, Cincinatti

Hackman, R, and Wageman, R (1995) 'Total Quality Management: Empirical, conceptual and practical issues', *Administrative Science Quarterly*, **40**, pp 309–42

Hanson, P, Voss, C, Blackmon, K, and Oak, B (1994) 'Made in Europe: A four nations best practice study', IBM Consultancy Group and London Business School, London
Prabhu, V B, Appleby, A, and Riley, M (1997) ' "Best Practice" Organizations in the UK: Preliminary survey results', University of Northumbria, Newcastle
Prabhu, V B, and Yarrow, D J (spring/summer 1998) 'A practice performance study of North East manufacturing and service-sector industry, *Northern Economic Review*, **27**
Spendolini, M (1992) *The Benchmarking Book*, AMACOM, New York
Watson, G (1993) *Strategic Benchmarking: How to rate your company's performance against the world's best*, John Wiley, New York
Ziari, M (1998) *Benchmarking for Best Practice*, Butterworth Heinemann, Oxford
Ziari, M, and Leonard, P (1994) *Practical Benchmarking: The complete guide*, Chapman & Hall, London

4

# Benchmarks and Templates – Some Notes and Queries from a Sceptic

*Sinclair Goodlad*

The object of this chapter is to raise some questions about the need for benchmarks and templates.

In raising some questions about the advisability of the Quality Assurance Agency for Higher Education (QAAHE) pressuring universities into producing 'benchmarks' and 'templates', this chapter notes that, since their inception, universities have valued the free flow of information. It also examines possible reasons for the current concern in England for audit and assessment and points up some problems. These include the danger of cycles of institutional reviews; the operational meaninglessness of credit units; confusion about the specification of programme templates, which can be too vague or too restrictive; concern as to whether or not they are really necessary; the danger of sliding into a national curriculum for higher education; and the danger of pretending to certainty about appropriate teaching methods.

To be against the efficient and effective flow of information to all who need it (students, employers, funding agencies and the providers of higher education themselves) would be nonsense. Freedom of communication has been of their essence since universities began in the Middle Ages. They were founded by guilds of foreign scholars who banded together when attending the medieval schools known as *studia generalia,* which were recognized places of study open without restriction to students from all parts of Europe. Indeed, in Bologna at the end of the twelfth century, there were four 'universities' of scholars attending the *studium generale* there. If the universities felt restricted, they moved. Hastings Rashdall, for example, describes how in the Dispersion of 1229 the masters and scholars of the University of Paris, resenting injustices meted to them by the ecclesiastical authorities, simply left Paris for nearly two years (Rashdall, 1936). Oxford profited from this migration, and, similarly, Cambridge began as a university in 1209 when some disaffected scholars moved there from Oxford. No doubt they (or, rather, their faculty and students) will migrate again if they become threatened; but they should not be put into a situation that requires this. Long before the advent of telecommunications or cheap and easy travel (or, for that matter, the invention of 'benchmarks' and 'templates'), and for hundreds of years since, universities have attracted to themselves people who make it their business to find out what they do.

There already exist admirable procedures by which universities communicate to all and sundry what they are and what they do. Why is it all so different now? Why is it that what appears at first glance to be a way of improving communication actually threatens to destroy the very institutions that it is designed to support?

The problem arises when the methods by which universities communicate become locked into some huge, centralized, system that purports to be about 'quality' – and who dares to say that they are against 'quality'?! The dividing line between advice and consent, between flexibility and tyranny, between facilitation and control, is a narrow one that is in grave danger of being crossed – particularly if the threat of withholding funding is used as an instrument to enforce conformity. (This is already an idea in play – see NCIHE, 1997, Recommendation 24; QAAHE, March 1998, Part I, paragraph 24.)

To understand the gravity of a situation in which England seems in danger of destroying some of its most revered institutions, it is necessary to see current developments in context. In England, the first step along a dangerous path towards State control of universities was taken in the Treasury Minute of 1919 that established the University Grants Committee (UGC; see Wolfenden, 1972; Carswell, 1985; Shattock, 1994). However, for many years, a remarkable system operated in which universities enjoyed considerable autonomy in ordering their affairs in exchange for responsible and accountable use of public funds. Some members of the UGC were from industry and commerce, but the majority were university professors, not administrators – no university vice-chancellor, secretary, registrar could be a member. The system, which attracted envious attention from abroad, worked well until universities started to cater for very large numbers of students. There are now, for example, more students taking university degrees in Church Associated Colleges of Higher Education (70,000+) than there were university students in the whole of Great Britain in 1951. With the incorporation in 1992 of the former polytechnics as universities, the proportion of the 18–24-year-olds receiving university education moved up to a third of the total, with many more mature students than previously coming forward for higher education.

The cost of all this to the public purse grew considerably. Accordingly, the National Committee of Inquiry into Higher Education was appointed by the Conservative government on 10 May 1996 to make recommendations on how the purposes, shape, structure, size and funding of higher education, including support for students, should develop to meet the needs of the United Kingdom over the next 20 years. The Committee was asked to report in the summer of 1997, neatly taking the gritty issue of the funding of students out of the 1997 election (no doubt to the relief of all parties).

Many people believed that the issue of student funding was what 'The Dearing Committee' was all about. However, the Committee's report (NCIHE, 1997) also dealt with other matters, including qualifications and standards. Although acknowledging that 'the systems in the United Kingdom for assuring the quality of higher education are among the most rigorous in the world' (NCIHE, 1997), the Committee devoted a complete chapter of its report (Chapter 10) to these matters, recommending (Recommendation 22, page 151) that 'the Government, the representative bodies, the Quality Assurance Agency, other awarding bodies and the organizations which oversee them, should endorse immediately the framework for higher education that we have proposed'. The present Labour Government's Department for Education and Employment (DfEE) eagerly endorsed the Dearing Committee's observations on quality and standards in 'The Learning Age: Higher education for the 21st century' (DfEE, 1998) and in its white paper 'The Learning Age: A renaissance for a new Britain' (DfEE, February 1998).

That issues of quality should arise is not in itself remarkable – debate about quality has been taking place worldwide for some years (see, for example, Craft, 1992; de Rudder, 1994; Frederiks, *et al*, 1994; Neave, February 1994). Much of the debate concentrates on the form rather than the content of university education. Huge quantities of people's time and effort has been devoted to quality assurance mechanisms, often with no reference to what exactly is to be assured. One early document (HEQC, June 1993) asked universities to provide documents exemplifying policies and practices relating to quality assurance. These, it suggested, might include undergraduate and admissions access policies; equal opportunities; credit accumulation and transfer; modularization; new course or programme design and approval; programme or course reviews; departmental reviews; resource allocation for courses and programmes; validation of other institutions' courses; franchise arrangements for courses/programmes taught off campus; postgraduate students' admission; students' work and progress; research students' supervision; student assessment and degree classification; examination appeals; external examiners' appointments; external examiners' reports; academic staff appointment procedures; academic staff probation; staff development and training; academic staff appraisal; academic staff promotion criteria; teaching and learning innovation; academic standards; interaction with accrediting bodies, such as BTEC, and professional organizations; securing students' views on academic matters; securing graduates' views on academic matters; securing employers' views on academic matters; Enterprise in Higher Education projects.

Being concerned with quality assurance, rather than quality control, most of these items concentrate on administrative procedures rather than on the stuff of the academic enterprise – its intellectual and academic content. What was not clear was how these procedures, without further exegesis of how they operated, could have any bearing whatever on the quality of what universities do. Indeed, some of the apparently approved items (such as modularization and Enterprise in Higher Education projects) seemed to signify the first signs of what could become a new orthodoxy. All this made for much work for audit teams and even more for universities that enjoyed (or endured) 'visitations' (a word previously used mainly in connection with the Plague).

Having decided that the provision of quality assurance documentation had not been very illuminating about what quality actually was, the Higher Education Funding Council: England (HEFCE) issued a further document (HEFCE, July 1993) concerning the actual assessment of the quality of education. To aid institutions in their self-assessments, the HEFCE offered a 'template' with six sections corresponding to the structure then used by the Council to give institutions feedback following an assessment visit. The sections were aims and curricula; students – nature of intake, support systems and progression; the quality of teaching and students' achievements and progress; staff and staff development; resources; academic management and quality control. Each section referred to 'evidence' that the Council was seeking, yet there was no indication at all of how this 'evidence' was to be judged!

Even the distillation of these matters into four basic questions avoided any indication of what 'quality' could conceivably be. The document indicated that an assessor would seek to answer the following four questions.

- Is there evidence of a systematic, self-critical approach within which the institution has: evaluated relevant issues; demonstrated, as far as possible, the quality of provision in the subject; and developed plans for the future?
- If yes, has the institution claiming excellence made a prima-facie case that it is providing excellent quality education in the subject? ... If no, are there grounds for concern that quality may be at risk? ...
- What are the main issues arising from analysis?

(The ellipses indicate that text, mainly unilluminating gloss, has been left out in my reproduction of the questions.)

The Higher Education Funding Councils of England and Wales helpfully commissioned a study of their own procedures, which was carried out by the Centre for Higher Education Studies of the University of London Institute of Education (see Barnett and Parry, 1994). This report rightly called for clarification of the criteria and procedures being adopted by teams visiting universities. For example, the report questioned the heavy focus on observation of teaching performance in the procedures used by the teams that visit universities, pointing out that procedures designed to foster responsibility among students for their own learning (such as problem-based or resource-based curricula) might be undervalued using this method of observation. In its recommendations, the report stressed that quality of learning should be the focus of concern.

Although all the fuss about the administrative shell of education had been causing a huge amount of time-consuming (and thus expensive) hassle to universities, it was only when (no doubt well-meaning) attention was paid to 'the quality of learning' and associated programmes of study that dangerous interference with the autonomy of universities intensified. Such interference is central to the document 'An agenda for quality' that formed the bulk of the March 1998 Bulletin of the Quality Assurance Agency for Higher Education (QAAHE). Because the QAAHE is the agency that looks set fair to cause most havoc in universities, and because 'benchmarks' and 'templates' are part of what it will be judging in the interests of 'quality', most of my notes and queries will refer to that document.

The first problem concerns the danger of cycles of institutional reviews – a procedure inherited from the HEFCE's Teaching Quality Assessments (QAAHE, March 1998). If the information to be scrutinized in a 'visitation' includes 'benchmarks' or 'templates' like those offered an Annexe A of the document, and if the QAAHE disapproves, an institution may be blighted by a possibly unfair or misguided judgement and suffer diminished funding for several years to come. (A similar problem, of course, vitiates an equally cumbersome procedure – the research assessment exercise.)

Second, there is a fundamental problem involved in developing the qualifications framework in the UK (QAAHE, March 1998). That is that, for the purposes of quality assurance or control, credit units are almost completely meaningless. In the huge edifices that are being constructed, it is taken that one credit represents ten hours of student study. Fine, but how does one account for the effectiveness and efficiency with which any given student uses his or her time? It is certainly very useful to have in mind a *notional* (note emphasis) amount of study required for a credit – if only to protect students from overly eager faculties burying them in work. At my own institution, for example, an undergraduate academic year represents a notional 1200 hours of work – 40 hours per week for 30 weeks, inclusive of lectures, laboratory work, seminars, tutorials, and private study. Only by judging what a student of modest ability could do in that time is it possible to decide on, for example, the length of reading lists or the number and complexity of problem sheets. The word 'notional' is used because such structuring can only be very loose – the time that a lower second class honours sort of student (whatever that might be) would need to spend to actually achieve a lower second class honours degree. 'Third class' students would have to run faster to keep up; 'first class' students would burn through comparable material in under 1200 hours and would undertake more challenging work, and, no doubt (because of interest, ability, even excellence of previous preparation), spend more than this notional quantum of time, progressing further. Although notional hours of study (and credits based on them) can give a very rough idea of how much time and attention should be devoted to what, the assigning of credit units tells the enquirer nothing about the standard of work achieved by the students. The Dearing Committee clearly recognizeses this when stating, 'It is fundamental to our approach that awards should be based on achievement rather than on the length of study required' (NCIHE, 1997). It is nonsense to use listings of credit units as anything but the vaguest intimation of what degree courses are all about.

Third, the confusion about the specification of programme templates (QAAHE, March 1998) is so elemental and so profound as to verge on naiveté. The problem resides in the degree of specificity involved. If templates are too specific, they are likely to cramp a university's style. Not only is there a danger (acknowledged by the QAAHE) of stifling innovation, but more particularly of inviting litigation. The time between, say, a third-year university course being created and students sitting examinations may be anything up to five years – one year (at least) for internal planning and validation by university and departmental committees; one year of being advertised in the university's prospectus; three years of learning and teaching before the student can check whether or not the 'outcomes' were what he or she might have been led to expect. If a student took a university to court, it might be difficult for the university to get away with a defence claiming that the lack of achievement was the student's fault.

If templates are too vague, like the illustrative example in Annexe A of the document, they are no more use (probably less) than the information commonly given in a university prospectus and calendar. In the example given, on sport, coaching and exercise science, there is liberal use of trendy phrases circulating (particularly those from the professional skills world) but a dismal failure in terms of being in any way illuminating. For example, in section 6 on 'What a graduate should know and be able to do on completion of the programme', under 'Knowledge and understanding in the context of the subject', there is listed 'The social and political context of sport, coaching and exercise'. Yet in section number 8 listing 'Main subjects, levels, credits and qualifications', there appear to be no modules at all touching on these matters. What, then, does the word 'understanding' mean here? Those of us who have been writhing for the last ten years on the Procrustean bed of writing objectives in the ways recommended by Rowntree (1988), for example, have learned to handle the word 'understanding' with caution. What would students actually do to demonstrate their 'understanding' of 'the social and political context of sport, coaching and exercise'? Describe three occasions on which the Olympic Games have been disrupted by political action and suggest what measures could have been taken by the IOC to prevent the disruption? Analyse and explain the nature of the debate leading to the change in the off-side rule in football? List and justify a set of rules for a suburban tennis club that seeks to avoid discrimination on the grounds of race, class, creed, or colour? Without some such detail, anyone studying the 'template' can have no idea how (if at all) the subject is to be treated.

The section on cognitive skills is equally unilluminating. What are we to make of 'Synthesize information/data from a variety of sources'? It is necessary to do this even to buy a palatable and affordable ice-cream at the seaside.

The general/transferable skills (including key skills) are equally vague. What, for example, would a prospective employer glean from reading that a job applicant had acquired 'Numerical skills appropriate to the scientist'? What skills? What sort of scientist? What is the meaning of 'appropriate'?

The fourth problem is a related one – what is the rationale for the subject grouping? The QAAHE reveals that its agreed starting point was the Dearing suggestion of 40, but they acknowledge that 'An approach is needed that can allow meaningful statements particular to the identified subject area to be made, accommodate innovation and development, and reflect the diversity of UK higher education, whilst avoiding the risk of curricular prescription' (QAAHE, March 1998). The exercise is doomed to inevitable failure. If the 'templates' are too vague and woolly (like the one in the QAAHE's Annexe A discussed above) they offer little useful information to intending students, other academic institutions or employers. If they go into the level of detail required for a statement of objectives to be meaningful, they will be the raw materials for the degree – and too cumbersome for wide circulation.

The dilemma points to the fifth problem, the basic question 'Are 'benchmarks' and 'templates' really necessary?' If a student is thinking about taking a degree, he or she no doubt starts by deciding what broad subject area to go into. Subsequent questions no doubt relate to the location of the university (travel distance from home, cost of accommodation, range of student societies, ambience and so on) and the likely ease or difficulty of gaining admission (in terms of A level grades required of entrants). The university's prospectus (and student union's 'alternative prospectus') will supply the former type of information; the UCAS booklet contains the latter. The concerned and diligent student may then need to do a bit of further investigation – such as speaking to someone who has recently attended the course/university, attending an open day, asking to see past examination papers, project reports and so forth. Reading a 'template', such as the specimen offered by the QAAHE, can be only a range-finding shot.

Likewise, employers must take their own responsibility for selecting the types of employees they want; they really cannot expect universities to do their selecting for them. Long ago, employers saw through the fiction that all universities are alike. The most shrewd among them will also have realized that the phrase 'graduateness' is fatuous nonsense – only when the idea is grounded in the detail of a particular subject can it have any meaning. Likewise, discerning employers will know that in some universities (such as research intensive universities), the natures of the disciplines are changing all the time to reflect the movement of research, and that the syllabus in the calendar is much less interesting than the type of individual or group project the student has done. If their companies are highly specialized, they will almost certainly know from which stables the racehorses they want are likely to come – 'templates' are not likely to help. Some of the most exciting new areas (such as information systems engineering and engineering in medicine) are not even included in the QAAHE list of 'Suggested subject areas for QAA work on benchmarking' (QAAHE, March 1998).

The sixth problem is that of the danger of sliding into a national curriculum for higher education. While a national curriculum may be defensible for junior schooling, and possibly even for GCE A level (to reduce, for example, the problems raised by there being 40 different mathematics A level syllabuses), it would spell death to university work. University study is not, nor ever could be, defined primarily in terms of its subject matter. Chemistry abstracts, for example, appear in such profusion that it is obvious to even the most casual observer that the discipline of 'chemistry' as taught for a university first degree can be but only a minute selection of all that could possibly be learned. Academic disciplines are intellectual procedures for focusing thought, accelerating learning, searching for significance. They are not so much taught as experienced – in that a student should be able to get a feel for how an historian thinks or how an experimental scientists works, by even a short, well-designed course. (The provision of humanities options for students of science, technology and medicine at Imperial College is, for example, based on this perception.) Subject 'benchmarking' groups would have to steer between the Scylla of overprescription of content and the Charybdis of listing only transferable skills. The chances of shipwreck are so high that they should not even attempt to embark on the voyage.

The seventh problem concerns the danger of pretending to certainty about appropriate teaching methods. I have argued at length elsewhere (Goodlad, 1995) that the tentativeness of educational research and the uncertainty implicit in our quest for knowledge (in universities an 'authoritative uncertainty' because it is based on profound scholarship), may make us aware of what not to do. Only preferences based on a personal philosophy can lead us to deem one idea or intellectual process of greater 'quality' than another. The sources of attachment and inspiration for learners are many, various and complicated, as Marjorie Reeves has strongly demonstrated (Reeves, 1988). Some students in some circumstances may work best on their own in resource-based learning or project work; others may take inspiration from seeing and hearing a subject expert thinking their way through a problem – even if this is more of the nature of an interior monologue by the lecturer than clear exposition. Again, interactive methods of teaching (currently much in vogue) can disguise a fundamentally limited, limiting and repressive curriculum, whereas straight lectures, if well-designed, can produce much more intellectual involvement than 'buzz groups', 'pyramids' and so forth. (I have set out elsewhere, for example, Goodlad, 1996, 18 strategies for making a technical lecture interesting and involving.) 'Benchmarks' and 'templates' cannot and should not attempt to prescribe content or procedures. 'Ignition' only occurs if the mixture of students, teachers, subject matter and modes of learning and teaching are in harmony.

I have not touched on other possible dangers of 'templates' and 'benchmarking' (such as that of 'dumbing down' by defining subjects in terms of minimal achievements with the associated danger of teaching to the syllabus) or of the huge cost of what is proposed by the QAAHE. Nor have I uttered Cassandra-like warnings of the coming doom of already vibrant and highly successful institutions being buried in paperwork or strangled in red tape designed primarily to bind the feet of a few villains. What I do detect, and especially in the nonsense that is talked about 'graduateness', is a throw-back to Plato's *Republic* with its quest for forms or ideals, valid for all time and offering truths for the philosopher/ruler, and leading to the totalitarian tendency that some (for example, R H S Crossman and Karl Popper) saw as latent in Plato.

Universities are complicated organizations; they can only be appreciated in complicated ways – usually involving detail that no quality control system can touch. In their relationships with those who pay for education and those who employ their students, universities must rely on trust, as they do with those whom they teach. Certainly let us all share best practice in trying to do what we do as well as we possibly can (most people I meet in universities already do this). Certainly, too, let us open ourselves to more contact with people from outside if that is necessary. But just as there is no 'ideal' (in Plato's sense) of '*the* university', so there is no ideal in any one of the multifarious subjects studied and taught in universities.

Plato is dead: let us bury him.

## REFERENCES

Barnett, R, Parry, G, Cox, R, Loder, C, and Williams, G ( 1994 ) 'A Review and an Evaluation Report for the Higher Education Funding Councils for England and Wales', Centre for Higher Education Studies, Institute of Education, University of London

Carswell, J (1985) *Government and the Universities 1960–1980*, Cambridge University Press, Cambridge

Cave, M, Hanney, S, Kogan, M, and Trevett, G (1988) *The Use of Performance Indicators in Higher Education: A critical analysis of developing practice*, Jessica Kingsley, London

Craft, A Z (ed) (1992) *Quality Assurance in Higher Education*, Falmer Press, London

De Rudder, H (1994) 'The quality issue in German higher education', *European Journal of Education*, **29** (2), pp 201–19

DfEE (1998)'The Learning Age: Higher education for the 21st century', response to the Dearing Committee, HMSO, London

DfEE (February 1998) 'The Learning Age: A renaissance for a new Britain', presented to Parliament by the Secretary of State for Education and Employment by Command of Her Majesty, Cm 3790, HMSO, London

Frederiks, M M H (1994) 'Effects of quality assessment in Dutch Higher Education', Westerheijden, D F, and *European Journal of Higher Education*, Weusthof, P.J.M.29.2. pp181–99

Goodlad, S (1995) *The Quest for Quality: Sixteen forms of heresy in Higher Education*, SRHE and Open University Press, Buckingham

Goodlad, S (1996) *Speaking Technically: A handbook for scientists, engineers, and physicians on how to improve technical presentations*, Imperial College Press, London

HEFCE (July 1993) 'Description of the template used in June 1993 to analyse the self-assessments and claims for excellence received in May 1993', Quality Assessment Committee, HEFCE, Bristol

HEQC (June 1993) 'Request for Briefing Documentation', HEQC, Division of Quality Audit, Birmingham

QAAHE (March 1998) 'An Agenda for Quality', *Higher Quality* (bulletin of the Quality Assurance Agency for Higher Education), pp 1–23

NCIHE (1997) 'Higher Education and the Learning Society', Report of the National Committee of Inquiry into Higher Education, The Dearing Committee (Ref NCIHE/97/850), HMSO, Norwich

Neave, G (February 1994) 'The politics of quality: Development in Higher Education in Western Europe 1992–1994', *European Journal of Higher Education*, pp 115–34

Rashdall, H (1936) in *The Universities of Europe in the Middle Ages*, eds M Powicke and A B Emden, Vol. I, Clarendon Press, Oxford

Reeves, M (1988) *The Crisis in Higher Education: Competence, delight, and the common good*, SRHE and Open University Press, Milton Keynes

Rowntree, D (1988) *Educational Technology in Curriculum Development*, Paul Chapman Publishing, London

Shattock, M (1994) *The UGC and the Management of British Universities*, SRHE and Open University Press, Buckingham

Wolfenden, J (1972) 'Great Britain' in *Higher Education: From autonomy to systems*, ed J A Perkins, International Council for Educational Development, New York

# Part II

## Operational Issues for Benchmarking and Threshold Standards in Higher Education

# 5

# Describing Higher Education – Some Conflicts and Conclusions

*Jenny Moon*

This chapter concerns a number of topical ideas in higher education – learning outcomes, generic level descriptors, thresholds, benchmarks and standards – and the relationship of these to another topical issue – the argument for more reflective and autonomous learning. It is the story of an intellectual journey, one that has woven its way around these ideas that centre on what we might see as the aims and nature of higher education in the late 1990s. The issues in question are not separate items in a list, but, rather, they interrelate and, in some cases, conflict in ways that must be resolved if we are to understand how to retain a coherent approach to higher education. The timespan of the intellectual journey has nearly reached five years, and it stretches across work in three separate projects, each of which has contributed to the thinking from its own stance. The first project involved UK-wide professional development work in the health field, the second was a credit development project based in Wales and the third is in teaching and learning support work in a traditional university.

While my ideas on reflection and autonomy in learning had been evolving in the work on professional development, the start of conscious deliberation on these issues began in a credit development project in Wales – the Higher Education Credit Initiative Wales, funded by the Department of Education and Employment (DfEE). A credit system generally requires that learning is given a currency value and, in current thinking, this is in terms of the achievement of learning outcomes that are ascribed to specific higher education levels (Moon, December 1995a, b and 1995 c); HECIW, 1996). My task on the project was to develop a set of guidelines for writing learning outcomes for higher education modules and, similarly, develop a set of generic level descriptors that would be both acceptable to and agreed by all of the higher education institutions in Wales. Both parts of the project involved working with higher education staff across Wales and, in the case of the level descriptors, another 33 institutions in the South East England Credit Consortium (SEEC).

At the time, the pressure to get through the work before the funding ended meant that, while there was no problem in justifying levels and learning outcomes in terms of their significance for a credit system, I had no time to consider their more general implications for practice in teaching and learning. I was aware of the mixed reactions of teaching staff to levels and learning outcomes from the many workshops that were involved in the development work. In terms of learning outcomes, there was a feeling that this initiative might represent the surreptitious introduction of national vocational qualifications. These suspicions were evident later in the staff development workshops aimed at cascading the use of learning outcomes throughout institutions. There was frequently an argument that learning outcomes 'pin down' teaching and learning too much. In what now seems a significant, but not a fully considered reaction, I would counter this by pointing out that learning outcomes are written at minimum – or 'just pass' standard. Because of this fact, they do not pin down learning too much. At the time, I did not see the importance of learning outcomes being set at minimum, but I return to this later.

The development of level descriptors involved senior higher education staff from a wide range of disciplines in meetings in Wales and London. Initially there was much scepticism about the possibility of drawing from the variety of higher education disciplines, a set of generic descriptors that were both sufficiently general and meaningful to be of use to all disciplines in institutions. I can recall the first London session when the only way to achieve our goal seemed to be a three-dimensional DNA look-alike. In the processes of writing, revision, arguing and then agreeing, the descriptors gradually emerged – fortunately in two dimensions.

One of the features of the level descriptors that had been written into the project brief was that they should be set at the threshold of each level. It was assumed that this was essential in order that they could match the learning outcomes for modules and facilitate credit. We were aware that the descriptors were meant to be at threshold level and every so often someone would put out a reminder of this across the table. The reminders often came from the HEQC staff who attended many of the workshops. They were particularly interested in thresholds because investigation of the possibility of defining threshold standards was a remit in the Graduate Standards Programme (HEQC, 1997).

I vividly remember the day on the train, travelling back from discussions on level descriptions in London, when I finally admitted to myself that the newly hatched set of generic level descriptors in my bag were not written at threshold, but were more like average expectations of student performance.

The question was, did it matter for the credit development work? After some discussion, we decided that it did not matter so long as learning outcomes were written at minimum acceptable standard for modules. Level descriptors that are appropriate for all disciplines are inevitably imprecise and at the time I felt that this inevitable imprecision was the main reason for our having failed to define threshold descriptors.

To finish this part of the story, the final report of the Graduate Standards Programme was published with the opinion of the HEQC from its research and observations that it is not possible to describe standards at threshold level (HEQC, 1997). I pick up this thread of the story later.

A new part of the story opens. The credit framework was launched in Wales with agreement of the guidelines for learning outcomes for modules and fair agreement on the generic level descriptors (HECIW, 1996). The funding for the credit project came to an end. In a new post in the learning support field in a traditional university, I was confronted with the task of facilitating the implementation of learning outcomes, but this time they could not be 'sold' on the basis of their role in credit developments. In this world staff did not see credit as a relevant issue. The new situation prompted some serious consideration of the implications of using learning outcomes for the teaching and learning process.

In the environment of a traditional institution, there is a faith that student learning goes beyond the 'given' in the curriculum's aims or objectives, that students at levels 2 and 3 become excited about their disciplines and learn for learning's sake, following topics because they are interested in them. It is easy to view the use of learning outcomes as opposing the expression of these values because they can appear to make learning simplistic, and, indeed, it is argued that the existence of outcomes enables students to aim for the minimum. On this basis it is paradoxical to note that the content of the generic level descriptors, the complementary development to the learning outcomes work, actually specifies these more sophisticated qualities of learning for level 3. For example, the level 3 descriptor suggests that the student should function in 'complex and unpredictable contexts', should be able to 'design novel solutions' in terms of synthesis and creativity, and should be manager of their own learning.

Personally I do not feel convinced that students will generally use learning outcomes as a guide to 'getting by' on the minimum – being strategic (Keane, 1997, and Moon, 1997). I think that some students will always choose just to scrape by while others are more engaged with their study. If a few more make the former choice now, it is likely to be related to their busy working lives in front of or behind the local bars. It seems fair and reasonable in an educational establishment to specify on what basis a pass or a fail is judged.

In the new learning support role, I had reading to do on student learning and in particular on the research that originally emanated from the

Gothenberg school in the late 1970s (such as Marton, Hounsell and Entwistle, 1997). The reading began to focus on the topic of reflection because this had long been of interest that had its origins in the context of learning in professional development situations. Reflection appears to play a substantial, but relatively unexplored, part in deep learning and, eventually, explorations of the role of reflection in student learning turned into major study and the manuscript of a book (Moon, 1999).

This meant that at the same time as I was promoting the use of learning outcomes to describe learning, I was also propounding enthusiasm for the greater role of reflective activity in learning. The aim of increasing the role of reflection in learning often, though not necessarily always, concerns the encouragement of students to come to use reflection with facility and regularity to enhance and deepen their learning. In more general terms, I view reflection as a means of increasing self-awareness in learning, enabling students to speak 'with their own voices' (Belenky, Clinchy, Goldberger and Tarule, 1986, and Barnett, 1997). However, the encouragement of these less tangible qualities and results of learning began to appear to oppose the apparent idea of learning outcomes as the specification of the results of learning in advance of the learning process itself.

A conflict was emerging. Which camp did I belong to? In some senses I was a supporter of precision and clarity in learning, with the learner being well informed about the nature of the learning that is expected of them and with clearly written learning outcomes for modules. In another sense I supported the notion of learning as a journey, as exploration, as unpredictable, an activity that is best directed by learners themselves, with guidance and facilitation from others and not principally as an activity directed by others.

I began to see this conflict in more general terms too. I came to see reflection, as I have described it above, as largely symbolizing development of divergent forms of thinking. Reflection is essentially a private process that can only be guided by another, and therefore learning with a greater reflective content is less under the control of others and less likely to conform to the ends prescribed by others. In contrast, the use of learning outcomes can be construed as influence towards convergence in learning, the attempt to control the results of learning. In this way I viewed the conflict between reflection in learning and the use of learning outcomes as one that could be described in terms of a tension between convergent and divergent influences in higher education.

Perhaps this is an aside, but I noticed that the tension between what might be called divergent and convergent forces also emerges in other places in higher education. I see the following as examples. Dearing (NCIHE, 1997) calls for depth and breadth in the higher education curriculum. He also calls for the celebration of diversity in higher education, but, at the same time, a concern for standards. We modularize to produce choice for learners and then become concerned with the lack of integration of programmes. Laurillard's 'paradox' is a further example of the same struggle. She suggests that while we want students to learn the same thing, we want them at the same time to make their learning their own (Laurillard, 1993).

I needed to see how I could favour both reflection and the use of learning outcomes. The underlying question in this regard seemed to be whether or not the influences towards convergence as illustrated by the use of learning outcomes can co-exist with the encouragement towards independent thinking and divergence in learning as epitomized by reflection.

I began to consider more closely the implications of setting learning outcomes and, in particular, the standard at which they are set. In the literature of the 1960s and 1970s on learning outcomes (often called 'learning objectives' then) the implication is usually that the standard is set at 100 per cent. In other words, a pass represents the provision of evidence of perfect attainment of the learning outcomes. This was termed 'mastery' and it completely 'pins down' the target of learning. On this view, the intention is to bring all learners to the point where they achieve perfectly all of the learning outcomes. The NVQ system uses the mastery model – learners are competent or not yet competent and require further learning. The NVQ approach 'fixes' the end point of learning but stresses that there may be many learning routes to the same end point. In most areas of higher education, it is not intended that learning should be related so precisely to the achievement of learning outcomes at the module level. In higher education it is as if we need 'room' for unpredictable or independent learning that may be realized that is beyond the curriculum or in terms of the quality or depth of the learning. The quality may be realized in grading that indicates how much the quality of given work is above or beyond the expected. Equally, there are some instances in higher education where particular areas of learning are essential, such as in health and safety issues, and the learner must display complete competence.

Most people seem to assume that learning outcomes describe the average expectations of the work of students. If learning outcomes are written at average standard and are deemed to be essential as opposed to desirable, they become more like a description of the curriculum in designating what must be learnt on the programme. There is also a problem in determining where average is when it comes to wording a learning outcome. It could be between the mark of the best student and the pass–fail mark or is it a point that the majority of students achieve? Placing learning outcomes at 'average' is guesswork because there is no definable standard at average. In practice, where learning outcomes are notionally average in standard, they are not usually treated as if they are essential, but only desirable outcomes and, in effect, students may be assessed on how many they achieve. Stones (1972) suggests that in situations like this, learning outcomes are often being treated as 'window dressing'.

If we need learning outcomes to be more than window dressing, and to be helpful as information to learners and other teachers, and if we want them to indicate to students what they need to know, the only logical standard for essential learning outcomes is at the minimum, just pass standard – or at threshold. On this basis, students should pass all the given learning outcomes and (theoretically) should not be awarded credit for the module unless they achieve the outcomes. Furthermore, we can locate minimum because we do it when we grade students' work. Placing learning outcomes at minimum actually separates them from grading, except at the pass–fail point. Grading is for quality above or below the minimum, or it may be based on some quite different assessment system in addition to judgement of attainment – or not – of the learning outcomes.

I think of the writing of learning outcomes that clarify the minimum acceptable learning as being like the development of a form of contract with students – 'if you attain this learning outcome, you will pass the module'. However – and here we bring in reflection again – with the learning outcome at minimum, there is all that 'room' above the minimum for recognition of different qualities of work in grading or for independent learning attainments.

It may be helpful for learners if this field of useful, but not essential, learning is described in terms of 'desirable learning outcomes', but these do need to be distinguished from those learning outcomes that will determine pass or failure of that module. Another possibility is that, while the essential learning outcomes are under the control of the teacher or validation panel, the learners themselves write desirable learning outcomes that they wish to attain. Figure 5.1 illustrates the suggested positioning of learning outcomes on a scale of the potential quality of learning – notionally 0–100 per cent.

Suddenly the conflict I had identified between the encouragement or celebration of independent learning and reflection and the use of learning outcomes was fading. So long as learning outcomes are written at minimum standard, there is plenty of room above that minimum to allow, and in which to recognize, expression of reflective learning. However, here I need to add some provisos. There may be times when it is essential that a student displays reflective activity as a condition of passing the module. Reflective learning is then an essential learning outcome. This can, however, pose problems of its own as we are not well organized in attributing criteria for reflective learning – but this is not an insoluble issue in my view.

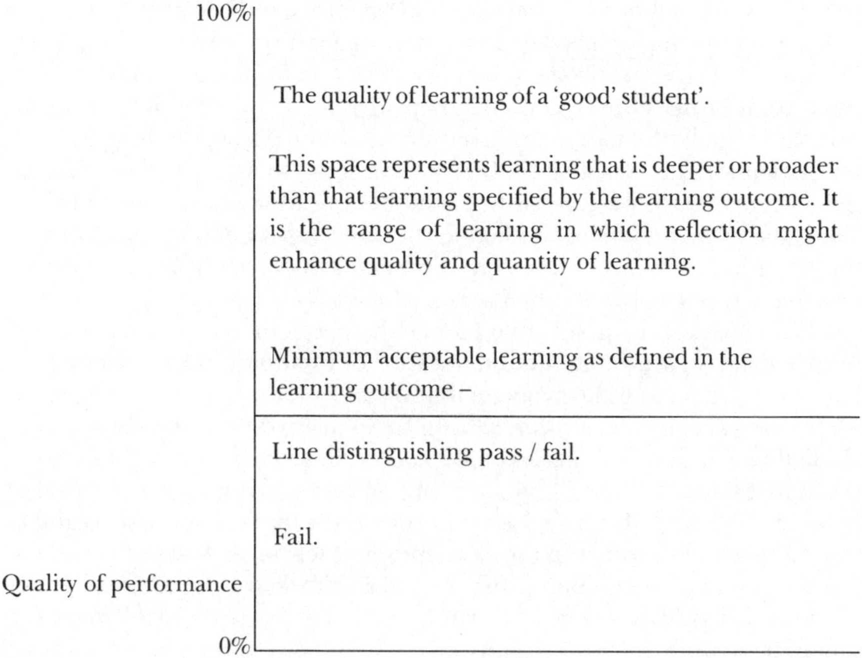

100%

The quality of learning of a 'good' student'.

This space represents learning that is deeper or broader than that learning specified by the learning outcome. It is the range of learning in which reflection might enhance quality and quantity of learning.

Minimum acceptable learning as defined in the learning outcome –

Line distinguishing pass / fail.

Fail.

Quality of performance

0%

**Figure 5.1** *A representation of the positioning of learning outcomes in relation to the quality of student performance*

In a similar way to the above is the need to think about the type of learning that is implied by the learning outcome. This is guided by the use of generic level descriptors (such as HECIW, 1996). While learning outcomes may imply that a surface approach to learning is acceptable at level 1, such as a memorizing approach, this should not be deemed acceptable in learning outcomes at level 3. Level 3 outcomes should imply that evidence of a deep approach to learning is necessary.

So, I arrived at a personal resolution of the conflict between learning outcomes and reflection in the higher education curriculum. They can live alongside each other if the extent to which the learning is prescribed in a learning outcome is limited to what is fair to both teacher and learner in terms of necessary communication about standards and expectations. Beyond that, the quality of divergence in higher education has room for expression.

I then reconsidered the other situations that I suggested to exemplify convergent and divergent influences in higher education. The first was Dearing's call for the expression of depth and breadth in the curriculum.

Depth is described in the generic level descriptors and where they are used to guide the writing of learning outcomes, adequate depth is assured. Along the lines of the model above, it seems reasonable to suggest that as long as some of the curriculum is covered in depth, there is room for broader study. The same would then be true for standards and diversity – so long as minimum standards are described in higher education, there is room to celebrate the diversity that is possible in this form of education above the minimum. The same principle can be applied to the other two examples given above – the provision of choice in the curriculum and the concern for integration, and the paradox expressed by Laurillard.

On the basis of the points that I am making, it is important that learning outcomes are written at minimum or threshold standard. I have thought on and discussed further the problem that we encountered in describing levels where we were unsuccessful in setting them at threshold standard. I conclude that, for purposes I can conceive, level descriptors do not need to be set at threshold so long as the learning outcomes for a module are set at threshold. This implies a slightly different, but I think potentially realistic, role for level descriptors in the description of learning. Instead of providing a basis like a benchmark for the writing of learning outcomes, they describe a fairly wide range of learning achievements around average, and guide the writing of learning outcomes. The precision rests in the learning outcomes, close to the subject matter of the module, instead of in the generic level descriptors.

However, as with a good story that does not want to end, there it might have rested, with the view of HEQC and the credit development projects that generic description of learning at threshold is difficult or impossible. Then, along came the Dearing Report with the suggestion that standards should be described in threshold terms (NCIHE, 1997).

I do not want to go into the ramifications of the Quality Assurance Agency's task of implementing the Dearing Report's recommendations via benchmarking subject groups and other initiatives, but, instead, I want to end on some thoughts about why we might find difficulty in identifying thresholds in generic learning terms, or in subject groups. I acknowledge that what is now coming to light in the subject groups is some difficulty in deciding what threshold itself is, but, for now, let us see it as learning at the minimum acceptable level for a pass.

The explanation for the difficulty in describing learning at threshold in the Graduate Standards Programme was that higher education staff do not tend to think in terms of failing students, particularly at level 3. Most failing students have, by then, dropped out and so there are few instances of such individuals' learning for consideration. However, there may be more to it than that. Thinking back to the kinds of words and phrases we thrashed about in our efforts to construct level descriptors, they were largely what I would describe as 'success' ones such as 'analyse', 'synthesize' and 'independent in learning'. They have connotations of efficiency and effectiveness in learning and the only way in which we could apply them to a failing student is to attach a negative to them – for example, 'not able to ...' or 'little evidence of ...'. In this way we would not be describing threshold learning as such, but threshold learning in relation to successful learning. I suggest that, in this situation we would be drawing on the wrong conceptual word bank.

Thinking more on the nature of student learning at threshold point, I wonder if it is that these failing students cannot analyse, synthesize or learn independently or if, in fact, these skills are not sufficiently expressed in them because there is an overwhelming failure in terms of motivation or personal organization, for example. In other words, functioning in learning at threshold standard may not work on a simplistic sliding scale from 'poor at', for example, 'analysis', to 'good at analysis', but, rather, it may be qualitatively different. Perhaps we need to look more carefully at what is happening to the learning of students at threshold standard. We might discover another word bank that will enable use to describe such learning. Alternatively, we may discover that learning at threshold is a process often distorted by extraneous factors that may mean that we at last abandon these attempts to describe generic learning at threshold, allowing the expression of minimum acceptable quality of learning to be declared through learning outcomes for modules.

## REFERENCES

Barnett, R (1997) *Higher Education: A critical business*, SHRE and Open University Press, Buckingham

Belenky, S, Clinchy, B, Goldberger, R, and Tarule, J (1986) *Women's Ways of Knowing*, Basic Books, New York

HECIW (1996) Welsh Higher Education Credit Framework Handbook, Wales Access Unit, Cardiff

HEQC (1997), 'Graduate Standards Programme Final report Volume 1: The Report', HEQC, London

Keane, P (1997) 'The rise of the 'strategic student': How can we adapt to cope?' in *Facing up to Radical Changes in Universities and Colleges*, S Armstrong, G Thompson and S Brown, Kogan Page, London

Laurillard, D (1993) *Rethinking University Teaching*, Routledge, London

Marton, F, Hounsell, D, and Entwistle, N (1997) *The Experience of Learning*, 2nd edn, Scottish Academic Press, Edinburgh

Moon, J (December 1995a) 'Levels in Higher Education', UCoSDA Briefing Paper 27

Moon, J (December 1995b) 'Learning outcomes for modules in Higher Education', UCoSDA Briefing Paper 28

Moon, J, (December 1995c), 'Credit in Higher Education: The implications for staff development' UCoSDA Briefing Paper 26

Moon, J (1997) 'Higher Education under pressure', *Italic* (3) Learning Support Project, University of Wales, Cardiff

Moon, J (1999) *Reflection in Learning and Professional Development*, Kogan Page, London

NCIHE (1997) 'Final Report of the National Committee of Inquiry into Higher Education', NCIHE, London

Stones, E, and Anderson, D (1972) *Educational Objectives and the Teaching of Educational Psychology*, Methuen, London

6

# Institutional Comparisons – Reality or Illusion?

*Harvey Woolf*

This chapter draws on reflections on work carried out informally over the past five years with a small group of colleagues from six other new universities. Collectively known as the Student Assessment and Classification Working Group (SACWG), the group comprises Bernard Bourdillon (Anglia), Paul Bridges (Derby), Debbie Collymore (Wolverhampton), Angela Cooper (Wolverhampton), Wendy Fox (formerly London Guildhall), Chris Haines (Middlesex), David Turner (Oxford Brookes) and Mantz Yorke (Liverpool John Moores). While the accounts of the SACWG's projects that follow represent the joint work and writings of all the members of the Group, the other views expressed in this chapter are my own. However, the Group's discussions have provided enormous stimulus and, thus, in many ways this chapter is as much a joint venture as SACWG'S previous work.

In that work, the Group concentrated initially on comparing assessment outcomes in the seven institutions. More recently, the Group's attention has been turned to methods of assessment. Inevitably, though, these activities have led to thinking about the broader question of the feasibility and value of making institutional comparisons. It is from these broader reflections and SACWG's detailed work that the structure and the central thesis of this chapter derive.

First, there is a consideration of some of the difficulties generated by published attempts to compare institutions by the creation of so-called league tables of universities in the United Kingdom. This draws in particular on the SACWG's explorations of subject and degree results. Then there is a brief description of the SACWG's work on the benchmarking of assessment to illustrate what can be usefully achieved by way of institutional comparisons. The final section adumbrates an answer to the question posed in the title of this chapter.

## PUBLIC COMPARISONS

Put baldly, the thesis is that, of course, institutions will be compared one with another. However, these comparisons are at such a level of generality that they have little or no meaning. Careers advisers, parents, partners, students, for example, will make generalizations about institutions based on memory or perceived reputation or direct experience when considering which higher education institutions to include in the Universities and Colleges Admissions Service (UCAS) application form. Newspapers enjoy devising league tables that rank universities according to a series of criteria. One, typical publication appeared in *The Sunday Times* (8 November 1998). These tables have been the subject of much trenchant criticism, for example, by Yorke (1997).

Universities have no more power to stop the publication of tables than any other type of organization, such as schools, further education colleges or hospitals, to take just some of the most obvious examples that have been the subjects of this kind of public interest. Indeed, even if organizations could prevent comparisons being made, there remains the crucial question of why, in an accountable society, such prohibitions should ever exist.

The issue is not one of whether or not institutional comparisons are made or should be made, but how to ensure that they are sensible and meaningful. Put another, way, comparing institutions can only be of significance if it is clear that like is being compared with like. All too often, the aggregate data or institutional averages that appear in the public domain obscure subtle but real differences between institutions. For example, how helpful is it to know the relative bookstocks or number of PCs per students in institutions? This can act as a general guide, but there are some real questions that lie behind the data. For instance, what kind of level of access is there to the resource? Do all subjects or courses operate at the same level of resources? As anyone who has been involved in validation panels or is an external examiner will know, generalizations only assume reality when translated into the day-to-day experiences of students and staff.

An often-cited statistic when making institutional comparisons is the average A level score achieved by students entering a university. The relationship between achievement at A level and subsequent degree performance and how to measure that relationship continue to be hotly debated, as Wagner (25 September 1998) demonstrates. There is, though, another, perhaps more pertinent and important question of the relevance of A levels for many higher education courses. For institutions that offer predominantly vocational programmes, emphasizing A level scores produces a somewhat misleading profile of those institutions' 'input standards'. For such courses there are likely to be more appropriate preparatory programmes than A level. Thus, if entry level indicators are to be published, it would be more useful to include data on EDEXCEL awards, GNVQ performance and other similar qualifications. How this input measure approach could deal with Access to Higher Education Certificates awarded under the Quality Assurance Agency for Higher Education (QAAHE) Kitemark is yet another conundrum. One of the principles of Access programmes is that the credits awarded to students are not formally graded. Until there are ways of incorporating the variety of entry qualifications into a model of institutional comparison, such comparisons will always be at best partial and at worst misleading.

The implication of the foregoing is that comparisons can be made across institutions but that they need to be made with sensitivity to the shortcomings of the published, and largely quantitative, data. The need for extreme caution when dealing with these data has been underlined during the SACWG's work on the comparison of degree classifications.

Even a cursory glance at degree performance data exposes problems at two levels:

1. subject level;
2. the level of the rules that determine the classes of degrees awarded to students.

It is well known that there are very significant differences in the marking cultures of the subjects studied in higher education. To take one very obvious example, students are some five times more likely to obtain a first class honours degree in mathematics than they are in law (HESA, 1998). SACWG's own work (Yorke, *et al.*, 1996) and Chapman's (1996) analysis of the classifications awarded between 1972 and 1992 reinforce the extent to which each 'academic tribe', to use Becher's (1989) graphic phrase, determines the performance levels of its students.

The subject 'mix' of an institution and the proportions of students taking each subject are essential pieces of information to have to be able to make valid interpretations of the proportions of firsts and upper seconds appearing in most of the university league tables. It may be that the traditionally high-scoring subjects in an institution cancel out the low-scoring ones and that subject differences even out over time. However, a bald aggregate figure will not tell a potential student or parent about a specific subject's performance in the institutions of their choice. In short, it would be valuable to publish sub institutional data alongside the overall proportion of firsts and so on for the institution. The creation of the Higher Education Statistical Agency (HESA) makes this task easier than it has ever been. Similarly, the ubiquity of the Internet allows for easy dissemination of readily comprehensible data. If governments, the QAA and the higher education institutions are serious about informed choice, then the detailed information on which that choice can be sensibly based must be more widely available than it is at present.

This is not to argue that publication of this type of information will necessarily affect the institution or the subject applicants choose. Nor should this suggest that some subjects are easier or harder than others. As academic disciplines are epistemologically different, it is not surprising that they will exhibit differences in what subject teachers perceive as appropriate standards. The varied ways in which chemistry, history and law have approached the task set by the QAA of establishing sectoral subject benchmarks is instructive in the search for finding a common baseline against which to measure institutions. What I am arguing is that, in order for cross-institutional comparisons to be meaningful, it is essential that more nuanced information about institutions is easily available.

That there are differences in the distribution of classifications between subjects will come as little surprise to those in higher education. It may, of course, be more unanticipated by those outside the system. What is perhaps less well acknowledged, both inside and outside the system, is the impact local institutional and course rules for the way in which honours classifications are calculated can have on students' degree results. In a small-scale study, SACWG recalculated the same set of genuine results according to the classification algorithms used by the member universities. We found that 15 per cent of the cases we used would have been awarded a higher or lower class of degree had another institution's examination board considered them. Extrapolating from this to the national level indicates that some 30,000 students who graduated in England and Wales at the end of the 1996/97 academic year could have achieved a different class of degree at a different institution.

These variations are not the consequence of different standards of achievement in the units of study on which a degree is based. They are not the result of intermarker variability or of the reliability and validity of different assessment methods and assessment tasks. The variations are the direct outcome of different institutions operating different, albeit consistent and legitimate, rules for the way in which students are classified. Because all the SACWG universities have institution-wide regulations, we can have confidence that examination boards in different departments operate in essentially the same way. The extent to which this is the case for those institutions that have faculty or departmental rules is a matter for speculation.

An institution or a department's academic regulations evolve because they embody a set of educational and academic principles that staff believe to be important. There is nothing wrong in this, not least because most regulations are designed to help students as they progress through their courses. The problem is, as I have already indicated, each set of regulations is (slightly) different from the regulations of other departments or institutions. Rules about whether poor performance in one or more units of study can compensate for good performance in other units can influence the class of degree a student is awarded. These rules can even determine whether a student qualifies for an honours or a non-honours degree. What constitutes poor and good performance can differ from one university to another. In some places, compensation may apply to near passes in the region of 36 to 39 per cent. In others, poor performance may be a mark one or two classes below the student's average grade. At the other end of the scale, a good performance might be defined as 60 per cent plus, while elsewhere it might be any grade above the student's average mark.

Borderlines, their recognition and resolution, are another source of critical variation. Some institutions do not recognize the concept of a borderline in their regulations – students either meet the criteria for a class of degree or they do not. If a higher class has just been missed, then that is a fact of academic life. Other universities have strict and sometimes elaborate criteria for determining whether or not someone has fallen into a border zone and how these cases are resolved. Others still leave the whole matter to the wisdom and judgement of the members of the examination board. Clearly, all assessment is ultimately a matter of academic judgement, but it is hard to conceive of an argument in support of a system that devolves decision making of this kind to such a local level.

On a more positive note, SACWG's studies give support to the view that there is little difference in the results generated by algorithms that base classification on all the units students take in their second and third years and those that select a subset of the units studied. (Another common feature of classification systems is that first-year marks rarely, if ever, contribute towards honours classifications.)

From both SACWG's work and my experience as an external examiner, I think the case can be made that it is the rules and regulations accompanying algorithms that are the most significant cause of the variations identified in SACWG's study on classifications (Woolf and Turner, autumn 1997). Certainly, because there is no consistency across the sector (Armstrong, Clarkson and Noble, 1998), it is difficult to make direct comparisons between institutions in respect of degree classifications, except in a very rough and ready way.

Encouraging compilers of league tables and their users to take a more sophisticated approach to their use of what I have characterized here as generalized institutional-level data is manifestly no easy task. The Teaching Quality Subject Assessments carried out under the auspices of, first, the Higher Education Funding Councils and now the QAA have adopted a profiling method of judging the quality of subject provision in higher education. Despite these efforts, league table compilers and, it must be said, institutions themselves aggregate the grades allocated to each of the six 'aspects of provision' to arrive at an overall grade. The overall grade then becomes the indicator of the quality of the subject offering in an institution. Thus, we have another example of trying to capture a complicated phenomenon by reference to a single figure. However, because this reductionism happens so often, there is an imperative to stress continually that all these kinds of data must be accompanied by a health warning. The data are the start, not the end, of enquiries about quality and standards in different institutions.

## BENCHMARKING GROUPS

So far this chapter has been concerned with the presentation of comparative data to a variety of publics and the importance of exercising caution in interpreting the data. There is, though, a dimension of institutional comparison that does not have a public face and has always occurred, at least in an informal way. It is the comparison of institutional practices to enhance the quality and effectiveness of those practices. In late 1997, the Higher Education Quality Council (HEQC), the QAA's forerunner, sponsored SACWG to undertake work on benchmarking assessment practices among its members as part of the Council's umbrella project on benchmarking academic standards (Jackson, 1999). The exercise had two distinct yet related goals:

- to exchange information about assessment practices at the subject and unit of study level in each institution;
- to reflect on the process of establishing and running a benchmarking group.

The timescale for the completion of the project and the limited resources available to SACWG necessarily limited the range of subjects that could be investigated. Therefore, it was important that the subjects chosen for the study were representative of wider academic constituencies. Eventually business, computing and history were selected as the case studies. Business was identified because it is a multidisciplinary subject that incorporates both qualitative and quantitative components. From previous work, it was known that marking behaviour in computing produced broadly bi-polar patterns of grade distribution with a wide spread of marks. It also represented a (relatively) new discipline with professional body involvement. Finally, history served as an example of a traditional qualitative discipline that used a fairly narrow spread of marks in its grading strategies. Each subject group determined its own approach to benchmarking within the generic project guidelines. This recognized the separate and different needs of the individual subjects and also maximized the opportunities for collecting evidence about different ways to run academic benchmarking clubs.

Each group used a common questionnaire appropriately adapted for its own discipline as the basis for collecting data about the contributing departments. The results of this part of the project provided a considerable amount of detailed information about departmental assessment strategies and methods that is only normally seen more publicly by external members of validation panels or external examiners. Moreover, the data were presented in forms that made institutional comparisons straightforward and systematic. Beyond this stage, each subject group pursued a different though complementary route. Business explored assessment results in the context of the similarities and differences between the aims and curricula of the modules that contributed to the BA Business Studies degree in each university. The computing group examined their institutional practices for the initial validation and subsequent quality control mechanisms of assessment methods. History concentrated on the range of assessment instruments used by the member institutions and started to examine the relationship between types of assessment and grading.

Although the project was a small one, sufficient evidence was collected to permit the conclusions that across the participating universities:

- the educational aims of nominally similar programmes are broadly comparable;
- the aims of nominally similar modules are generally comparable;
- the intellectual demands made by assessments on students are broadly comparable;
- the variations in the distributions of marks can be explained by the interaction of subject and institutional cultures.

In themselves, these conclusions might have been expected. What is significant for comparing institutions is that they are the outcome of a systematic analysis based on comparing similar processes and characteristics. In the cliché, apples were being compared with apples.

Even this small project demonstrated the value of setting up benchmarking clubs; it also pointed to many of the difficulties entailed in such ventures. They do not happen of their own accord, but, rather, need to be prepared for and managed. Participants have to understand and own the process (Price 1994) and to believe their departments are gaining from the effort and resources they are contributing to the exercise. Contributors need time to establish mutual trust and understanding. People need to meet together to share experiences. E-mail, mailbases or video- and telephone-conferences are at best complements to face-to-face discussion. Group sizes need to be limited to 10 to 12 members if there are to be effective contributions from all participants. Making comparisons in this way self-evidently carries with it a cost. The gain, however, is that institutions and all other stakeholders in higher education will have a greater understanding of both the processes and outcomes of the system. In its turn, this understanding will lead to improvements in the way in which departments operate.

## TOWARDS AN ANSWER

In one sense, the answer to the question of whether or not institutional comparisons are illusory or real is relatively simple. They are illusory if they are made on the basis of unqualified, unexplained institutional-level data. Because these data do not necessarily compare like with like, they distort comparative pictures. Comparisons can be real if they are made on the basis of sharing information, knowledge and experience of commonly defined activities within institutions.

It is difficult to envisage a total solution to the institutional-level issue. Funding agencies, government departments and newspapers publishing league tables want simple, instant snapshots of institutions. None the less, the current tables could be made less crude by the kind of contextual and analytical reviews *The Guardian*, for example, provides alongside the publication of GCSE and A level results. (For example, why not give the proportion of entrants who hold each type of entry qualification?) While these commentaries may be read in detail only by a small proportion of readers, the very fact that they are available alerts people to the dangers inherent in an unquestioning reading of the raw figures.

The development of sub-institutional benchmarking groups offers greater scope for optimism. There are already numerous groups in the sector representing all manner of functions and activities in the institutions. Many probably already benchmark, although they may not call it that. It would not require an enormous shift in their work to establish more formal benchmarking groups. The outcomes of their work might then inform institutional-level comparisons. The specific tasks of the groups would inevitably vary one from another. Some would be more straightforward than others. For example, the benchmarking of academic standards by the chemistry, history and law groups referred to earlier indicates the complexity of the undertaking for academic disciplines. None the less, by benchmarking thresholds, standards and best practice across the sector at the level of academic and service departments, it should be possible to arrive at institutional comparisons that are well-founded and meaningful.

These comparisons must be truly cross-sectoral. At present, most of the published league tables include information only about universities. The university sector colleges and their equivalents and those further education colleges that offer a substantial amount of higher education are omitted from many comparative analyses. The inclusion of four university sector college representatives among the 43 members of the QAA's subject benchmarking groups underlines the necessity of incorporating all higher education providers into the framework of institutional comparisons.

Comparing institutions is not easy. The sector must take responsibility for ensuring that it is done with sensitivity to, and understanding of, the full complexity of the task. If that responsibility is not seized, the flawed comparisons we have currently will continue to be made for higher education in the United Kingdom.

## REFERENCES

Armstrong, M, Clarkson, P, and Noble, M (1998) *Modularity and Credit Frameworks*, NUCCAT, Liverpool

Becher, T (1989) *Academic Tribes and Territories*, SRHE and Open University Press, Buckingham

Chapman, K (1996) 'Inter-institutional variability of degree results: An analysis in selected subjects', HEQC, London

HESA (1998) 'Students' Qualifications', Higher Educational Statistical Agency, London

Jackson, N (ed) (1999) *Pilot Studies in Benchmarking Assessment Practice*, QAA, Gloucester

Price, I (1994) *A Plain Person's Guide to Benchmarking*, Unit for Facilities Management Research, Sheffield Hallam University, Sheffield

*The Sunday Times* (8 November 1998) 'University Guide', *The Sunday Times*

Wagner, L (25 September 1998) 'Made to Measure', *The Times Higher Education Supplement*

Woolf, H, and Turner, D (autumn 1997) 'Honours classifications: The need for transparency', *New Academic*, pp 10–12

Yorke, M, *et al.* (1996) 'Module mark distributions in eight subject areas and some issues they raise', in *Modular Higher Education in the UK*, ed N Jackson, HEQC, London

Yorke, M (1997) 'A good league table guide?', *Quality Assurance in Education*, **5** (2), pp 61–72

# 7

# Benchmarking Across Subjects in an Institution

*J P Margham and S Jackson*

## QUALITY AND STANDARDS

The terms quality and standards are often used interchangeably to refer to the value and reputation of an institution's programmes of study. The HEQC defined academic standards as 'explicit levels of academic attainment that are used to describe and measure academic requirements and achievements of individual students and groups of students' (HEQC, 1995). This definition provides a starting point for the specification of subject threshold standards (benchmarks), which are referred to by the QAA as 'the intellectual attributes associated with successful study of a discipline to degree level' (QAA, 1998).

The difference between institutional quality and standards is a significant one. 'Quality' may be taken to refer to the quality of the student experience – that is, the level of service provided for students – and refers to such things as whether or not a programme meets its stated objectives, whether students receive adequate support or whether assessments are conducted in accordance with required procedures and so on. Quality can be measured and assured and forms the basis of programme validation, monitoring and review. 'Standards', on the other hand, are less easily defined and measured. They relate both to the perceived reputation of the subject, in relation to other subjects, and to the reputation of the institution. Together these reputations are a measure of the 'worth' of an award.

It is possible to have a programme of study that maintains high levels of quality (for example, learning materials are well-produced, essays are regularly marked and returned to students within two weeks), but only achieves modest 'standards' as defined in terms of the intellectual development of students and the standing of the programme curriculum. Ideally higher education institutions should strive to achieve both high quality and high standards in all programmes. However, whereas procedures can be put in place and monitored to assure the maintenance of quality, it is very much more difficult for an institution or a subject team to drive-up the 'standards' of awards.

## Variations in standards between subjects

One of the fundamental features of the British higher education system is the assumption (if not belief) that there is a parity of standards between academic subject areas within individual institutions. A first class degree in fine art is considered of equal 'worth' to a first class degree in biology; even though the students of these subjects will have received very different learning experiences. The differences are not just in subject content but also in the whole approach to study – one being studio-based with an emphasis on the assessment of the 'final product', the other, traditionally, relying on lectures and laboratory classes with the accumulation of marks for individual pieces of assessment.

There is no set of standardized performance indicators that higher education institutions can use to measure the comparability of awards between subjects. Standards are defined within subjects by a variety of mechanisms – principally by the involvement of professional bodies, where appropriate, and by peer group evaluation. The external examiner system is designed to ensure comparability in standards within subject areas between institutions. This system perpetuates the existence of subject 'cultures' where the allegiance of individual staff may be to the subject peer group – both within the institution and elsewhere – rather than to an institution. The conformity to subject culture rather than institutional standards is evident in the fact that a biologist, for example, will feel comfortable in assessing the quality of a student's work in biology from any other UK institution but would be totally unable to pass judgement on the work of a student from the same institution studying a different subject.

## Differences between higher education institutions

The same problem applies to differences between institutions. The current view is that the higher education sector is typified by a wide diversity of different types of institution but all conform to some undefined and undefinable notion of common standards. What should matter to students – and potential employers – is the grade of award achieved and not the name of the institution from which it was received. However, there is clearly a 'reputational' hierarchy table of institutions made explicit by league tables and such organizations as the Russell Group. This implies that the value of an award is determined both by the level of performance of a student and by the regard in which an institution is held. An 'upper second' may define the level of achievement, but some upper seconds from some institutions, apparently, are better than others.

## Variability and standards

This notion of 'ranking amongst equals' highlights a basic dilemma in the organization of higher education. The responsibility for the award of qualifications rests with accredited institutions, but the standards of qualifications are defined by subject disciplines. Although institutions can take measures to ensure a degree of commonality of practice between subjects, ultimately the guarantee of the value of a student's award is determined by subject assessors operating under the watchful gaze of an external examiner from another institution who, in turn, operates to an intuitive code of practice defined by an understanding of the essential characteristics of the subject (See Figure 7.1).

**Institutional procedures for Quality Assessment:**
assessment regulations
external review (audit)
modular scheme regulations

**Subject Quality Assessment:**
peer evaluation
professional body monitoring
external review (TQA)

| | Higher Educational Institution | Higher Educational Institution | Higher Educational Institution |
|---|---|---|---|
| *Subject A* | | | |
| *Subject B* | | | |
| *Subject C* | | | |

**Figure 7.1** *Matrix of Institutional and Subject Responsibilities for Quality Assurance*

Subject disciplines that involve professional or vocational qualifications are also subject to being overseen by professional bodies. Some bodies take an active interest in standards and define requirements for programmes of study. Invariably these requirements relate to the 'practice' of the profession – that is, they are intended to ensure that practitioners are 'competent' in the profession.

## BENCHMARKING ACROSS SUBJECT DISCIPLINES

The need to establish a degree of commonality in standards between subject disciplines within a single institution is implicit in the structure and organization of modular programmes of study. In theory, if not in practice, the individual modules in an integrated scheme carry a credit tariff that is defined in terms of a standard 'currency' – credits in fine art have the same value as credits in biology. Students have the ability to combine modules from different subject disciplines in their individual programmes of study. The achievement of standardization is based on common procedures and common definitions. For example, there is a need for all subjects to conform to institutional regulations for the management of assessment. Similarly, there is a need to define modules in terms of a common language with attention to a standard set of parameters. Modules defined in terms of learning outcomes provide an opportunity for comparability – for, although the specific outcomes will differ markedly between subjects, it is possible to identify common 'levels' of performance.

In operating a well-established modular scheme, Liverpool John Moores University is regularly producing data that may inform the principle of commonality of standards between subject disciplines. From the inception of the scheme, all modular results have been held on a single database and, in most years, an annual report of assessment outcomes has been presented for analysis by the Academic Quality and Standards Committee on behalf of the Academic Board. This report contains a wealth of information on each of the John Moores University's Schools, including mean marks for all its modules (around 4000), module pass rates, completion rates for each level of undergraduate programmes and a summary of degree results achieved.

We have taken data from a typical year –1995/96 – and examined a number of issues around standards (JMU, December 1996). Thus, in this analysis, we are defining benchmarking not so much as the matching of a subject area with a common set of subject descriptive parameters, but, rather, as a comparison of performance variability in cognate and non-cognate subject areas. Our basic premise is that, if standards are similar in cognate areas, we should expect similar student outcomes, as measured in terms of assessment results. We also wanted to test whether or not comparing results from non-cognate subject areas would produce dissimilar outcomes and, if so, to ask whether or not such a result might indicate a different approach to standards or tangible differences in the level of student performance.

We have taken three groups of cognate subject areas – science, engineering and humanities – for our subject comparisons

## Biological and Earth Sciences (BES) and Biomolecular Sciences (BMS) Schools

This pair of science-based Schools offers a range of programmes that contains many common modules, each owned by one or other of the Schools. Student profiles at entry are similar (see Table 7.1).

**Table 7.1**

| *School* | *Under-graduate level* | *Number of modules* | *Proportion of mean Module Marks in various mark bands* | | | | |
|---|---|---|---|---|---|---|---|
| | | | *Marks of <40%* | *Marks of 40–49%* | *Marks of 50–59%* | *Marks of 60–69%* | *Marks of =>70%* |
| BES | 1 | 26 | 4% | 54% | 35% | 8% | 0% |
| | 2 | 39 | 3% | 39% | 54% | 5% | 0% |
| | 3 | 29 | 0% | 0% | 79% | 21% | 0% |
| BMS | 1 | 22 | 5% | 41% | 32% | 18% | 5% |
| | 2 | 28 | 0% | 50% | 25% | 18% | 7% |
| | 3 | 40 | 0% | 5% | 65% | 27% | 3% |

Here we see a similar set of outcomes in the two Schools: lower average performance at lower levels and a gradual reduction in the spread of average marks as the level increases.

**Table 7.2**

| *School* | *Under-graduate level* | *Number of modules* | *Proportion of modules with pass rates (first attempt plus referral) in various pass rate bands* | | | | |
|---|---|---|---|---|---|---|---|
| | | | *=>90% pass rate* | *80-89% pass rate* | *70-79% pass rate* | *60-69% pass rate* | *<60% pass rate* |
| BES | 1 | 26 | 31% | 46% | 19% | 0% | 4% |
| | 2 | 38 | 55% | 29% | 11% | 3% | 3% |
| | 3 | 30 | 87% | 3% | 7% | 3% | 0% |
| BMS | 1 | 22 | 64% | 18% | 14% | 0% | 5% |
| | 2 | 28 | 57% | 25% | 18% | 0% | 0% |
| | 3 | 40 | 80% | 8% | 5% | 8% | 0% |

The gradual improvement of scores with increasing level is reflected loosely in the higher pass rates aligned with the higher levels. However, there are differences in pass rates between modules offered by the two Schools, especially at the lowest level. Comparing these two Schools with another science-based School, Pharmacy and Chemistry (PAC), introduces another parameter of standards: the requirements and expectations of a professional body, in this case the Pharmaceutical Society of Great Britain. The BSc Pharmacy undergraduate programme within the School's programme range has ensured that PAC regularly maintains an enhanced entry profile as compared to BES and BMS.

The results for PAC are shown in Tables 7.3 and 7.4.

**Table 7.3**

| *School* | *Under-graduate level* | *Number of modules* | *Proportion of mean module marks in various mark bands* | | | | |
|---|---|---|---|---|---|---|---|
| | | | *Marks of <40%* | *Marks of 40–49%* | *Marks of 50–59%* | *Marks of 60–69%* | *Marks of =>70%* |
| PAC | 1 | 31 | 3% | 58% | 16% | 19% | 3% |
| | 2 | 23 | 0% | 39% | 48% | 4% | 9% |
| | 3 | 24 | 0% | 8% | 67% | 21% | 4% |

**Table 7.4**

| *School* | *Under-graduate level* | *Number of modules* | *Proportion of modules with pass rates (first attempt plus referral) in various pass rate bands* | | | | |
|---|---|---|---|---|---|---|---|
| | | | =>90% *pass rate* | *80-89% pass rate* | *70-79% pass rate* | *60-69% pass rate* | *<60% pass rate* |
| PAC | 1 | 30 | 43% | 27% | 13% | 17% | 0% |
| | 2 | 23 | 43% | 39% | 9% | 9% | 0% |
| | 3 | 23 | 65% | 30% | 4% | 4% | 0% |

Here the PAC students were performing similarly to those in the BES and BMS Schools in terms of average performance per module, indicating, perhaps, a similar range of standards being applied across the three science Schools. However, the pass rate per module for PAC students was clearly less skewed towards the higher end, especially at higher levels. Thus, in the other sciences (and the other examples given below) there may be an expectation that a large majority of level 3 students will pass their modules; this is less clearly evident in the PAC profile of results.

## Engineering and Technology Management (ETM) and Built Environment (BLT) Schools

These two engineering Schools share almost no modules. Each has a significant proportion of programmes accredited by professional bodies, including Civil Engineering in BLT. Each has also been actively promoting recruitment from a wider range of student abilities, with the outcome reflected in the entry profiles.

**Table 7.5**

| *School* | *Undergraduate level* | *Number of modules* | *Proportion of mean module marks in various mark bands* | | | | |
|---|---|---|---|---|---|---|---|
| | | | *Marks of <40%* | *Marks of 40–49%* | *Marks of 50–59%* | *Marks of 60–69%* | *Marks of =>70%* |
| ETM | 1 | 47 | 21% | 45% | 26% | 6% | 2% |
| | 2 | 58 | 0% | 24% | 55% | 19% | 2% |
| | 3 | 61 | 8% | 8% | 62% | 21% | 0% |
| BLT | 1 | 101 | 3% | 22% | 51% | 20% | 5% |
| | 2 | 105 | 0% | 17% | 55% | 20% | 1% |
| | 3 | 94 | 1% | 9% | 60% | 30% | 1% |

While the results vary between the two Schools, they appear similar in trend to those of the three science-based Schools presented above (see Table 7.6).

**Table 7.6**

| *School* | *Under-graduate level* | *Number of modules* | *Portion of modules with pass rates (first attempt plus referral) in various pass rate bands* | | | | |
|---|---|---|---|---|---|---|---|
| | | | =>90% *pass rate* | *80-89% pass rate* | *70-79% pass rate* | *60-69% pass rate* | *<60% pass rate* |
| ETM | 1 | 46 | 22% | 28% | 17% | 17% | 15% |
| | 2 | 58 | 62% | 28% | 5% | 5% | 0% |
| | 3 | 61 | 67% | 20% | 3% | 2% | 8% |
| BLT | 1 | 101 | 59% | 28% | 7% | 3% | 3% |
| | 2 | 105 | 86% | 12% | 2% | 0% | 0% |
| | 3 | 94 | 87% | 10% | 2% | 1% | 0% |

Similarities in average module performance between the two engineering Schools are not matched in pass rates per module, particularly at level 1. Indeed, there are very real differences, with ETM having a much longer 'tail' of lower pass rates, possibly reflecting the entry profile.

## Law, Social Policy and Social Work (LSW) and Media, Critical and Creative Arts (MCC) Schools

These two humanities-based Schools have much in common in terms of styles of teaching and a successful history of student recruitment. The LSW School has a majority of professionally accredited programmes, unlike the MCC School where there are some vocational programmes but none that is linked to professional bodies. Their assessment data are as shown in Table 7.7.

**Table 7.7**

| *School* | *Under-graduate level* | *Number of modules* | *Portion of mean module marks in various mark bands* | | | | |
|---|---|---|---|---|---|---|---|
| | | | *Marks of <40%* | *Marks of 40–49%* | *Marks of 50–59%* | *Marks of 60–69%* | *Marks of =>70%* |
| LSW | 1 | 23 | 9% | 43% | 35% | 13% | 0% |
| | 2 | 42 | 0% | 31% | 50% | 19% | 0% |
| | 3 | 36 | 0% | 3% | 61% | 36% | 0% |
| MCC | 1 | 48 | 0% | 4% | 85% | 10% | 0% |
| | 2 | 51 | 0% | 0% | 69% | 31% | 0% |
| | 3 | 49 | 0% | 0% | 51% | 49% | 0% |

There are some remarkable differences between the two humanities Schools. The LSW School's results show a wider spread of average marks, although, like the MCC School, none is in the highest possible band, and there is an increasing overall average module mark up through the levels. In the MCC School, the average module marks are almost entirely limited to two mark bands (50–69 per cent), with a gradual shift to the 60–69 per cent band up through the three levels.

The overall results from the LSW and MCC Schools clearly are different from those presented in the science and engineering areas, particularly in the high proportion of average module marks in the 60–69 per cent band, and, perhaps surprisingly given these overall high average results, the complete absence of mean marks in the 70+ per cent band, even at level 1.

Table 7.8 shows that the results are broadly similar in the two Schools in that the vast majority of students are passing their modules at the first cycle, although the success rate is more pronounced in the MCC results, even from level 1.

**Table 7.8**

| *School* | *Under-graduate level* | *Number of modules* | *Proportion of modules with pass rates (first attempt plus referral) in various pass rate bands* | | | | |
|---|---|---|---|---|---|---|---|
| | | | *=>90% pass rate* | *80-89% pass rate* | *70-79% pass rate* | *60-69% pass rate* | *<60% pass rate* |
| LSW | 1 | 23 | 57% | 30% | 4% | 4% | 4% |
| | 2 | 42 | 71% | 19% | 10% | 0% | 0% |
| | 3 | 36 | 94% | 0% | 0% | 6% | 0% |
| MCC | 1 | 48 | 94% | 4% | 2% | 0% | 0% |
| | 2 | 51 | 98% | 2% | 0% | 0% | 0% |
| | 3 | 51 | 96% | 0% | 0% | 0% | 0% |

## CONCLUSIONS FROM THE ANALYSIS

In crude terms, we can conclude that results are more homogeneous in the humanities than in science and engineering. The spread of marks is greater in science and engineering, at least at lower levels of the undergraduate programmes and the module pass rate is lower. What is unclear is whether this reflects real differences in student performance or differences in marking practice. If we disregard entry profiles, then, all other things being equal, we might conclude that a student is more likely to be successful if they choose to take a non-professionally orientated humanities programme rather than one in science and engineering.

Perhaps this point about entry profile can be re-evaluated by looking at results from another John Moores University School – Human Sciences (HUM). This School is rooted in two main science curricular areas – psychology and sports science. Both are extremely attractive to potential candidates and the entry profile is high. What can we predict from the previous analysis? From the results in science and engineering, we might expect a wide spread of module marks (and, therefore, of student achievements) at undergraduate levels 1 and 2, with a narrowing of average marks at level 3 around the 2:2 area. Further, we might expect a fairly wide spread of module failure that narrows and improves with increasing level. Tables 7.9 and 7.10 show the actual data.

**Table 7.9**

| *School* | *Under-graduate level* | *Number of modules* | *Portion of mean module marks in various mark bands* | | | | |
|---|---|---|---|---|---|---|---|
| | | | *Marks of <40%* | *Marks of 40–49%* | *Marks of 50–59%* | *Marks of 60–69%* | *Marks of =>70%* |
| HUM | 1 | 40 | 0% | 15% | 75% | 10% | 0% |
| | 2 | 53 | 2% | 0% | 70% | 28% | 0% |
| | 3 | 74 | 0% | 1% | 74% | 24% | 0% |

**Table 7.10**

| *School* | *Under-graduate level* | *Number of modules* | *Portion of modules with pass rates (first attempt plus referral) in various pass rate bands* | | | | |
|---|---|---|---|---|---|---|---|
| | | | *=>90% pass rate* | *80-89% pass rate* | *70-79% pass rate* | *60-69% pass rate* | *<60% pass rate* |
| HUM | 1 | 40 | 88% | 13% | 0% | 0% | 0% |
| | 2 | 53 | 98% | 2% | 0% | 0% | 0% |
| | 3 | 74 | 97% | 1% | 1% | 0% | 0% |

In fact, rather than reflect the situation in science and engineering, the results are very similar to those of the MCC School, with a strong recruitment profile. Can we conclude from this that subject standards are being maintained in science and engineering and that the lower recruitment profiles are the cause of the wider spread of marks and the lower pass rate in modules? Alternatively, could the wider spread of marks be a result of a higher proportion of criterion-referenced assessment in the more objective sciences and engineering areas? If the latter point were true, what is this indicating about the basis of assessment in the applied psychology and sport science courses and about the contrast in results between the courses in the LSW and MCC Schools?

The differences in the typical marks profiles of subjects is of particular importance in areas where non-cognate subjects are linked in joint subject awards. Our evidence indicates that a typical students who links law with media can expect to gain higher marks from the media half of the programme (especially at levels 1 and 2), while those linking humanities with sciences can expect to gain lower marks from the science side. While we can debate the relevance of these comments to standards, we certainly are entitled to question the equity of such outcomes if they are proven true when variables have been taken into account in a more detailed analysis.

Evidence has been presented that suggests that where programmes are linked to professional bodies there may be an effect on results, namely a lowering of the overall average marks obtained and a spread in the proportions of module pass rates. These types of result were discernible even where there were cohorts with a higher entry profile (LSW and PAC), but were less clear in BLT where the average entry requirement may not be as high. Does this possible effect of professional bodies drive-up standards in that these types of courses are more challenging? Is a first class pharmacy degree different in standard than a non-professional science degree? Our results are not conclusive, but are certainly thought-provoking and controversial. What can be said with confidence is that the link with professional bodies does give courses a link with standards that are being compared nationally. In one example, pharmacy, graduates are required to take a national examination following a year of professional training after graduation. The results from this national assessment are likely to be used as a means of judging the quality and standards of the different institutional courses, just as much as of the individual students.

Our final conclusion concerns the challenge of reconciling the institutional search for quality with the national search for standards. On the one hand we are clear that subject standards are most likely to be maintained, and hopefully driven upwards, by a cross-institutional culture that needs to be proactively encouraged by institutions in all manner of ways, including external examining. On the other hand we remain convinced that, in the final analysis, the degree-awarding powers of universities impose on higher education institutions the responsibilities for the standards of their awards. Institutions must ensure that their regulatory and monitoring systems are of a nature that encourages individual subject areas to feel ownership of, and involvement in, the institution's quality assurance processes.

## REFERENCES

HECQ (1995) 'Graduate Standards Programme Interim Report', p 2, HEQC, London

QAA (October 1998) 'The Way Ahead', *Higher Quality*, **1** (4), QAA, Gloucester, p 11

JMU (December 1996) 'Assessment outcomes in 1995/96: A report to the Academic Standards and Quality Committee', JMU, Liverpool

8

# The Business Approach to Benchmarking – An Exploration of the Issues as a Background for Its Use in Higher Education

*David Yarrow*

This chapter records some practical experiences of benchmarking in the business world by the author at the University of Northumbria at Newcastle over a period of eight years, and attempts to draw lessons from them. It will focus on experiences that can be described at first hand, 'warts and all', in the belief that useful lessons are drawn from what went wrong at least as much as they are from what went right.

In this context the definition of the word 'business' should be a flexible one. The experiences on which this chapter is based have involved assisting a wide range of organizations to learn about and apply benchmarking principles. That range encompasses many commercial operations, including manufacturers of all sorts of products and providers of services in fields such as transport, communications, hospitality and professional services. It also encompasses organizations that may not regard themselves as 'businesses' (though some are seeing this conventional wisdom challenged), such as hospitals and local authority departments. The participants of the study have also included a number of colleges and universities. Of the 700 participants in the current 'diagnostic benchmarking' project in North East England, 24 are from higher education (faculties, colleges and service departments from four universities) and 12 are from further education. One of these is the Business School at the University of Sunderland, the then Director of which, Professor Graham Henderson, commented in informal discussions:

> The benchmarking process provided us with an invaluable opportunity to both reflect upon the recent progress that had been made within the

> School and identify key areas for further development in the future. The outcome has been used within the School as a major focus for the determination of future strategy in a number of key areas, most particularly those related to aspects of customer service and the development of associated systems and processes.

It is also worth pointing out that some of the best examples of learning and improving through benchmarking occur across sectoral boundaries. If you run a bus company, you could no doubt learn a lot by studying other bus companies; but you shouldn't stop there. With some lateral thinking, there may be more to learn by looking at rail companies and airlines, and if you can really think laterally then pick a specific business process that you need to improve and study how it is done by people who are not in the transport business at all. A good example of lateral thinking is the ambulance service that studied the operation of a pizza delivery company to learn how it dealt with the difficulties posed by traffic congestion.

In an earlier chapter, Alex Appleby has described several types of activity that are all labelled as benchmarking. This chapter will comment on practical achievements and limitations to these specific types, distinguishing between metric, diagnostic and process benchmarking as three linked but rather different approaches. Figure 8.1 depicts these three modes.

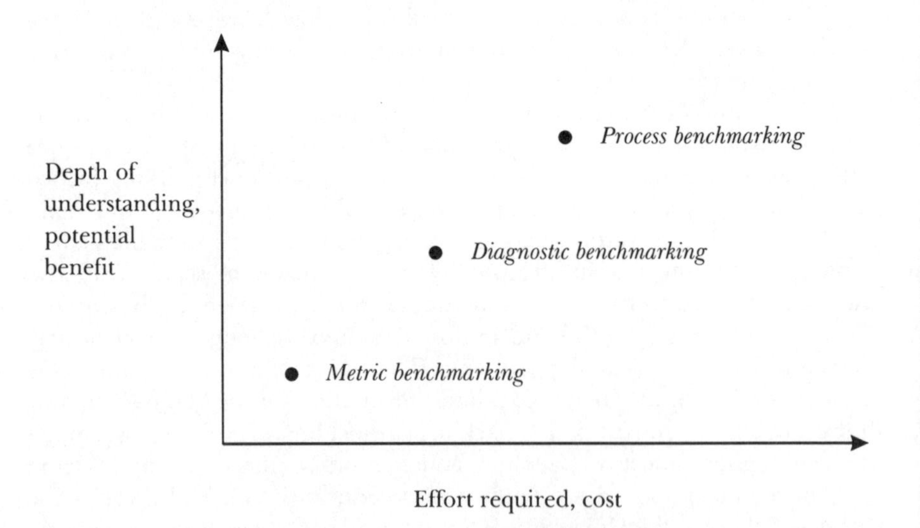


**Figure 8.1** *The three benchmarking modes*

## METRIC BENCHMARKING – A VERY GOOD PLACE TO START

The discussion begins with the experiences of a well-known manufacturing company with a factory in the North East of England. In the early 1990s, the company's head office requested each factory to submit data returns so that they could be benchmarked. Among other measures, they were asked to report numbers of people employed in various roles. The factory in the North East was then informed that the number of people it employed on quality assurance was high. The implications were clear – do something about it!

Investigation revealed a flaw in the argument. Other factories actually employed just as many quality assurance people, but had different interpretations of the definitions. Rather than all being grouped together in a quality assurance department, some were categorized as employees of other departments – inspectors working within a production department, for example. The person who tells this story is the Quality Manager in the factory and both he and the company have since moved on to better things in benchmarking terms. As an aside, the same company has since done away with quality assurance as a separate function, preferring to place responsibility for quality in the hands of those who are making the products.

The example illustrates something important about metric benchmarking – that it can work, to an extent. Analysis of the numbers identified an aspect of the factory that warranted further investigation. In this case, the investigation revealed that the problem was one of measurement. However, it does not take much imagination to see that a similar scenario in a less enlightened company might have resulted in an instruction to reduce headcount, or at least in harsh judgements being made about management of the offending factory or department.

Metric benchmarking, then, has its pitfalls, but it is not suggested for a moment that it is not a useful technique. Carefully applied, so that valid 'apples-with-apples' comparisons are made, it can provide an invaluable 'wake-up' call. A good example of this thought process is the set of comparisons presented by Womack, Jones and Roos in their book *The Machine That Changed the World* (Womack, *et al.*, 1990). In it they compared the performance of Japanese and Western car manufacturers, and identified dramatic performance gaps. The impact of that book on the Western manufacturing community is testament to the power of benchmarking. It triggered a wave of enthusiasm for emulating the performance of the high achievers, and the authors have responded by teaching many companies the principles of 'lean thinking'.

This example, as well as highlighting the potential power of metric benchmarking, illustrates some of its limitations. Metric comparisons may indeed provoke the thought 'We'd better do something about it!', but this in itself is not enough to help us to make our organization more successful.

Two other questions should also occur once it has been discovered that somebody else performs better than we do in terms of a particular measure. First, and perhaps this is the most important question, we should ask 'So what?' Does our poorer performance on this particular measure really matter? Should its improvement be a high priority for us? The 'So what?' question may at first sight seem strange. An example can be used here to explain why it is important. Imagine a supermarket chain that compiles comparative statistics on space utilization discovers that one store's figure is 25 per cent lower than the average. The manager is instructed to act, so initiates a project to buy more shelving and pack it with saleable goods. What the manager and head office have both missed is the fact that this store has another weakness, in an area no one has yet thought to measure – the level of repeat business. The store has fewer regular customers than the other stores, and performs particularly poorly in terms of the long-term loyalty of its customer base. This performance gap may not be as dramatic as that for space utilization – maybe the difference is only a few per cent – but perhaps if the manager knew the numbers and thought through their implications, they would conclude that, in the interests of the long-term profitability of the store, the loyalty issue was both more important and more urgent than improving the use of space.

This, of course, would be a judgement call, as are so many managerial decisions. There is no magic formula that proves that improving one figure (the number of loyal customers) will increase another figure (the store's profitability this year and next) more than increasing a third figure (the utilization of space). If it was that easy, managers wouldn't be paid such high salaries! However, the example illustrates a point, which could be summarized as 'think before you leap into action!'

The second question that should occur to us once we've studied the outputs of metric benchmarking is, quite simply, 'How?' We've discovered that someone else performs better on measure 'x'. We've asked 'So what?' and concluded that improving this aspect of performance is a priority for us. Metric benchmarking has done its job; it can take us no further. It has been able to tell us what we need to improve (in performance terms), but it can't tell us how. To answer that question, we need to move into more sophisticated measures.

## DIAGNOSTIC BENCHMARKING

Such sophisticated measures need to be described in benchmarking terms. However, this is not the only way to respond to the alert provided by a successful metric benchmarking exercise. It is quite possible that, having pinpointed a performance figure that needs to be improved, an organization's people can readily identify what they need to do to improve it. Alternatively, they may apply other techniques to tease out the necessary understanding (using problem-solving techniques, for example), without necessarily considering or needing progression to another form of benchmarking.

What is clear is that, in order to improve performance, we need to change practice. This is the rationale behind diagnostic benchmarking, which is akin to an organizational health check. The technique builds on the idea of comparing performance figures, but recognizes the limitations of such comparisons in isolation, and therefore adds another dimension. The organization is invited to compare its practices (or processes) to those of other organizations, as well as the results that those practices deliver.

This is a simple principle, but not quite so easy to put into practice. How will we know which set of practices to benchmark, and how they are linked to the performance measures we have decided are important? And how will we make sure that, in moving between organizations, we are comparing like with like? This is difficult enough when comparing performance measures that (in theory at least) are quantifiable. How much more difficult will it be when we try to compare the way an organization goes about the practices that comprise its day-to-day work?

These difficulties have not stood in the way of some very credible initiatives to put the principles of diagnostic benchmarking to work. These have been based on empirical work, building on the achievements of leading organizations and studies of the approaches they have adopted and developed. Management is itself still as much an art as a science, and for as long as this is the case, the same will be true of a technique such as diagnostic benchmarking. Indeed, over time, it should contribute to the development of the science of management.

Diagnostic benchmarking is a close relation of self-assessment, which has become very popular among progressive organizations during the 1990s, as well as in institutions of further and higher education. Self-assessment in business contexts often makes use of the business excellence model (BEM), developed by the European Foundation for Quality Management. This model provides a blueprint for the excellent business, describing the practices that should be in place (grouped under five headings described as 'enablers') and the performance that should follow (under four results headings). The aspects of performance considered include financial measures, but also some less tangible outcomes including customer satisfaction, people satisfaction (that is, employee satisfaction) and impact on society. It is interesting to compare these with some of the areas covered in the UK by the QAA within self-assessment documents for subject review, including student satisfaction measures and quality management and enhancement.

Self-assessment involves comparison between an organization's practices and performance, and the standards that the BEM describes. This involves a combination of quantitative comparisons and qualitative judgements, and could itself be described as a form of benchmarking. However, it is helpful to distinguish self-assessment from diagnostic benchmarking in that the focus of self-assessment is comparison with the absolute standards of the model, rather than with the standards achieved by other organizations. In QAA self-assessments, by comparison, subject staff are judged on their effectiveness in achieving their self-defined aims and objectives within a broad quality template articulated by the QAA and currently being further refined by codes of practice.

A good example of diagnostic benchmarking is PROBE (you will recall that this stands for PROmoting Business Excellence). This is an international benchmarking scheme, managed by the Confederation of British Industry (CBI) in partnership with the London Business School and the IBM Consulting Group. It has grown out of a series of studies that set out to discover what best practice and world-class performance really look like and to benchmark hundreds of companies in several countries against these standards. The findings have appeared as a set of reports (Voss, *et al.*, 1997; Hanson, *et al.*, 1994; CBI, 1997) and they make fascinating reading. For example, a comparison of the service sectors of the UK and the USA. (in Voss, *et al.*, 1997) reveals that, while 5.3 per cent of the UK sample were categorized as world-class organizations, the US sample performed rather better, with 13.2 per cent. On the other hand, the US has a longer tail of poor performers than the UK. The comparisons of specific sectors are also interesting. For example, the UK's public sector (the sample includes local government, schools, police and government agencies) 'generally came out ahead of the US in overall service practices, being higher than the US in all areas except leadership' (Voss, *et al.*, 1997).

Setting aside the benefits of analysing characteristic strengths and improvement opportunities for a particular country or business sector, this scheme and others like it represent an opportunity for the individual organization to benchmark not only against a tried-and-tested model of business excellence, but also against the standards achieved by hundreds of others within and beyond their own sector. A team is formed to make judgements about the organization's practices and performance that represents a diagonal cross-section of the organization (about ten people covering a range in terms of seniority and functions). Each team member scores the organization on some 90 scales that form a fairly holistic picture of what the organization does and what it achieves – from relationships with customers to approaches to managing employees; from design and development of new services and products to measures of financial and non-financial performance. The team then meets for two sessions, spending a day in total developing consensus scores, assisted by an external facilitator who acts as an independent, objective stimulus and custodian of the benchmark standards.

The tangible outcome of this process is a set of charts, comparing this organization's practices and performance with those of other service or manufacturing companies in general and of those that inhabit the same sector at a more specific level. Figure 8.2 illustrates the nature of the analysis.

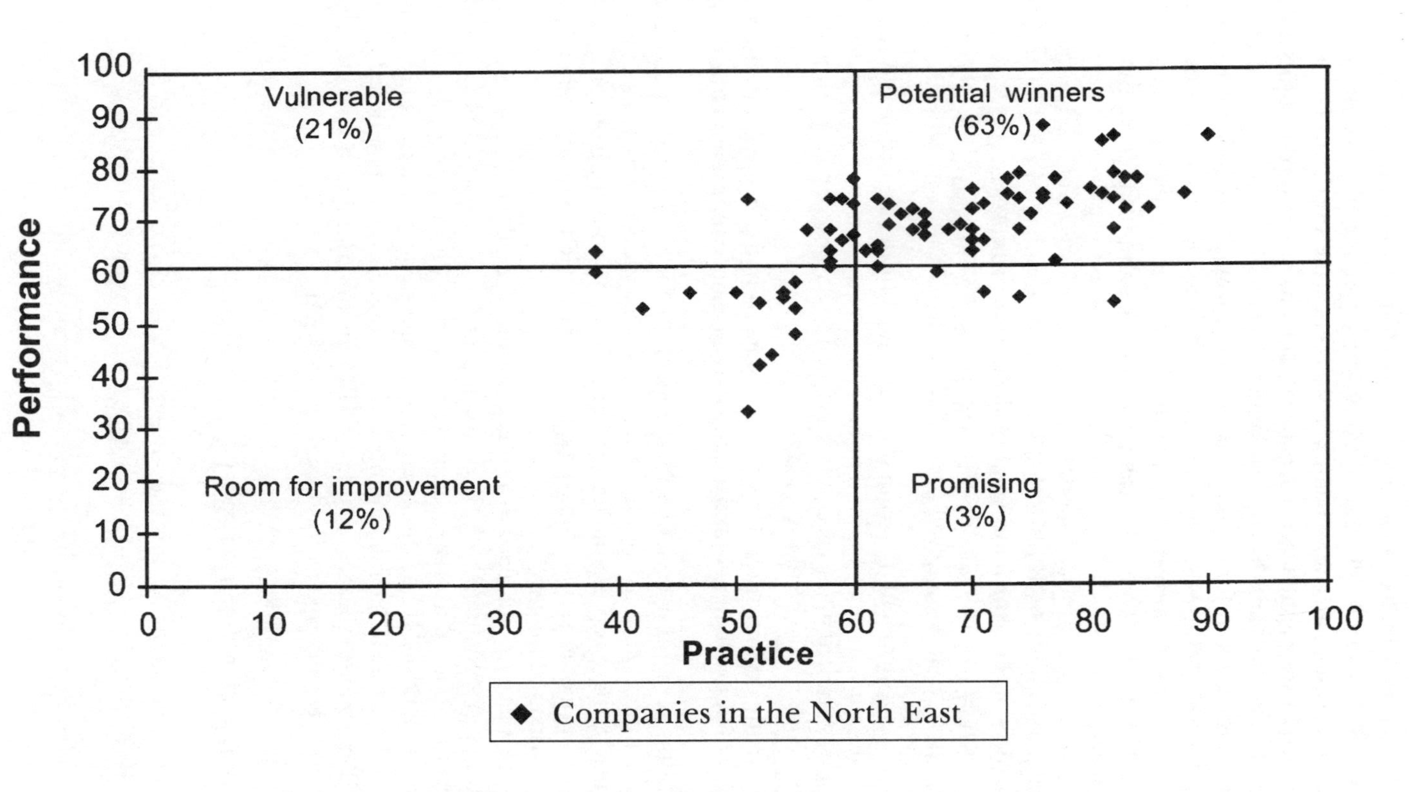


**Figure 8.2** *Scatter plot produced in diagnostic benchmarking*

A project was undertaken in the North East of England that, during 1997 and 1998, assisted 700 organizations in completing the PROBE process or, in most cases, an abbreviated version known as PILOT. The project has helped the region to learn a great deal about its business population, and the results (Prabhu and Yarrow, summer 1998) are being put to good use in drawing up plans for business support. In terms of the benefits to the businesses themselves, the almost unanimous response (measured by an independent follow-up survey) is that this kind of diagnostic benchmarking is a worthwhile exercise. The demonstrable benefits can be summarized as follows:

- participants have been challenged and stimulated to judge their practices and performance against demanding standards;
- they have been helped to do this in an objective, structured and generally non-threatening way;
- the involvement of a team stimulates healthy debate within the organization, often about topics that have not been examined previously in this way, and, in many cases, some surprising differences of opinion and perception have been revealed;
- many organizations have been prompted to dig deeper into the apparent improvement opportunities that have been pinpointed by the study.

Another emerging benefit is the opportunity for companies to make contact with others who are doing certain, specific things better than they are. Clearly, there is potential for such organizations to learn from one another, and the diagnostic benchmarking process is an aid to knowing where to look and what to look for.

This latter point leads to a consideration of the third and last of the three modes of benchmarking. It is worth pointing out that PROBE is one of several tools that have been created for the purpose of diagnostic benchmarking. It has the advantage of being one of the most credible and well-established, having built up a large and growing international database. Other notable schemes include the UK Benchmarking Index and the British Quality Foundation's tools based on the BEM.

## PROCESS BENCHMARKING

Process benchmarking is the subject of most of the books and articles that have been written about benchmarking. In essence, it consists of:

- identifying a specific process within an organization (organization A) that needs to be improved;

- comparing the way this process operates within organization A with the way it operates in another organization (or organizations);
- learning lessons and bringing them back to organization A, where they are put into practice;
- enjoying the fruits of these labours in the shape of improved performance.

This sounds simple enough but, predictably, it isn't necessarily so in practice. In Chapter 3, Alex Appleby has provided a thorough exploration of the theory of process benchmarking. This chapter concentrates on the practice and the experiences described feature a particular approach, called group benchmarking, with which a group of staff at the University of Northumbria has experimented over the last few years. It differs from the approach adopted by many organizations in that group benchmarking involves several organizations clustering around a common interest, whereas the more usual approach is a one-to-one exchange. However, it seems likely that many of the lessons we have learned have general applicability.

The experience of benchmarking on which this chapter is based dates back to 1990, arising from involvement in creating a business club. The idea was simply that many organizations in different sectors were wrestling with their own internal problems, unaware that many of these problems were common and that they might be spending valuable time reinventing the wheel. In particular, many people were trying to implement TQM and apparently all encountering similar patterns of achievement and difficulty. It seemed sensible to try to discover whether or not they could benefit from sharing these experiences.

The initial membership of the Best Practice Club was 20 organizations drawn from 20 different sectors, including a hospital, university, mail courier, brewery and manufacturers of cars, power tools and electrical goods. Managers attended presentations by visiting speakers and 'see for yourself' meetings hosted by other members.

The Club has proved its worth and now has 50 members. The benefits are many and varied, albeit fairly intangible and members have learned much from each other. Despairing lone voices have been reassured by their peers from other companies that they are not alone in facing difficulties and that perseverance is worth while. As the networking aspects of the Club developed, members learnt who to contact for help on specific topics and, in some cases, unearthed helpful ideas in quite surprising places.

Having said all of that, some devotees of benchmarking would suggest that the Club's activities leave much to be desired. They would describe them as 'industrial tourism' and see this as an inferior form of benchmarking, perhaps not worthy of the name at all. To an extent, this view was shared by some of the Club's members, especially after a presentation in 1993 by a speaker with extensive experience of process benchmarking. Their reaction was to suggest that the Club needed to evolve to support more sophisticated and detailed exchanges, and this led in time to the creation of The Benchmarking Network.

The Network's creation was demand-driven and the members played a major part in designing its structure and practices. A facilitator was appointed and a code of conduct was drafted, covering confidentiality and 'rules of engagement'. A study of the benchmarking literature provided guidance on how process benchmarking should be approached. Training was provided to bring members up to speed with the theory and with the experiences of organizations that had used benchmarking successfully.

The crunch came when the Network's structure was in place and the members were invited to make use of it. They were asked to pinpoint processes that they wished to benchmark and offered guidance on how to select these processes. The logic was clear:

- refer to the organization's strategic plans to discover its priorities and identify development needs;
- use existing knowledge of strengths and weaknesses to pinpoint performance targets that are not being achieved and processes with improvement potential;
- select the processes that are most in need of improvement;
- start looking for benchmarking partners willing to share their expertise in relation to these processes.

This is simpler than it was in practice. Every organization should have some form of strategic planning and review process in place, the outputs of which should include the raw material for selecting priorities for process benchmarking. However, it didn't work like that in practice. Some network members followed this logic and duly tabled their benchmarking plans, but the majority were either unwilling or unable to follow this path. Some became impatient with the facilitator's requests that they should do so and in the end many produced their benchmarking 'shopping lists' in a far more *ad hoc* manner. Some lists were fairly long and it was difficult to avoid the feeling that, for some participants, the opportunity to start benchmarking was more important than the irritating requirement to select a process to improve!

Pressing on, we attempted to find matches between strengths that members claimed for their organizations and processes that others wanted to benchmark. Groups of organizations were identified with some common ground – generally they contained several people who wanted to benchmark the same process (broadly speaking) and one or two who claimed to have strength in the same area. The focal points of the groups were many and varied. 'Measuring customer satisfaction' and 'Managing change' were two of the themes.

The common interest groups were brought together at an introductory meeting, and invited to exchange views. They explored the potential for mutual benefit and decided whether or not and how to proceed. Most agreed to meet again to begin the benchmarking process, and did so. Nevertheless, the success rate was low. Eight groups were formed, but only two lasted beyond a second meeting. These enjoyed modest success, but were far from being exemplars of effective transfer of better practice from one organization to another.

The experience gained from this first attempt was invaluable and a few months later the process of forming common interest groups was repeated, with a rather different approach being adopted and improved guidance offered to the groups regarding how they should proceed. The second round was more successful, although some groups again fell by the wayside. Two of the groups in particular achieved encouraging results. Following this second round, a review was conducted, involving most of those who had participated. The general consensus was that:

- all had benefited from the experience;
- for most, the prime benefit was that they had learned a lot about benchmarking, rather than that they had been able to significantly improve their processes or performance;
- a few were able to say that such improvements had been achieved;
- all felt better equipped to make future judgements on the usefulness of benchmarking as an improvement tool in a given set of circumstances;
- for a few, the experience had convinced them that they were unlikely to try process benchmarking again – they had realized that it was not a quick fix, and were not convinced that further attempts would be worth while for them.

The Network is still in existence, and has supported a number of further benchmarking initiatives since the review described above. The lessons learned from the exercise can be summarized under the following headings.

- **Think seriously about what you want to benchmark**
  - Common sense doesn't seem to be common practice. We believe that our experiences in forming the common interest groups are typical of many organizations' approaches to benchmarking – the appeal of trying out the technique clouds the judgement and resources are devoted to benchmarking a process that doesn't deserve to be a high priority. Questions need to be asked at the outset about whether or not this process

actually needs to be improved? If it is improved, which aspects of performance will benefit? Will it be worth the effort? These questions aren't easy to answer in advance, but should at least be considered. If the organization has sound strategic processes, it should not be too hard to identify priorities for improvement and an investment of time in diagnosis at an early stage could pay dividends.

- **Is there a commitment at a senior level to take benchmarking seriously?**
  - The initiator of a benchmarking project may not be very senior in the organization. How successful will they be unless they have the backing of senior management to invest substantial resources in benchmarking and to make changes to processes if the results suggest this? Our experience is that some benchmarking projects reveal improvement opportunities, but the individuals involved end up frustrated that they cannot put the lessons learned to good use.

- **Are the right people involved?**
  - We have seen examples of benchmarking enthusiasts (commonly the quality manager, or similar) benchmarking processes that belong to colleagues and learning valuable lessons, but then struggling to implement them because they encounter internal resistance. Is this surprising? If one of your colleagues announced to you that they'd seen examples elsewhere of people doing your job better than you do it, would your natural reaction be to reply, 'Oh good. Do tell me more. Perhaps you can tell me what I have been doing wrong all these years?' This is unlikely to be a typical reaction. Surely it makes sense that the process owners should be directly involved in the benchmarking process?

- **'Homework' is vital**
  - It is tempting but erroneous to think that benchmarking begins with a visit to another organization to view their better practices. It begins with a study of your own processes. Anyone who has done this will probably confirm that it is surprising how difficult it is to formally map one of their own processes in sufficient detail to really understand how it compares with its equivalent in another organization. If you haven't really achieved a full understanding of your own process, how will you know what to look for in someone else's?

- **'Best is the enemy of better'**
  - Our own preconception of benchmarking was that it involved finding a world-class organization and persuading them to open their doors. This argument is flawed. First of all, how do you find world-class organizations? They are not listed in the *Yellow Pages*! Second, do we really want to find an organization that is excellent at everything? Perhaps not – one

that is excellent at the specific process we are trying to improve would do. Third, do we really need to find the organization that is best at this particular process? Our experience is that finding better practice is a pretty good starting point.

- **The benefits are usually mutual**
  - It is easy to think of benchmarking as a one-way street. The benchmarker learns from the benchmarkee, who magnanimously gives away their secrets. However, if it is done well, process benchmarking is normally a matter of mutual benefit. The act of thoroughly reviewing your own process and comparing it with someone else's will inevitably reveal opportunities to improve, whatever the apparent overall superiority of one party's process over the other.

- **Think outside the box**
  - Another common belief is that benchmarking is about gleaning ideas from your competitors. This is not only quite difficult for most people, it is also very limiting. The chances of finding significantly better practice are far better if you do some lateral thinking and cross sectoral boundaries. One useful tip is to think of an organization for which this particular process is central to its success, even though for yours it might not be quite so crucial. It's a safe bet that it'll be managing the process rather well.

- **Find a compatible partner(s)**
  - As in life, so in benchmarking! Finding compatible partners isn't easy, but it is vitally important. Do they share your understanding of what this process is all about? Are their objectives for the benchmarking project compatible with your own? Are they as willing as you are to devote resources to the task? Do they share your sense of urgency and timescale? Do you trust each other? If your answer to all of these questions is 'yes', then you may be on to a winner!

To summarize, process benchmarking can be an effective tool that contributes to improvements in an organization and its performance. However, it is not as easy as it sounds, and it should perhaps carry a health warning – 'benchmarking can damage your wealth!' There are quite a few challenges to overcome if benchmarking is to deliver on its potential. For the conscientious benchmarker, willing to invest the time and effort and be patient and persistent, there is a pot of gold at the end of the rainbow. However, experience suggests that, for every benchmarker who fits this description, there are several who will end up disappointed. The danger of benchmarking as a technique is that these people will tend to tell others 'benchmarking doesn't work'.

## CONCLUSION

This chapter has outlined some practical experiences of benchmarking in the business world and drawn some lessons from them for the higher education sector. In a nutshell, the lessons are that:

- benchmarking is not one technique but three (at least!);
- the simplest form, metric benchmarking, can be a useful starting point but has some pitfalls and limitations;
- used appropriately, diagnostic benchmarking can help to pinpoint priorities and provide a 'call to action';
- process benchmarking has the greatest potential to deliver organizational improvement, but also the greatest potential to absorb resources with no guarantee of easy success.

One other lesson, important in the context of this book, is that benchmarking is every bit as applicable to higher education as it is to more commercial organizations, both in terms of benchmarking standards of student achievement and in benchmarking the performance of institutions in the same sector. Indeed, if providers of higher education want to significantly improve some aspects of their performance that are often, and perhaps justifiably, criticized, then benchmarking with organizations in other sectors may prove very fruitful – if it is done properly. Benchmarking, then, is like any other tool. Used appropriately to tackle the right task, it can be very effective. However, it is not a panacea and it is not a quick fix, but that is, of course, an entirely expected conclusion.

## ACKNOWLEDGEMENTS

I would like to acknowledge the contribution of many others to the work described in this chapter. They include people who work for the many companies and agencies involved in the various benchmarking projects, colleagues at Newcastle Business School at the University of Northumbria at Newcastle and our partners London Business School, IBM Consulting, The CBI and West London TEC.

## REFERENCES

CBI (1997) 'Fit for the Future: How competitive is UK manufacturing?', CBI, London

Hanson, P, Voss, C A, Blackmon, K, and Oak, B (1994) 'Made in Europe: A four nations best practice study', IBM UK and London Business School, London
Prabhu, V B, and Yarrow, D J (summer 1998) 'Best practice within North East Industry', *Northern Economic Review*, (27)
Voss, C, Blackmon, K, Chase, R, Rose, B, and Roth, A V (1997) 'Achieving world-class service: An Anglo-American benchmark comparison of service practice and performance', Severn Trent PLC, Birmingham
Womack, J, Jones, D, and Roos, D (1990) *The Machine That Changed the World*, Rawson Associates, New York

# Part III

## UK Perspectives in the Development and Use of Benchmarks and Threshold Standards

9

# UK Experiences in the Development of Benchmarking and Threshold Standards

*Ian Haines*

## THE BROAD CONTEXTUAL ISSUES

As has been indicated in earlier chapters, the driving force for the creation of a benchmark against which all UK chemistry degrees could be measured was the report by Sir Ron Dearing (DfEE, 1998) on the future of higher education and the Government's response to it. Dearing's report listed a number of issues that gave rise to concerns that there might be considerable variability in the standards of degree courses in the UK. One such concern related to a small number of well-publicized cases where procedures for the assurance of quality and standards had been seriously deficient. In addition to this, employers and professional bodies were also perturbed about the standards of some degree qualifications. However, many of these concerns were not supported by any quantitative data, but grade inflation evidenced by the increased proportion of students obtaining higher degree classifications (for example first and upper second class honours) in the context of large increases in the student population and the lowering of entry requirements for some courses, was used to indicate that there must have been a lowering of standards.

### External verification

These varied factors led Dearing to conclude that the external examiner system as currently operated was incapable of ensuring consistent standards of awards in the expanded and more diverse higher education system. It is worth noting that the HEQC had previously commissioned an evaluation of the external examiner system (Silver, *et al.*, 1995), but this had failed to provide any useful solutions. The Dearing Report thus proposed the extension of the conventional functions of external examiners to include verification of:

- the attainment of academic standards by the development of threshold standards using benchmarking statements;
- programme objectives, as defined by individual institutions.

## From an élite to a mass higher education system

Reducing entry requirements and expanding access need not necessarily lead to a reduction in output standards. Before 1962, fewer than 4 per cent of school-leavers were able to benefit from higher education. The university expansion in the 1970s increased access to 1 in 8 students (the start of the alleged reduction in standards?) and current participation rates are around 30 per cent in England and Wales, though it is worth noting that in Scotland, with its rigorous educational system and standards, 47 per cent of school-leavers are judged currently to be at the appropriate level for entry into higher education.

Any explanation as to why a reduction in entry standards inevitably leads to a lowering of the threshold level of a particular classification of degree has yet to be established satisfactorily. In all other aspects of human endeavour it is fully accepted that progress can be made and higher standards achieved. For example, in 1953 only one man was able to run a mile in under four minutes, but those watching an international athletics event now will expect most of the field to achieve this. No one has argued that the standard of chronometry has become less accurate. Why should it not be possible for the increases in access and opportunity and developments in teaching and learning to achieve similar increases in abilities alongside changes in participation provided that the measurement made is one of the outcomes – that is, what a student is capable of at the end of a course?

## Degree classification creep

It is only fair to note, however, that in the past ten years many universities have made changes to the regulations governing the award of degrees and these have sometimes increased the ease with which higher degree classifications can be obtained. Such changes have included:

- allowing students to discount some of their worst marks;
- introduction of a greater variety of assessment methods;
- giving a higher weighting to course work marks – generally many percentage points greater than the marks obtained in traditional examinations that previously had been the predominant contribution to degree classification.

While these factors may have had relatively little effect in some universities, they have led, in some institutions, to almost no students being awarded a third class honours or unclassified degree. However, a check of the overall assumption that there has been a significant upwards drift in the proportion of students obtaining first and upper second class honours degrees in chemistry shows very little grade inflation (see Table 9.1). Any long-term comparison is somewhat difficult to carry out as, until relatively recently, a number of students took examinations for Graduateship of the Royal Society of Chemistry Part II (GRSC) rather than for the award of an honours degree. These examinations were at least the equivalent of a lower second class honours degree and there is no doubt that the performance of a significant proportion of students was of first or upper second standard. If one allocates half of the GRSC cohort to the lower second category and half to the first/upper second level, a reasonable comparison can be made of degree classifications in chemistry over the last decade (see Table 9.1). The percentage increase (from 40.7 to 44.5 per cent) in first and upper second class degrees awarded is probably much less than most people would have expected and certainly not in itself sufficient cause for alarm about falling standards.

**Table 9.1** *Degree classifications in chemistry 1987 and 1997*

| *Degree classification*<br>*Year* | *1st/2.1* | *2.2* | *3* | *P* | *Total awards* |
|---|---|---|---|---|---|
| 1987 | 40.7% | 30.4% | 19.0% | 9.9% | 3181 |
| 1997 | 44.5% | 31.3% | 16.9% | 7.2% | 3753 |

*Notes:* In 1987, there were 294 awards of GRSC that have been split equally between the 1st/2.1 and 2.2 classifications for the purpose of calculating percentages (*see text*).
1987 calculated from 1991 Review of Chemistry: Courses and Teaching, Council for National Academic Awards.
1997 calculated from UCAS Annual Report.

## PERCEPTIONS OF THE QUALITY AND STANDARDS OF HE CHEMISTRY

This chapter will not suggest that the UK's university sector has been achieving perfect calibration of standards within and between subjects, but it is worth considering how much the perception of standards, both in the UK and overseas, has been affected negatively by the publication of data, including assessment of quality, that were subsequently used in inappropriate ways. The use of such data in the production of league tables and their publication – with little or no explanation or interpretation – was bound to suggest a wide variability in standards.

### Assessing quality

In the methodology for assessing quality of teaching in England and Northern Ireland between 1992 and 1995, the descriptors used to describe the quality of provision were excellent, satisfactory or unsatisfactory. In all subjects other than chemistry, which were assessed between 1992 and 1995, the percentage of excellent grades was 26 per cent (HEFCE, 1995a). However, as usual, the chemistry community was extremely harsh in its self-assessment (HEFCE, 1995b) with the result that in England and Northern Ireland only 18 per cent of institutions were judged to be providing an excellent education in chemistry, with the remainder – a total of 59 institutions – considered to be merely satisfactory. It made no difference to public perception of chemistry courses that the definition of 'satisfactory' meant that there were 'many elements of good practice. Aims and objectives are being met and there is a good match between these, the teaching and learning process and the students' ability, experience, expectations and achievement.'

A further illustration of the ability of the UK chemistry community to judge itself harshly is shown in the most recent research assessment exercise (HEFCE, 1996). This produced judgements suggesting that chemistry was well behind other scientific disciplines as the assessment panel concluded that only 45 per cent of funded departments were worthy of the upper three ratings whereas, for example, the physics panel judged that 75 per cent of departments were within that category.

## CONTEXTUAL ISSUES FOR THE BENCHMARKING OF CHEMISTRY

### Views of employers

There is much anecdotal evidence that although the chemical and allied industries have continued to employ new chemistry graduates and postgraduates there have been considerable concerns about their knowledge and skills. However, an in-depth survey of employers (Mason, 1998) indicated a very high level of satisfaction (about 90 per cent) in most of the scientific skills of chemistry graduates who were recruited (the main complaints being about others who had been rejected). There was some lack of satisfaction of graduates' interpersonal skills, commercial understanding and so on. Mason also found that almost 80 per cent of graduates felt that the chemistry content of their first degree was adequate for their current job. These facts suggest that, in terms of subject knowledge and direct subject-related skills, the content and level of chemistry degrees has been about right, though there is a need for more attention to be given to the other transferable skills.

## Flexibility

The view of the Government is that there must be a productive dialogue between universities and industry. Specifically, according to the Minister of State for Science, Energy and Industry, 'A closer match is needed between undergraduate course choices and the projected needs of industry, especially at the local level' (Battle, 1998). It is unclear how some less vocational subjects could be expected to take up this challenge, except in the development of transferable skills. However, the need to meet this challenge means that any benchmarking statement must be sufficiently flexible in its application' so that individual chemistry programmes:

- are not restricted to a narrow, prescribed range of content;
- can reflect important specializations and applications of the subject;
- can meet the aspirations of individual institutional missions.

## The relationship with professional bodies

All of those involved in the further development of quality and standards assurance are aware of the risk of escalating the costs of such activities. In its consultation exercise, the Quality Assurance Agency (QAA) indicated its wish to create processes that:

- are less resource-consuming than the previous methodology;
- are cost-effective;
- avoid placing unreasonable burdens on institutions.

As most institutions tend to have a five- or six-year cycle for the internal review of programmes of study – and many disciplines receive accreditation from professional bodies on a similar timescale – there is a real opportunity, in simple planning, to reduce the number of such resource-intensive events from three to two, or even one. Most institutions, with sufficient notice, could adjust the timescale of their internal review processes to coincide with those of the QAA. However, the arrangement with professional bodies is potentially more complicated, at least until all levels of courses have been benchmarked. This is due to the number of different degree programmes available – three-year honours (single subject and joint), four-year higher honours, exit points below three-year honours courses and so on, and their equivalents in the Scottish system. In addition, for a subject that is offered in most universities, the parallel processes of professional accreditation and national checking of standards and quality will almost certainly need to be spread over several years as most professional bodies do not have the resources to commit to a concentrated period of accreditation.

## Applying standards – entry or exit?

The accepted accrediting body for chemistry – The Royal Society of Chemistry (RSC) – is currently considering how it might change its membership structure to reflect the constantly evolving nature of the subject. Although discussions are, as yet, incomplete, it is likely that within two years there will be considerable changes to the categories and requirements for membership. At the moment, two broad categories of membership are being proposed. These are Chartered Chemist (designated CChem.), for those operating as professional chemists, and Member (designated MRSC). This latter category is being designed to be as inclusive as possible, so that, for example, those who operate in a more extensive range of roles requiring the application of some aspects of chemical (or molecular) sciences would be included. The criteria for both these categories will involve consideration of academic training as well as work as a practitioner. It is likely that the achievement of Chartered status will require meeting the outcomes of an enhanced first degree course (MChem. or MSci.), possession of appropriate practitioner experience and evidence of updating by means of continuing professional development activities. The Membership category will be available to those with a much broader interest in the application of chemistry – those who, perhaps, have achieved the outcomes in chemical/molecular science normally found in a joint or combined honours BSc course of the type defined by the title 'Chemistry with… '. This less specialist requirement will open up membership to graduates from a range of related disciplines – biochemistry, materials science, food science and so on. The current exercise in chemistry of benchmarking a three-year single honours Bachelors degree (and its Scottish equivalent) clearly falls between these two sets of academic requirements and cannot be allocated automatically to either category of membership.

A major requirement for any benchmarking statement is that it is easy to understand, unambiguous and straightforward in its application. When the new professional accreditation requirements of the RSC are finally agreed, they are likely to provide relatively brief and not overly prescriptive criteria and will concentrate on specified outcomes. This approach contrasts sharply with the Engineering Council's position on accreditation (Engineering Council, 1998). Its documentation (weighing in excess of 1kg) concentrates essentially on specifying the entry requirements for accredited courses. These requirements state that, by 2002, courses leading to Incorporated

Engineer (IEng) status will have an intake in which at least 80 per cent of the A level cohort has achieved a minimum of 10 UCAS points. Such a course does not even have to be an honours degree programme. The equivalent academic requirement for an accredited MEng. course (which is the fast route to Chartered Engineer status) is that 80 per cent of entrants have a minimum A level score of 24 UCAS points.

The interpretation of the Standards and Routes to Registration (SARTOR) requirements by the British Computer Society (BCS) is contained in a mere 40 pages. However, the 40 pages do not even specify course content, except to note the need for appropriate underpinning of mathematics and the use of formal and semi-formal design methods and the identification of generic and subject-specific skills. The BCS does, of course, still have the SARTOR entry requirements based on UCAS points with limits on non-standard entrants.

By adopting an outcomes approach (as opposed to entry restrictions) the strategy of the RSC should be straightforward in operation and, unlike the Engineering Council's, will ensure equality of opportunity and access to courses. The RSC will therefore be able to utilize the chemistry benchmarking statement if it wishes to assist in its accreditation activities as that, too, is written in terms of outcomes. Indeed, this is essential if benchmarking and accreditation activities are not to operate separately with the consequent additional burden this will put on institutions. It is unlikely that the decision of the benchmarking group (see later) that it was QAA and not the Society that would have to own the benchmarking statement will create any difficulties.

## THE PROCESS

### Production of a benchmarking statement for chemistry

As described earlier, the QAA decided that chemistry, history and law were to be the first three discipline areas to investigate and produce benchmarking information on subject threshold standards. The RSC agreed to coordinate nominations to the Chemistry Benchmarking Working Group and the Association of British Pharmaceutical Industries, Chemical Industries Association Ltd, Higher Education Chemistry Conference and Society of Chemical Industry were asked for nominations (the final membership of the benchmarking group is given at the end of this chapter). The Group met on four occasions over a period of six months.

### Initial actions and decisions

At its first meeting, the group received a small amount of background material on the topic and an oral report by the Chief Executive of the QAA on a benchmarking consultation exercise that was nearing completion. Despite some scepticism about the concept of benchmarking and other associated issues (at that stage, the QAA was offering for discussion radical – and impractical – proposals redefining the role of the external examiner) the group began its task with an open mind. This, perhaps, reflects the nature of the subject and its practitioners – whatever the challenge, chemists are willing to seek, and attempt to develop, practical solutions!

## Diversity and flexibility

The chemistry community has a wide range of opinions on the content, delivery and assessment of chemistry courses. At one extreme, the traditionalists require courses to have fixed, detailed syllabi containing substantial proportions of inorganic chemistry, organic chemistry and physical chemistry as well as major elements of ancillary physics and mathematical science. This approach is seen by others as protecting academic specialisms and preventing change by attempting to ensure that every chemistry course has to employ several chemists who specialize in each of these areas. A more modern approach views chemistry as the enabling science, encompassing a variable range of molecular science content together with appropriate applications of the subject (for example, biological, medicinal or environmental aspects). Thus, initially, the group debated the extent to which benchmarking statements should concentrate on the subdisciplines of inorganic, organic, physical and analytical chemistry or on an approach emphasizing atomic and molecular science based on integration across the discipline.

To progress the debate, each Group member was required to produce a statement, within two weeks of the first meeting, giving their own interpretation of the skills and knowledge expected of a chemistry graduate at the lower second/upper second borderline.

The first meeting of the Group also agreed that any statement of the standard of graduate attainment for a single honours chemistry degree should:

- be specified in terms of subject knowledge, subject-specific skills and transferable (key) skills;
- concentrate on a definition of the threshold point at the lower second/upper second borderline for a three-year honours programme, including consideration of the Scottish equivalent;
- refer specifically to chemistry in its curriculum content, but not in such detail as to prevent course teams from developing a varied range of courses;
- emphasize the acquisition of problem-solving skills and laboratory-based practical skills;

- be owned by the QAA and not the professional body or higher education chemistry community.

At the second meeting, copies of individual members' proposals and ideas relating to assessment issues were passed round. A summary of the proposals, produced by the Group secretary, was discussed. Itcontained a set of statements, generated from the individual proposals, that grouped the perceived main aims/outcomes of a chemistry degree programme under the broad headings of subject knowledge, subject-related skills (including those related to practical work) and transferable skills. The summary also included a consideration of possible assessment processes. At this stage, the Group agreed to:

- emphasize degree outcomes rather than course entry requirements;
- consult widely when the benchmarking statement was complete among employers as well as academia using a structured questionnaire;
- avoid the use of the current degree classifications (first, upper second and so on) in further development of the benchmarking statement;
- emphasize the value of chemistry as a vehicle for the development of transferable skills;
- include a statement on appropriate assessment methods for the measurement of the proposed outcomes;
- consider descriptors for five levels of ability of a chemistry graduate instead of concentrating only on the lower second/upper second border.

Following the meeting all members were required to:

- comment further on the various aspects of the proposals;
- produce a statement of their views on the essential subject content of a chemistry honours degree (using no more than one A4 page);
- produce brief descriptors for five levels of ability of a chemistry graduate.

## Consensus

At this point in the process, the written submissions produced by individual contributors demonstrated significant divergence of approach to defining the curriculum content. Some members generated examples of syllabi, fitting comfortably into the traditional mould and clearly identifying inorganic, organic and physical sections. Others had attempted a much more radical and integrated approach and had completely avoided the traditional compartmentalization of the discipline. However, a summary of the views was discussed vigorously at the next (third) meeting, a consensus obtained and a draft benchmarking statement generated.

### The final stages

Prior to the fourth and final meeting of the Group, a final draft of the benchmarking statement and a structured questionnaire were circulated to all members of the Higher Education Chemistry Conference, a wide range of industrialists and other interested individuals and groups. A summary of the views obtained was discussed at the meeting and the statement amended to incorporate some of the comments received. The final version of the benchmarking document will reflect the outcomes agreed at this meeting. For those who are not familiar with the subject, it is important to point out that it is a statement of a very small core of essential knowledge and nowhere near the national curriculum for higher education that many had feared might be imposed on them.

## EVALUATION OF THE PROCESS

The benchmarking proposals have yet to be tested for widespread acceptance and applicability and it is unlikely that all other subject and multidisciplinary areas could (or would wish to) use exactly the same approach as that employed by the Group. However, it is possible to offer some lessons for consideration by other disciplines about to embark on the benchmarking process.

### Group composition

It is suggested that the members are chosen so that the group:

- has a high level of acceptability across the sector – the Chemistry Group included individuals who were present or past senior officers of The Royal Society of Chemistry, held senior appointments in their own institutions and were highly active in research and/or other professional activities;
- can represent as wide a range of stakeholders as possible – such as the professional bodies, commercial and other employing organizations (including small to medium enterprises), and relevant trade associations (unfortunately, the Chemistry Group was unable to recruit industrial members, despite strenuous attempts to do so, but some Group members did possess recent industrial experience and several were involved in large commercial research contracts and the distribution of the draft benchmarking statement and associated questionnaire to a range of industrialists ensured their views were obtained and considered);
- is chaired (and led) by a professional who can command the respect and confidence of members of the discipline and can bring about agreement when differing, strongly-held opinions are being expressed (the Group

was fortunate in being chaired by Professor Eddie Abel who was just completing his two-year term as President of The Royal Society of Chemistry);

- is comprised of individuals who are committed to carrying out, and completing to deadlines, any work required between meetings, and to attending the meetings (the quality of the work the Group produced was high and members' full participation demonstrated a determination to seek a solution, or range of solutions, to the issues being considered);
- has the services of a subject specialist to distill members' views into the production of objective discussion documents and produce other documents for consideration at the formal meetings.

### The process

While it is possible that the statement could have been generated more rapidly during, say, an 'away' weekend, it was helpful to have time to consider and reflect in depth the implications and requirements of the process over the course of weeks. Spreading the process over this period also allowed group members to discuss the work with colleagues and receive further views and input into the development of the benchmarking.

The pace of the exercise was brisk and, as all Group members have heavy workloads and professional commitments, keeping the number of meetings to a minimum was essential. The process was progressed rapidly by requiring members to undertake a considerable amount of work between meetings. Further, the collation of this information, by a subject specialist, for presentation at the meetings allowed the meetings to be highly focused and productive.

It is important to have administrative support for the Group from someone who is also a subject specialist as then the issues being discussed are fully understood and accurate documentation is produced at each stage.

Obtaining and recognizing the views of all relevant stakeholders is essential if the final statements are to have widespread credibility. The organizations that might be consulted include higher education institutions and appropriate educational establishments, professional bodies, commercial/non-commercial organizations (especially small to medium enterprises) and trade associations and trade unions, where appropriate.

## THE FUTURE

### Comparability

The Higher Education Chemistry Conference, in its response to the Dearing Report, had accepted that, alongside the increase in the age participation rate and the varying needs of employers, there had been a variation in the aims of degree programmes. It considered this variation as acceptable given the differing needs, for example, of a course intended to prepare students for entry into a research degree programme compared with a programme that produced practitioners for advanced technical employment in industry. Agreement with this argument hinges on whether or not there is an agreed threshold level that is achieved by both types of courses. It is essential that the benchmarking system can accommodate such variations and not require the development of two different sets of threshold levels for courses with differing, planned outcomes.

## Generic outcomes

The Chemistry Benchmarking Group expended considerable time and thought in producing a benchmarking statement for a single-subject honours degree. Its proposals had a mixed reception when circulated for consultation, indicating that, even in the case of a single-honours programme in an apparently well-defined scientific discipline, there is no universal agreement about the core knowledge base of the subject. This issue will be magnified for joint honours programmes and is likely to lead to generic, non-content-based statements for interdisciplinary and multidisciplinary programmes. It will also challenge those developing new degrees in non-traditional subject areas to articulate clearly what is meant by the new degree title and to specify what graduates of the discipline can be expected to demonstrate.

## A dilemma for the Engineering Council – SARTOR; Suppressing Access Routes to Registration?

As mentioned previously, the Engineering Council has decided that a main requirement for courses leading to professional accreditation will relate to the entry qualifications of the majority of students. Unlike in Chemistry (see Table 9.1), there has recently been significant grade inflation in degree courses in engineering and technology subjects. Table 9.2 shows significant increases, in just two years from 1995 to 1997, in the percentage of upper second (25.8 to 30.9 per cent of the total) and lower second (26.5 to 29.3 per cent) degrees awarded, while at the same time the percentage of students obtaining unclassified degrees reduced by more than 50 per cent (18.2 to 8.1 per cent). Whether or not these changes were accompanied by an increase, or decrease, in the average A level points possessed by students on entry is unclear, but the degree classification changes have been produced and sanctioned by the engineering community itself, through its internal and external examination procedures.

**Table 9.2** *Degree classifications – all engineering and technology (% of total)*

| | 1st | 2.1 | 2.2 | 3rd | U | Total |
|---|---|---|---|---|---|---|
| 1994–95(%) | 16.6 | 25.8 | 26.5 | 12.9 | 18.2 | 1695 |
| 1995–96(%) | 16.0 | 30.0 | 29.2 | 10.6 | 14.2 | 1862 |
| 1996–97(%) | 16.6 | 30.9 | 29.3 | 15.0 | 8.1 | 1876 |

*Sources:* 1995, 1996, 1997, 'Students in Higher Education', Higher Education Statistics Agency

## A levels – the 'gold standard'?

Despite the Engineering Council's insistence on specifying A level grades for entry to its accredited courses, there is little evidence to demonstrate that these are a consistent, unchanging measure of the knowledge required for degree entry. A longitudinal survey, carried out between 1989 and 1996 and involving A level chemistry students who had attained various A level grades, measured the ability of the students to answer simple multiple-choice questions on very basic, core aspects of the subject. The average percentage of correct answers for students with different A level grades (see Table 9.3) shows, for example, that the average result of a grade D student in 1989 was attained by the average grade B student in 1996.

**Table 9.3** *Percentages of correct answers by A level chemistry grade*

| Year/Grade | A | B | C | D | E | N | F |
|---|---|---|---|---|---|---|---|
| 1989 (%) | 82 | 73 | 64 | 56 | 51 | 49 | 37 |
| 1996 (%) | 68 | 56 | 48 | 44 | 37 | 26 | 16 |

*Source:* 'Research in Assessment XIII', The Royal Society of Chemistry, 1996

Obviously, over time, A level syllabi have changed and may not prepare students so thoroughly in all core concepts, but the results do indicate that A level grades are not necessarily the fixed 'gold standard' some may believe them to be. (The decline in scores for some individual questions are even more disconcerting than the averages quoted here.) However, if the Engineering Council is to continue to view A levels as the entry determinant, then, from the above results, entrants to MEng. courses will surely need to possess 30 points by the year 2005 (currently required) and to have gained three A* grades by 2010!

## Outcomes or entry qualifications?

The three subject areas that have produced benchmarking statements to date have all concentrated on expected degree outcomes. Outside the Engineering Council and its constituent institutions, it is difficult to find anyone who believes its SARTOR requirements are appropriate. If the Council maintains its present position, however, there is a real danger that many students who have the potential to benefit from higher education, but who have been socially or educationally disadvantaged will be prevented from joining accredited engineering courses. If the engineering subject groups follow the path established by the first three disciplines and develop benchmarking statements that ignore entry requirements, concentrating instead only on outcomes, the Council may just be persuaded to reconsider its position, and its stance on the requirements for courses leading to professional accreditation.

## Accountability and competition

It is essential that public funding is properly accounted for and fully and thoroughly audited. While governments have demanded quality and standards auditing, they have also created, in the higher education funding mechanisms, a climate of commercial rivalry between institutions that potentially invalidates any form of peer review and assessment. We have reached a point where a competitive advantage – in teaching, research and other activities – that can be sustained by a particular university for a year or two may have a very significant effect on the 'business'. In an increasingly commercial environment, it may be considered unreasonable for universities to expose their activities in public reports to the scrutiny of professionals from competitor institutions. This is neither an argument for a return to a national group (comparable with Her Majesty's Inspectors who inspected the previous polytechnic sector) nor for a lack of accountability. However, the notion of Ford bringing in staff from Vauxhall and BMW to study its products, interview its workforce and dealers, interrogate its customers and then publish their report in public must surely be a long way off. It is difficult to believe that such peer review can continue much longer in the competitive, commercial world of universities.

## THE MEMBERS OF THE CHEMISTRY BENCHMARKING GROUP

Professor Edward Abel, University of Exeter (Chair), Professor Peter Atkins, Lincoln College, Oxford, Professor Ian Haines, University of North London, Professor Raymond Jones, Open University, Professor Richard Kempa, University of Keele, Professor Michael Page, University of Huddersfield, Professor Barry Parsons, North East Wales Institute of Higher Education, Professor David Phillips, Imperial College of Science, Technology and Medicine, Professor David Rice, University of Reading, Professor Keith Smith, University of Wales, Swansea, Professor Peter Tasker University of Edinburgh, Professor Alan Townshend, University of Hull, Professor John Winfield, University of Glasgow.

Others normally in attendance were:

Dr Sepp Gruber (The Royal Society of Chemistry) and Dr Charlotte MacKenzie (Quality Assurance Agency).

## REFERENCES


Battle, J (1998) 'Annual Conference', Council for Industry and Higher Education, London

DfEE (1998) 'The Learning Age: A Renaissance for a New Britain', HMSO, London

DfEE (1997) Higher Education in the Learning Society, HMSO, London

HEFCE (1995a) 'Quality Assessment of Chemistry: 1993–94', HEFCE, London

HEFCE (1995b) 'Report on Quality Assessment: 1992–95', HEFCE, London

HEFCE (1996) 'Research Assessment: The outcome', HEFCE, London

Great Britain Engineering Council (1998) 'SARTOR – Standards and Routes to Registration', Engineering Council, London

Mason, G (1998) *Change and Diversity: The challenges facing Chemistry Higher Education*, The Royal Society of Chemistry and Council for Industry and Higher Education, London

Silver, H, *et al.* (1995) 'The External Examiner System: Possible Futures', Quality Support Centre and Open University Press, Buckingham

# 10

# Benchmarking in law

*John Bell*

Law is not a national subject. The United Kingdom has three legal systems – in Scotland, England and Wales, and in Northern Ireland. What is presented here is the development of benchmarks in England, Wales and Northern Ireland, though the Scots have produced benchmarks of their own that are only subtly different from those south of the border.

This chapter sets out the reasons behind the particular standards that were produced for law and the processes that have been used. It also identifies potential problem areas.

## BACKGROUND – MOTIVATIONS SPECIFIC TO THE LAW BENCHMARKING EXERCISE

The setting of standards in law is not a new activity. Professional bodies have long set criteria for what they will treat as a 'qualifying law degree' permitting students to embark on vocational training. These days, the vocational training involves both a course and a period of traineeship (called 'pupillage' at the Bar). The traditional way in which the professions have defined the criteria for the qualifying law degree has been in terms of content. There are certain prescribed subjects (in England and Wales described as 'the foundations of legal knowledge') that any law student must pass in order to proceed to take the vocational course, and these subjects must occupy a minimum amount of time in the law programme. In the past, there have also been requirements by the professions as to the form of assessment, restricting the amount of course work assessment that can be used. Benchmarking represents a key moment in the increasing autonomy of the academic degree in law or legal studies in relation to professional requirements. For the first time, there will be a rival standard against which law degrees can judge themselves and that can be the focal point for a discussion of the academic aims of legal education, rather than just the requirements of the legal professions.

In England and Wales, the activity of creating initial benchmark standards coincided with a revision of the minimum content of qualifying law degrees established by the professional bodies (the 'Joint Announcement', Bar Council for England and Wales and the Law Society, January 1995 ). The revision of the Joint Announcement (1998) was intended to take account of the first report of the Lord Chancellor's Advisory Committee on Legal Education and Conduct (ACLEC) on the initial stage of legal education. That report, published in April 1996, suggested a radical change in emphasis from a focus on the content of the law curriculum to one on learning outcomes (ACLEC, April 1996). The suggestion was that a university programme would satisfy the requirements for being a qualifying law degree if certain outcomes related to general transferable intellectual skills and some broad definitions of subject content were demonstrated in a programme that contained at least two-thirds of law subjects. This was welcomed by legal academics as providing much greater freedom to define the content and the assessment of the legal curriculum. The secretariats of the professions also welcomed this as a way forward and the revised Joint Announcement was drafted in discussions between the professions and representatives of academics on that basis.

Among legal educators, the idea of benchmark standards fitted into the same approach as ACLEC in focusing on generic outcomes, rather than predominantly on specific content. All the same, there was a concern that law schools would be subjected to conflicting demands – one set of standards deriving from the legal professions and one from the QAA. Given that the majority of law students have the aspiration to enter the legal professions, the professions' standards would inevitably dominate the law curriculum. The QAA has also been concerned to use law as a pilot subject for benchmarking in order to demonstrate that the new processes of quality assurance can meet the concerns of professional bodies. Professional bodies are thus a constituency integral to the trial process but are not to dominate the shape of academic legal education. Throughout, there has been a concern both to free the law curriculum from undue restriction arising from professional requirements and to ensure a consistency in the external demands that are placed on it.

The professions themselves have wished to be more flexible in their requirements of the law curriculum. They recognize that there is a certain inconsistency in making very specific demands on the law curriculum and then recruiting a very significant number of students into the legal professions with no law degree at all. These latter students take the one-year Common Professional Examination (CPE) before joining the law graduates on vocational courses. The content of the CPE is tightly regulated by a body established by the professions. The outcomes of law degrees have come under scrutiny from vocational course providers who are concerned about the knowledge and skills that students have on entry into the Legal Practice Course and the Bar Vocational Course. Similar concerns about skills on entry come from recruiters in the professions. These voices do affect the views of the professional bodies.

Within academic institutions and the professional bodies, there are internal tensions between the different interests of law schools as providers of undergraduate degrees and vocational courses, and between the concerns of the professions not to over-regulate and yet secure appropriate entry standards. These internal tensions have been played out in the debates on standards. In brief, the likely result is going to be an articulation of professional requirements directly in relation to the benchmark standards, but at a higher level of achievement and with more specificity as to content. The lesson for other subjects is that, in relation to professional subjects, it is important to recognize the educational policy issues as well as the pedagogical issues in articulating standards.

## THE PROCESS

Like any academic process, benchmarking has been based on research and discussion. This has been supplemented by consultation. The development of benchmarks brought together expertise developed in four separate exercises in recent years. In the first place, the ACLEC's first report (ACLEC, April 1996) was produced by a group of people who had experience in producing outcome statements in relation to law and trying to shape the law curriculum in this way. Given that this had been well received, the approach, structure and terminology was an obvious starting point for further work. All the same, this work had focused on general intellectual skills and was really more suitable as a modal statement than as a minimum, threshold statement. The Graduate Standards Report on degree classification by Phil Jones, *et al.* (HEQC, 1997) had examined marking criteria and helped to present an understanding of assessment practice. In particular, the lack of articulated criteria in many institutions was recognized, as well as the reliance on shared assumptions that were increasingly under threat from changes in the system. These brought out clearly the description of the third class student in deficiency terms (for example, 'misses key points, contains important inaccuracies'). The Graduate Standards Report had led to work done by consortia of subject associations. In law, a feasibility study was conducted producing a report within four months. The group conducting this work had developed some broad criteria of graduate standards at modal level based on consultation with a group of experienced external examiners. This demonstrated clearly that conceptions of graduateness were set at modal level, but were largely implicit. All the same, when confronted with actual scripts, there was much similarity among law examiners, for whom accurate content was a major criterion for marks. There was a view, common among many colleagues, that there was not a progression of levels as in standard CATS systems, but a single standard to be applied – that of competence in the subject, which was applied to all law students, such that a student studying contract law in the first year would be distinguished from a third-year student doing that course by the marks achieved rather than by a distinct level of achievement. There was also some sense that there were differences in the expectations of students on law programmes and non-law programmes attending the same modules. The fourth element was the DfEE-sponsored Discipline Network in Law on General Transferable Skills in the Law Curriculum. This had produced a report in March 1998 (see also Bell, 1997), after two years' work, that set out some basic statements of requirements in relation to core general transferable skills the law curriculum might develop. This study had involved both questionnaires and workshops with a wide range of law schools.

The combination of these materials gave the subject benchmarking group some background research and information on opinions in the sector and materials encapsulating ideas on standards with specific reference to law that could be discussed. Although there had been some consultation or enquiry with the sector that had produced feedback on the 'Graduate Standards in Law' report (Bell, 1997) and the 'General Transferable Skills in the Law Curriculum' ( Bell and Johnstone, 1998), it would be wrong to say that the ideas were widely shared and applied in the sector. On the one hand, there were quite well-developed ideas produced by a small group of law colleagues that were the basis of drafts produced. While there was consultation with the law schools and their associations as part of the process of developing benchmarks and their reactions did influence the texts produced by the Benchmarking Group (particularly the Guidance Note), the character of the process was not widely understood. The report of the feasibility study 'Graduate Standards in Law' did note the need for wider education, which was not met by the process available to the Benchmarking Group.

In the end, the Academic Standards subcommittee of the ACLEC held preliminary discussions before the benchmarking group was set up and I prepared drafts for these meetings. This body contained representatives of the professions, law schools and wider interests. There was also a Scots observer. The draft from this process was then disseminated among academics via the subject associations. The actual nomination process for the benchmarking took some considerable time, such that the first proper meeting did not take place until July with a different composition and full representation of the professions and academics in the three jurisdictions. A revised draft was presented that was then sent out for consultation and discussion among professionals and academics. It would be fair to say that there was not a large number of responses to the consultation exercises. In part this was because of unfamiliarity with the kinds of statements produced and also because they did not seem to be broadly inconsistent with existing practice (a feature achieved as a result of the previous work done in this area). The final version produced after this period of consultation was presented in a different form and was then available for trials. Despite the iterations with the sector both before and after the creation of the Benchmarking Group, the process was essentially one of drafts being produced by a single individual that were then commented on by, first, the Group and then the wider community, mainly the subject associations. This may have been appropriate to get a coherent text and proceed at speed, but it does not help to build ownership of the standards, which is what was originally envisaged to be part of the process.

## PROBLEMS

The first problem in the consultation process was the lack of familiarity among many in the sector, notably in the old universities, with statements of learning outcomes and criteria. It was interesting that the majority of those who thought the initial statement produced by the Benchmarking Group in July 1998 was pitched at a 2.1 level or above came from that section of the community, whereas those from former CNAA-tradition institutions argued that, if anything, it was pitched too low.

The principal difficulties were with statements about outcomes in relation to intellectual attributes – analysis, synthesis, evaluation and creativity. Whereas the ACLEC's statements set at a modal level attracted little criticism, something less ambitious set at a minimum attracted criticism. Despite the suggestion that the criteria were pitched too high, no one was able to reformulate these at what they considered an appropriate level (even though they were able to perform this task in relation to other elements of the statement).

This aspect of the process demonstrated that benchmarking requires a minimum degree of common understanding within the sector. Clearly, within law, there were two groups of problems. On the one hand, the legal academics (despite their acceptance of the ACLEC's proposals) were not sufficiently familiar with the use of learning outcome statements and criteria to contribute to a debate that used these as a baseline for judging law degrees. When institutions did provide examples of their own marking criteria, they were very general and treated anything below a 2.1 as some form of deficiency. Second, among the professionals, educational terminology, such as 'learning outcomes', 'credits', 'modules' and so on, was not easily understood by those whose experience was predominantly of Oxbridge degrees. The second point was met by a radical simplification of the content of the benchmark statement to say in ordinary language what an employer could expect. All commentary was then hived off to a separate Guidance Note for institutions, for which a more precise, technical statement was appropriate.

The second problem was more difficult. The lack of expertise in using learning outcome statements made it difficult to be sure that the Group had reached a genuine point of consensus within the sector. The Group was reluctant to become more prescriptive by setting its statement at a modal level. It was thought that such a statement would have to be more prescriptive in terms of content and more intrusive in terms of approach. The draft of the benchmarking statement for chemistry seemed to bear this out. The Panel therefore persisted in its approach of setting the standard at the bottom of the honours classes. In order to explain itself more fully, it had to draft illustrations to be included in the Guidance Note that were deliberately not prescriptive, but could help explain the sorts of criteria that institutions might develop.

The third problem was the issue of the appropriate level at which to pitch the threshold statement. The Benchmarking Group took as its remit to set minimum standards for law degrees – a statement of 'the least that a law student is able to do'. The Group was concerned to address the wider public concern that degrees could be obtained too easily, such as in overseas franchises or validated degrees. It recognized the findings of the Graduate Standards Programme that academics think in modal terms and so was concerned to identify the typical student and define achievement in relation to that person. The Group considered that, with the diversity of law programmes, a modal statement might be difficult to write in a non-contentious form. It took the view that the minimum could be defined in prescriptive terms, and then, in future, modal descriptions could be produced for illustrative purposes. Given the concern among law schools to obtain greater flexibility in the design of their programmes, they were wary of anything equivalent to a national curriculum for Key Stage 7. A prescriptive modal statement might appear too close to a national curriculum for a first step in the circumstances. Furthermore, there was concern about how a modal statement could be used to judge a degree programme. If a modal statement means that 'a student is typically able to ...', then what public reassurance does it provide? The employer who is told that law students from Leeds are usually able to work with primary legal sources is not going to be amused to be told that the student he has recruited and who can't begin to work with primary sources is one of the unfortunate minority of students who cannot perform what typical Leeds students can do! The matter to be judged by benchmarking is the actual performance of students, rather than the aspirations of law schools.

Naturally, the professional bodies would wish to pitch their minimum requirements for entry at a higher level of achievement than the threshold. This matches their practice of setting a 2.2 as a minimum entry qualification for entry to the Legal Practice Course and, in practice, operating with a 2.1 requirement to obtain entry to major law firms and chambers. It was not felt that this level of achievement should be the focus of discussions about who should obtain an honours degree, however.

For a number of institutions, the development of programme specifications alongside benchmarks posed a problem. The programme specification did require institutions to develop their own statement of what a graduate should be able to do (albeit this could be at modal level). Given that the piloting of programme specifications was conducted by different QAA officers according to a different timetable and in only some of the institutions that would be involved in the benchmarking pilots, the scope for confusion was inevitable. The idea of bringing the two initiatives together into the piloting of the academic reviewer system was obviously an improvement. All the same, this did cause confusion among those involved in the initial pilots.

## PEDAGOGICAL ISSUES

Given the starting point of the minimally acceptable honours graduate, the process of definition was difficult. To begin with, very few law schools encounter such students. There are students who fail to proceed to obtain a degree, but most drop out in the first year. The A level entry requirements for law degrees are very high and so weaker students are not admitted (Wilson, 1993; Harris and Jones, 1996). Where a student is admitted who ends up on the pass–fail borderline, this is often the result of language or personal problems. A typical student who fails would have a number of passes at 2.2 level and a few fails. Thus, experience of identifying and dealing with students on the pass–fail borderline is limited in both new and old universities. The process of testing any standards against actual students was difficult and more hypothetical than real. For the professionals, the process was unreal in that they would not even consider employing a student who had got a third class degree.

The use of outcome statements, though appropriate, did not help the process of relating the standards to what law academics were used to. Staff would traditionally decide whether or not a student obtained a degree on the basis of a number of credits passed on a range of modules. While some institutions are used to mapping intellectual and other skills on their modules and developing a holistic view of a student's achievement, most are not. A student achieved a degree (and, in particular, a qualifying law degree) by passing a range of modules defined by their content (contract law, torts, and so on), rather than by their skills (analytical ability, independent research and so on). The working concept of a bare honours pass for most law lecturers is thus experienced in terms of individual modules, rather than in terms of the students' performance as a whole. But, when writing references for students, law lecturers are often required to comment on the skills students have in terms of communication, analysis, evaluation, teamworking and so on. The law degree is thus a process in which a variety of judgements are being made on the abilities of students and these are reported to the non-academic world – choices are made that are not solely based on examination performance. Benchmarking tries to make coherent sense of these claims being made for law graduates and encourage law schools to make more explicit the claims that they do wish to make for their graduates and the evidence on which they base them.

In this context, it was difficult to 'touch bottom' with a formulation that captured the qualities of the bare honours pass student. By and large, it was relatively easy to set minimum standards in key skills or in the range of knowledge that had to be exhibited. The problem area was the intellectual skills. How much ability to integrate material in a coherent way is it reasonable to expect when incoherence is one of the traits associated with the student at this bottom level? Issues such as 'creativity' were a problem. Original and creative thinking are associated with high performance. Thus, originality is a particular merit of the first class candidate. On the other hand, the research of Harvey and others associates 'graduateness' with 'transformation potential' (1997) and this is reflected in modal statements produced by the feasibility study. In these it is suggested that a graduate in law should be 'able to create new or imaginative solutions through approaching a problem or using material in different ways'. The law lecturers have a tendency to use the first class or upper second class students as a reference point and so think how far the bare honours pass student falls below that, rather than distinguish the graduate from the non-graduate. As many law lecturers have no experience of teaching at non-degree level, their ability to define what is special about graduates is limited and this perhaps means that they undersell the value of graduates. A benchmark statement is meant to indicate what students can do at the end of their degree-level education and this serves to justify the public expenditure involved in that process. The benchmarking statement and the individual institutions' own statements of standards are meant to articulate the value-added by academic legal education.

Describing threshold honours pass students in positive terms was a marked departure from the various classification criteria that were available to the Group. These criteria were at their least precise in describing the third class student. The effort to identify a third class student's abilities provides a platform on which to build the model of achievement of the better students. The initial work of the Goup in defining the bare pass student in a prescriptive form was then built on in the Guidance Note by the provision of an illustration of how better levels of performance might map on to this. Like the chemists, the lawyers did not wish to focus too precisely on the traditional classes. By describing the higher levels as 'proficient' and 'very proficient' there was sufficient scope for flexibility in the use of class boundaries as appropriate to the different kinds of degree scheme. If the future work of the Benchmarking Group is to develop further criteria beyond the threshold level, then the clear relationship to the threshold in terms of additional characteristics or higher levels of performance will be crucial. It may be that this in itself helps to publicize the value of a graduate beyond the legal profession.

One major issue that was much debated concerned assessment. If institutions were to claim that students had achievements in certain areas, did they have to assess all these areas? The answer from the Group was that there needed to be evidence on which an institution could state with confidence that a student had reached the right level, but that this need not be assessed in a conventional way. A report in a student progress file would be sufficient for many of the areas. The lack of familiarity with this idea, despite its currency for many years, led law schools to limited thinking in the area of assessment.

There is much validity in the comment that the benchmarking statement produced by the Benchmarking Group has relatively little in it that is subject-specific. Before embarking on the feasibility study and the writing of the threshold standard, I had been involved with Dr Chris Butcher of the University of Leeds' Staff and Departmental Development Unit in producing level statements for the University of Leeds, based on pilot activities in biochemistry, philosophy, mechanical engineering, geography and law. In that work, we produced generic-level statements influenced by the work of the South East Consortium for Credit Transfer and Accumulation. Much of the work done specifically for the benchmarking of law was influenced by that work in that the level descriptors and areas of performance for level 3 were a point of reference for checking out what should be contained in the law statement (see Table 10.1). It is not surprising that the key skills (including communication) should be similar. Nor is it totally surprising that much of what is said on analysis, synthesis, evaluation and critical judgement are similar. There are obvious differences in the expression of what is required under 'knowledge', but there is much that is similar. It would seem that there is good reason to think that, couched in terms of general intellectual skills, there is only limited merit in having distinct benchmark statements in relation to each of the 42 subject areas.

**Table 10.1** *Law benchmarks in relation to level descriptors devised previously*

| Area of performance | Law threshold benchmark | Law GSP pilot modal statement | Leeds generic (modal)<br>level 3 statement |
|---|---|---|---|
| *1. Knowledge* | A student should demonstrate a basic knowledge and understanding of the principal features of the legal system(s) studied, viz. He or she:<br>• should be able to demonstrate knowledge of a substantial range of major concepts, values, principles and rules of that system;<br>• should be able to explain the main legal institutions and procedures of that system;<br>• should be able to demonstrate the study in depth and in context of some substantive areas of the legal system. | A student should know:<br>• the principal features of the legal system studied, including general familiarity with its institutions and procedures;<br>• the principles and values of a wide range of topics extending beyond the core;<br>• in-depth, some specialist areas;<br>A student should also be able to demonstrate an insider's understanding of how law fits together and operates. | A student should:<br>• demonstrate a comprehensive and detailed knowledge and understanding of concepts, information and techniques of the discipline, with areas of in-depth specialization;<br>• be able to work confidently with abstract concepts;<br>• have an awareness of the provisional nature of the state of knowledge. |

*Table 10.1 continued*

| | | | |
|---|---|---|---|
| *2. Application and problem-solving* | A student should demonstrate a basic ability to apply her or his knowledge to a situation of limited complexity in order to provide arguable conclusions for concrete problems (actual or hypothetical). | A student should be able:<br>• to apply knowledge to situations which engage with doctrinal disputes; problems conceived as opportunities to demonstrate familiarity with doctrinal and conceptual difficulties and to provide own solution to unresolved debates;<br>• to demonstrate this application over a wide number of legal areas. | A student should be able:<br>• to identify and define confidently and flexibly complex problems and apply appropriate knowledge and skills to their solution. |
| *3. Sources and research* | A student should demonstrate a basic ability:<br>• to identify accurately the issue(s) which require researching;<br>• to identify and retrieve up-to-date legal information, using paper and electronic sources;<br>• to use primary and secondary legal sources relevant to the topic under study. | A student should be able:<br>• to identify and use primary legal sources and journals relevant to topic under study;<br>• to identify contemporary debates and engage with these while accurately reporting the law in an area. | Covered under ('Knowledge') |

*Table 10.1 continued*

| | | | |
|---|---|---|---|
| *4. Analysis, synthesis, critical judgement and evaluation* | A student should demonstrate a basic ability to:<br>• recognize and rank items and issues in terms of relevance and importance;<br>• bring together information and materials from a variety of different sources;<br>• produce a synthesis of relevant doctrinal and policy issues in relation to a topic;<br>• make a critical judgement of the merits of particular arguments;<br>• present and make a reasoned choice between alternative solutions. | A student should be able to:<br>• identify issues in terms of policy and doctrinal importance; able to produce clear doctrinal synthesis and summary of policy issues;<br>• evaluate law both independently in terms of doctrinal coherence and in relation to other policy perspectives which have been taught specifically;<br>• create new or imaginative solutions through approaching a problem or using material in different ways. | A student should be able to:<br>• analyse new and/or abstract data and situations without guidance, using a wide range of specialist and general techniques, tools and literature appropriate to the subject;<br>• with minimum guidance,transform abstract data and concepts towards a given purpose and can design novel solutions;<br>• make an independent personal contribution to the subject by gathering new information, engaging in new projects or offering insights not dependent on what has been given. Can identify own new perspectives review critically evidence supporting conclusions and/or recommendations including its reliability, validity and significance;<br>• investigate contradictory information and identify reasons for contradictions. |

*Table 10.1 continued*

| | | | |
|---|---|---|---|
| *5. Autonomy and ability to learn* | A student should demonstrate a basic ability, with limited guidance to:<br>• act independently in planning and undertaking tasks in areas of law which she or he has already studied;<br>• be able to undertake independent research in areas of law which he or she has not previously studied starting from standard legal information sources;<br>• reflect on his or her own learning, and to seek and make use of feedback. | A student should be able to:<br>• act independently in planning and managing tasks with limited guidance in areas which they have studied;<br>• identify own resources;<br>• reflect on own learning; can seek and make use of feedback. | A student should be able to:<br>• act independently in planning and managing tasks with minimum guidance, using full range of available resources;<br>• seek and make use of feedback; to be confident in application of own criteria of judgement;<br>• reflect on actions and learning. |
| *6. Communication and Literacy* | Both orally and in writing, a student should demonstrate a basic ability to:<br>• understand and use the English language (or, where appropriate, Welsh language) proficiently in relation to legal matters; | A student should be able to:<br>• engage in academic debate in a professional manner;<br>• use a range of formats, mainly written, to present specialist material; | A student should be able to:<br>• engage effectively in debate with specialists in a professional manner;<br>• present specialist material clearly and without distortion to a non-specialist audience; |

*Table 10.1 continued*

| | | | |
|---|---|---|---|
| | • present knowledge or an argument in a way which is comprehensible to others and which is directed at their concerns;<br>• read and discuss legal materials which are written in technical and complex language. | • write fluent and complex prose, using legal terminology correctly;<br>• read a range of complex works within and about law and to summarize their arguments accurately. | • structure a coherent and lengthy presentation dealing with complex issues;<br>• make a presentation with short notice (eg 1 day) on a topic which has been studied;<br>• relate material to the concerns of an audience;<br>• write clear but complex prose making appropriate use of technical vocabulary and constructions and to conform to requirements of a specialist genre of writing;<br>• read complex specialist works within one's discipline and to summarize their arguments accurately. |
| *7. Other key skills: numeracy, information technology and teamworking* | *A student should demonstrate a basic ability:*<br>• where relevant and as the basis for an argument, to use, present and evaluate information provided in numerical or statistical form; | *A student should be able to:*<br>• identify and collate relevant statistical or numerical information and use in a report; | *A student should be able to:*<br>• identify and collate relevant standard statistical information and make use of it in a report; |

*Table 10.1 continued*

| | | | |
|---|---|---|---|
| | • produce a word-processed essay or other text and to present such work in an appropriate form;<br>• to use the World-wide web and e-mail;<br>• to use some electronic information retrieval systems;<br>• to work in groups as a participant who contributes effectively to the group's task. | • demonstrate proficient use of word-processing; standard library and information retrieval systems, and WWW resources;<br>• specify technological tools needed for personal support;<br>• work in groups as a participant who contributes effectively to the group's task (low priority area). | • demonstrate familiarity with: standard word processing package for short pieces; use of library and standard information retrieval;<br>• use of e-mail and WWW;<br>• take the initiative in a team either as a member or, more usually, as a leader within it;<br>• set deadlines and identify resources which others will need to perform their tasks;<br>• perform a team role in a professional manner, recognizing the roles and responsibilities of others. |

## CONCLUSION

The process of producing benchmarks has moved the agenda of law schools towards examining learning outcomes in more depth. The move has been one that they have welcomed as a result of the ACLEC's report, but the benchmarking has required more flesh to be put on the outcomes that were expected. It will be a process that encourages the development of assessment criteria. In that sense, the process is one that renders more explicit the criteria for graduateness implicit in the actual practice of law schools. All the same, this will also lead to some changes in practice. At the very least, institutions will have to make more explicit how they assess or report on issues.

The work of the Group confirms much of what has been said on standards in the Graduate Standards Report. These are both modal and implicit among many law academics. The attempt to be more explicit but less prescriptive led to a threshold statement. There are advantages, but also problems in this starting point. In many ways, this idea requires more staff development than has been encouraged hitherto.

## REFERENCES

ACLEC (April 1996) 'First Report on Legal Education and Training', ACLEC, London – see also: http://www.law.warwick.ac.uk/ncle/html/alt96_report

Bar Council for England and Wales and Law Society (January 1995) *Joint Announcement on Qualifying Law Degrees*, Bar Council for England and Wales and Law Society London, (for earlier versions see P Birks (ed) (1992) *Examining the Law Syllabus: The core*, Oxford

Bell, J (1997) 'General transferable skills and the Law curriculum' (1997) II *Contemporary Issues in Law* (1)

Bell, J and Johnstone, J (March 1998) 'General Transferable Skills in the Law Curriculum', available on the Internet: http://www.law.warwick.ac.uk/ncle/ldn

Bell, J (1997) 'Graduate Standards in Law', available on the Internet: http://www.Law.warwick.ac.uk/ncle/html/grad_standards

Harris, P, and Jones, M (1996) 'ALT Survey of Law Schools 1996', available on the Internet: http://www.law.warwick.ac.uk/ncle/html/alt96_report

Harvey, L, *et al.* (1997) Graduates' Work: Organizational change and students' attributes, CRQ, Birmingham

HEQC (1997) 'Assessment in Higher Education and the role of "graduateness"', HEQC, London

Wilson, J (1993) 'A third survey of university legal education in the UK', *Legal Studies* (13) p 143, especially Table 8

# 11

# Collaborative Accreditation – Benchmarking in a Professional and Academic Partnership to Recognize Programmes of Continuing Professional Development – a Case Study

*Sally Gosling*

Between 1991 and 1996, the Chartered Society of Physiotherapy (CSP) and the University of Greenwich (formerly Thames Polytechnic) undertook collaborative work to accredit continuing professional development (CPD) programmes for chartered physiotherapists. The arrangement arose from the realization that, while it was not always practicable for programmes of learning for chartered physiotherapists to be based in the university sector, many were, nevertheless, worthy of academic recognition.

This chapter considers the development and refinement of quality assurance procedures that underpinned this joint accreditation work, particular attention being paid to the challenges posed by applying the principles of credit accumulation and transfer to programmes run outside the higher education sector; appraising clinically based and clinically focused programmes of CPD for the award of masters level credit; and developing flexible, but robust, processes for conferring credit to complicated and differently structured programmes. It also briefly outlines the way in which work was taken forward after 1996 and the CSP's reasons for encouraging teams to seek accreditation via other channels.

## CONTEXTS AND STARTING POINTS

The move from diploma to degree courses in physiotherapy in the early

1990s created increasing demand for opportunities for postgraduate-level study and influenced the profession's general approach to learning. Undergraduate physiotherapy students became exposed to more student-centred styles of learning, involving a greater focus on evaluating practice, clinical problem-solving and research. These developments informed the expectations of newly qualified physiotherapists and changed the interests and aspirations of more senior members of the profession (CSP, 1994a; CSP, 1995a; CSP 1996a; Gosling, 1997).

Initial discussions between the CSP and the then Thames Polytechnic highlighted the scope for CPD programmes run by, and for, chartered physiotherapists to be considered for joint academic and professional recognition. Such an opportunity fitted well with the CSP's development of a new framework – physiotherapy access to continuing education (PACE) – and complemented other collaborative projects of the polytechnic (Walker and Humphreys, 1994; Thomson and Hall, 1994).

The two organizations formed a memorandum of association for joint accreditation activity in 1991, following the scrutiny and approval of proposed working arrangements via a validation event (CSP and Thames Polytechnic, 1991). A committee, comprising representatives of each body, was formed to undertake accreditation business. This reported to the CSP's education committee and the polytechnic/university's academic standards committee. The CSP formed the locus of activity. The joint post-registration education panel comprised mainly CSP representatives and the management of accreditation business (including advice and support to programme teams) rested with the professional body. At the same time, academic staff played a key role in developing and implementing the accreditation process. As the academic partner – Thames Polytechnic/University of Greenwich – conferred credit ratings. The CSP endorsed them.

The objectives of the memorandum of association between the two bodies were to:

- ensure that educational activities included in PACE were given academic and professional currency in accordance with the national credit accumulation and transfer scheme (CATS);
- encourage chartered physiotherapists to pursue post-qualifying study by offering academic credit (CSP and Thames Polytechnic 1991).

The minimum requirements of programmes submitted for accreditation were that they:

- were designed for State-registered, chartered physiotherapists (or physiotherapists and other healthcare professionals);
- involved a minimum of 40 hours' student effort or workload;

- focused on developing knowledge and skills recognized as lying within chartered physiotherapists' scope of practice;
- involved formal assessment of students' learning;
- were monitored by an external examiner.

The panel's approach was predicated on current thinking on adult learning. It revolved around promoting a student-centred, outcomes-based approach, within which evidence-based clinical practice, the evaluation of the links between theory and practice, and developing assessment procedures that formed an integral part of the learning process were strongly encouraged (Allen, 1996; Barnett, 1992). The initiative was concerned as much with enhancing CPD opportunities and promoting models of good practice as providing a route to accreditation.

## LEVELS

At the outset of its work, the Panel endorsed the following criteria for each CATS level:

- *Level 1* – the 'building blocks' – in terms of core science subjects and clinical sciences – for subsequent professional education;
- *Level 2* – a greater emphasis on professional development and skills, with less emphasis on the clinical sciences, and involving a greater integration of subjects and application of knowledge and skills to the treatment of patients;
- *Level 3*– an increased focus on professional studies and the development of broader cognitive skills applicable to clinical practice (such as the evaluation of clinical practice, problem-solving and the justification of professional action);
- *Masters level* – specialization in a particular area of professional practice, involving implementing problem-solving skills and powers of critical analysis to advance the profession, innovation and the ability to plan and implement change (CSP, 1994b).

The criteria had been formulated during workshop sessions held prior to the enactment of a formal memorandum of association. The CSP's then curriculum of study for qualifying programmes formed the basis for this exercise, together with consideration of chartered physiotherapists' professional development after qualification (CSP, 1991).

In appraising a programme to determine its level, the Panel considered several aspects of its design:

- its aims and learning outcomes;
- how the learning process would enable students to fulfil the learning outcomes;
- how the assessment procedures would enable students to demonstrate fulfilment of the learning outcomes and the extent to which they formed an integral part of the learning process;
- its target group and the nature and amount of prior knowledge and experience required of students;
- its overall structure to ensure it created a coherent learning experience and that students had time to reflect on, and apply, their learning.

The panel reviewed whether or not the criteria formed a fair reflection of its expectations midway through its activity. While resolving that each criterion was sufficient, it produced additional guidelines on its approach to masters level accreditation (CSP, 1995b). The Panel was concerned to ensure that it gave sufficient recognition to the integration of cognitive and psycho-motor skills in advanced-level clinical learning. The guidance produced included advice on appropriate learning and teaching styles and assessment procedures, particularly in relation to developing advanced clinical knowledge and skills. Preparation of the guidelines was informed by broader thinking on academic levels (Universities Council for the Education of Teachers, 1994; Winter, 1993; Winter, 1994).

The key qualities that the Panel expected masters level programmes to develop were:

- questioning conceptual and contextual frameworks, underlying assumptions and established principles;
- applying critical judgement in analysing arguments and hypotheses;
- evaluating professional practice in light of research-based knowledge and analysing accepted theories in light of practice;
- handling complicated issues and situations and different perspectives and viewpoints;
- enhanced abilities in clinical decision making, justifying decisions and evaluating clinical outcomes;
- creativity in clinical practice;
- improved capacity for critical and independent enquiry (CSP, 1995b; Gosling, 1997).

The Panel encouraged teams to consider seeking masters level accreditation where this appeared in keeping with a programme's style, purpose and target group. Nevertheless, masters level accreditation raised questions about placing heavy academic demands on students who were learning outside the university sector. Of the six programmes accredited by the panel at this level, five had strong links with a university (for example, members of the team were members of academic staff). The other was subsequently developed with a university to form a postgraduate diploma.

The Panel reviewed whether or not it should continue to use all the CATS levels, given the lack of academic currency of level 1 and level 2 credit for chartered physiotherapists (CSP, 1994c; CSP, 1996a). It resolved that its primary function was to support the profession's development and contribution to patient care by providing a quality assurance system for CPD programmes. It saw enabling physiotherapists to gain academic awards as secondary. The panel therefore upheld the value of using the lower CATS levels. In practice, level 1 was not used, while several programmes that were initially accredited at level 2 were subsequently developed to level 3. Other teams on level 2 programmes developed their provision to a higher level either by developing their existing programme or by creating a new one.

## POINTS

The Panel produced guidelines on its information requirements and procedures for awarding credit points (CSP, 1995c). These made clear that it took account of the total student workload demanded by a programme and that its credit point recommendations were calculated on the basis of 1000 hours learning attracting 120 points. The Panel also issued a pro forma to help teams provide information on the notional student workload demanded by the programmes. It was keen to acknowledge and recognize the value of learning achieved in the workplace. It therefore stressed the importance of teams supplying detailed information on programme-related activity that students were expected to undertake in the workplace and in private study. The following details regarding work-based learning were required:

- its desired learning outcomes;
- the timescale in which students were expected to fulfil the outcomes – both in terms of the number of hours that should be devoted to programme-related activities and the period in which the hours should be completed;
- strategies for developing students' learning, such as keeping a reflective diary or gathering data for a case study;
- support arrangements, such as the appointment of mentors or clinical educators and links with the programme tutors;
- assessment procedures;

- links with other parts of the programme;
- resource requirements.

A focus on student workload enabled consistency in the Panel's consideration of a broad range of programmes. Submissions varied substantially in their structure and length. Some were delivered on a block release, modular basis over a substantial period (up to two years), while others were run over a matter of weeks; some included placements in specialist clinical centres, while others developed students' learning in their normal workplace; some made heavy use of distance learning, while others revolved around tutor–student contact. The Panel was concerned to establish the learning that students should achieve and the timescale within which this should occur. It therefore focused on 'output' rather than modes of programme delivery and contact hours. However, it required details of how students' learning was developed to substantiate information on workload and outcomes.

## CREDIT RATING RECOMMENDATIONS

The joint post-registration education panel accredited 58 programmes. It made 66 credit rating recommendations and considered a total of 72 submissions. (Some programmes were re-accredited on one or more occasion, while six programmes were not accredited on their first submission, hence the differing totals.) Of the 58 programmes, 38 (65.6 per cent) were not run in their accredited format by 1996. On the surface, this suggests a high rate of attrition. However, 19 of these (50 per cent) moved directly into the university sector and were developed to a higher CATS level, while 6 (15.8 per cent) were developed and submitted to the joint panel for re-accreditation at a higher level: 4 were developed from level 2 to level 3 and 2 were developed from level 3 to level M. On the six occasions that the Panel felt unable to make a credit rating recommendation, it gave detailed advice to the team concerned on how to make the programme suitable for accreditation. In all but one case, teams resubmitted their programme and secured a credit rating (CSP, 1996d).

The Panel's accreditation business gradually declined. The number of programmes submitted reduced both in real terms and in proportion to the number of formal CPD opportunities that became available to chartered physiotherapists. The amount of initial business was bolstered by a backlog of submissions and by the Panel's consideration of a large number of programmes for retrospective accreditation. For example, 25 programmes (38.5 per cent) had previously been validated in the CSP's former system of recognition and were submitted solely to gain credit for previous student intakes. Of these, 14 (56 per cent) formed the basis for new programmes, while 12 (48 per cent) eventually moved into the university sector.

Of the 58 programmes, 33 (56.9 per cent) were accredited at CATS level 3. As this formed an academic progression for the majority of the profession at that stage, this level came to be seen as the standard to which most teams aspired. (All students qualifying as chartered and State-registered physiotherapists did so by gaining a degree by 1994.) Some teams perceived securing level 2 accreditation as a failure to achieve accreditation at level 3. Others expressly developed programmes at a lower level to meet the perceived needs of their target groups. This was seen as appropriate for some programmes that covered clinical subject areas that students would not have addressed in their qualifying education. Masters level came to be seen as a natural progression for experienced teams who wished to meet a growing demand for advanced clinically focused learning opportunities.

## PROCEDURAL DEVELOPMENTS

The Panel kept under review how it could implement its accreditation processes most effectively and best support teams. Its work was also considered as part of a Higher Education Quality Council audit. The structures in place for joint accreditation were commended (HEQC, 1996). It became apparent to the Panel, however, that teams required significantly more guidance on preparing programme documentation than had initially been anticipated. The practice was therefore adopted of appointing two members of the Panel (one CSP and one university representative whenever possible) to advise teams on programme design and documentation preparation. This both increased the guidance teams received and enabled panel members to develop an in-depth knowledge of individual programmes. The scrutineers also monitored the delivery of accredited programmes by considering team and external examiners' reports on individual student intakes. Any significant issues arising from these were debated at Panel meetings. Feedback was then sent to the teams, with conditions set if any remedial action was required to retain accreditation (CSP, 1993a; CSP, 1994d).

The Panel's guidelines both formalized its approach to accreditation and helped ensure that teams were well-briefed on the Panel's procedures and expectations. New materials were produced when it became apparent that additional information could usefully be provided on the Panel's expectations and requirements. The guidelines addressed programme development and delivery issues – including the role of tutors in student-centred learning and developing effective assessment procedures, –and the quality assurance mechanisms of the Panel's own procedures; for example, on the additional requirements for programmes run on a satellite basis (CSP, 1993b; CSP, 1994e; CSP, 1996b). The sequential production of documents was partly counter-productive as it appeared to some teams that the Panel kept 'changing the goal posts'. However, the documents were generally welcomed.

CSP and university representatives worked well together, achieving a good level of integration of expertise and experience. The Panel considered programmes from a unified perspective, rather than from distinguishable 'academic' and 'professional' viewpoints. Its approach to accreditation also matured. It built up a case law, enabling it to compare individual submissions and ensure that it considered programmes consistently and with equal rigour. Panel membership naturally changed over time, with only two members (both university representatives) sitting on the Panel for the whole period. Induction sessions were held to familiarize new members with procedures and policies, while the guidelines helped to develop new members' understanding of the Panel's approach.

## SUPPORT AND DEVELOPMENT

The accreditation process formed a valuable framework for programme development. Seeking accreditation generally required teams to give greater consideration to the educational process of their programmes than they had done previously. In particular, they had to pay closer attention to their programme's structure, learning and teaching methods and assessment procedures and how these enabled students to fulfil – and demonstrate their fulfilment – of the programme's aims and learning outcomes. Some teams radically reviewed their approach to student assessment and role as tutors, and significantly developed their approach to teaching, learning and assessment. Some made particular progress in increasing students' understanding of research and their ability to engage in critical enquiry and evaluation. They helped students develop these skills by means of a range of activities and assignments, including small-scale research projects, reflective diaries, and critical literature reviews and case studies.

The Panel's support for, and contact with, teams was enhanced by introducing the scrutineer system, producing guidelines, convening an annual conference and housing copies of accredited programme documentation in the CSP's information resource centre. On some occasions, meetings were held with individual teams to provide in-depth advice and guidance. Support to teams could extend over a long period (up to 18 months) before a programme was ready for submission. Not all teams to whom scrutineers were appointed pursued accreditation. Although this raised questions about the best use of resources, the advice these teams received should have helped them provide better learning opportunities than had been achieved before.

Despite the decline in the Panel's business over the five-year period, the CSP continued to receive a lot of queries about the accreditation process.

There are several reasons that may explain why there were not greater numbers of submissions:

- the Panel necessarily imposed standards and requirements in keeping with its status as an accrediting agent of a university and professional body, but some teams were daunted by what was required to achieve accreditation, not least because they were trying to do so on top of a full clinical or managerial workload and in a climate of increasing work pressures;
- some teams found it difficult to articulate the nature of their programme in the manner required for accreditation and produce documentation in the format required by the Panel;
- some teams wished to achieve accreditation at a level that did not match the nature of their programme, which led to frustration and may have deterred some from pursuing a claim;
- many programmes were run on an *ad hoc* basis and lacked security – some teams decided against investing time and effort in seeking accreditation when the future of their programme was uncertain;
- conversely, other programmes recruited well regardless of whether or not they held a credit rating – teams for such programmes may have decided that pursuing accreditation was not the best use of their resources.

The pressures on busy clinicians and managers – who were generally new to the preparation of documentation for higher education recognition procedures – should not be underestimated. Attitudes towards validation/accreditation within the university sector highlight the additional difficulties for those trying to comply with them from outside (Woodman and Redman, 1996). The sheer demands of accreditation go a long way towards explaining why more teams did not make use of the collaborative arrangements. They also reinforce the substantial achievements of those who did.

## CURRENCY, ACHIEVEMENTS AND DEVELOPMENTS

The arrangement enabled chartered physiotherapists to gain academic recognition for their clinically based learning and to accrue credit towards academic awards. An additional collaborative venture between the CSP and the University of Greenwich was the creation of a 'top-up' degree programme for diplomate chartered physiotherapists, leading to the award of a BSc. (Hons) Physiotherapy Studies (Humphreys and Ham, 1994). Between 1992 and 1996, 51.5 per cent of those registering for this degree had completed a programme accredited by the Panel. Other physiotherapists who completed accredited programmes used their credit towards academic awards offered elsewhere. Some who gained M level points used them towards a masters degree.

Physiotherapists' primary reason for undertaking accredited programmes was to enhance their professional knowledge and skills. Many of the accredited programmes (particularly those run by the CSP's clinical interest and occupational groups) formed the principal CPD opportunity in this subject area. Members were also keen to follow a programme that had undergone a rigorous process of recognition and that was subject to ongoing monitoring. Informal feedback indicated that these factors were more important to physiotherapists than a programme's carrying academic credit. This has been confirmed by a recent study of physiotherapists' attitudes towards CPD opportunities in clinical audit and research (Dolan, 1998).

Fulfilment of the memorandum's objectives needs to be seen within the context of wider developments in physiotherapists' CPD:

- the accreditation activity undertaken as a result of the joint arrangements between the CSP and University of Greenwich contributed a relatively small proportion (10.5 per cent in 1995) of PACE-recognized programmes (CSP, 1995d);
- 1991 to 1996 witnessed a substantial expansion in the number and range of higher education opportunities available to physiotherapists, particularly at postgraduate level, and, during that period, most higher education institutions that hosted a qualifying programme in physiotherapy developed a masters level study route for the profession, while many others expanded their provision of more general postgraduate programmes for healthcare professionals (Gosling, 1997);
- the Society strengthened its links with the higher education sector by convening a consortium of universities with an interest and involvement in physiotherapists' CPD and by its growing involvement in university validation/accreditation across the United Kingdom (CSP, 1996e; CSP, 1998a);
- the original concepts and aims of PACE were subsumed within a broader CSP strategy on CPD, reflecting a keenness to promote all types of learning relevant to physiotherapists' professional development, not only that which enabled them to gain academic credit (Gosling, 1996; CSP, 1998b).

These wider developments both underscored the achievements of the memorandum of association between the CSP and University of Greenwich and provided an impetus to modify the arrangements between the two bodies.

The CSP reviewed PACE and considered its arrangements with the University of Greenwich in 1995/96 (CSP, 1996c; CSP, 1996d). It decided to encourage teams to make direct links with universities wherever possible. This was informed by the factors that militated against teams seeking accreditation under the joint arrangements, and rested on the belief that teams, their programmes and their students would benefit from a full integration with the university sector. The percentage of programmes that the panel had accredited, and for which direct links had then been secured with a university (34.5 per cent), indicated that this was already a strong trend. The development also fitted with the CSP's wish to broaden the focus of its work on CPD and to explore how it could develop a more formal and expansive framework for its members' professional development (Gosling, 1996; Walker, 1996; Powell, 1997).

The CSP recognized that it would not be possible for all teams to make direct links with universities, at least in the short term. It provided support to teams, by convening meetings and producing guidelines, to ensure that none was disadvantaged by its change in policy (CSP, 1996f). After formal discussions with the University of Greenwich, the business of the joint post-registration education panel transferred to the institution's faculty of human sciences credit-rating group, enabling programme accreditation and monitoring to be integrated into similar university business. For the CSP, it achieved parity between its relationship with the University of Greenwich and that which it had established with other universities throughout the UK.

## CONCLUSION

The accreditation activity of the two bodies was successful in a number of ways:

- it promoted the principle of joint academic and professional recognition of CPD programmes;
- it formed an effective quality assurance mechanism and helped raise the standard of CPD opportunities available to chartered physiotherapists;
- it developed the CSP's thinking on accreditation and informed the University of Greenwich's work with other organizations (Quinn, *et al.*, 1997).

Its limitations were that:

- the route to accreditation was not used by as many teams as had been hoped;
- the rigour and requirements necessarily attached to the academic recognition of learning made the process unattractive to some prospective users;

- although the process provided a framework for recognition, it could not offer a secure basis for programmes' development and delivery;
- the scrutineer system had distinct merits, but could not provide the kind of support that teams could gain from more direct links with a university.

The collaborative activity was not embarked on explicitly as a benchmarking exercise. However, in retrospect, it rehearsed benchmarking principles – not least because of its strong focus on learning outcomes (Race, 13 November 1998). It involved setting standards, trying to fulfil these and reviewing whether or not they were fulfilled – elements defined as key benchmarking principles in higher education (Higgs and McMeeken, 1997). The activity both set and implemented standards for physiotherapy CPD, enabling qualitative and quantitative judgements and comparisons to be made, and was itself subject to ongoing review, evaluation and scrutiny (Alstete, 1996).

The partnership between the CSP and University of Greenwich significantly developed the quality of opportunities for chartered physiotherapists' CPD. It formed one of the most tangible achievements of PACE and successfully combined the academic and professional recognition of clinically based learning. The decision to disband the Panel represented a maturation in the CSP's approach to accreditation and reflected broader and rapid developments that had occurred in physiotherapy education since the Panel's inception. The Partnership enabled clinical experts in the profession to become familiar with the demands and processes of university accreditation and use this experience as the basis for stronger links with the university sector. For both the CSP and the University of Greenwich, it provided a useful model for further projects and initiatives.

## REFERENCES

Allan, J (1996) 'Learning outcomes in Higher Education: The impact of outcome-led design on students' conceptions of learning' in *Improving Student Learning: Using research to improve student learning*, G Gibbs, Oxford Centre for Staff Development, Oxford Brookes University, Oxford

Alstete, J W (1996) 'Benchmarking in Higher Education: Adapting best practices to improve quality', ASHE-ERIC Higher Education Report No.5, The George Washington University, Washington

Barnett, R (1992) *Improving Higher Education: Total quality care*, SRHE and Open University Press, Buckingham

CSP and Thames Polytechnic (July 1991) 'Memorandum of co-operation between the Chartered Society of Physiotherapy and Thames Polytechnic', CSP and Thames Polytechnic, London

CSP (1991) 'Curriculum of study', CSP, London

CSP (1993a) 'Monitoring procedures for courses accredited by the Joint Post-registration Education Panel', CSP, London
CSP (1993b) 'The changing role of tutors in post-registration courses', CSP, London
CSP (1994a) 'PACE and postgraduate education', *Physiotherapy*, **80** (4) pp 228–30
CSP (1994b) 'Guidelines for course teams on the Joint Post-registration Education Panel's accreditation procedures', CSP, London
CSP (1994c) 'Accreditation activity of the Joint Post-registration Education Panel below level 3', CSP, London
CSP (1994d) 'Scrutineer system of the Joint Post-Registration Education Panel', CSP, London
CSP (1994e) 'The management and monitoring of course package delivery', CSP, London
CSP (1995a) 'Postgraduate study pack', CSP, London
CSP (1995b) 'M-level accreditation by the Joint Post-registration Education Panel', CSP, London
CSP (1995c) 'Credit-point tariffs: Procedures and information requirements of the Joint Post-registration Education Panel', CSP, London
CSP (1995d) 'Review of PACE, 1994/95', CSP, London
CSP (1996a) 'The academic status of physiotherapy qualifications and opportunities to gain academic awards', CSP, London
CSP (1996b) 'Developing effective assessment procedures', CSP, London
CSP (1996c) 'Final report of the PACE review working party', CSP, London
CSP (1996d) 'Critical appraisal of the memorandum of association between the Chartered Society of Physiotherapy and the University of Greenwich, 1991–1996', CSP, London
CSP (1996e) 'Involving the CSP in the validation/accreditation of post-qualifying programmes: Guidance for higher education institutions', CSP, London
CSP (1996f) 'Guidelines on collaboration: Linking with a Higher Education institution for post-qualifying programme development and delivery', CSP, London
CSP (1998a) 'CSP compendium of CPD opportunities', CSP, London
CSP (1998b) 'CSP policy statement on its approach to continuing professional development for qualified members', CSP, London
Dolan, M J (1998) 'A study of demand and need for CPD courses in clinical audit and research', *British Journal of Therapy and Rehabilitation*, **5** (10) pp 11–34
Gosling, S (1996) 'From PACE to CPD', *Physiotherapy*, **82** (9) pp 499–501
Gosling, S (1997) 'Physiotherapy and postgraduate study: A discussion paper', *Physiotherapy*, **83** (3) pp 131–5
Higgs, J, and McMeeken, J (1997) 'Benchmarking in physiotherapy education: A collaborative project', *Australian Physiotherapy*, **43** (2) pp 83–9
HEQC (1996) 'University of Greenwich: Quality audit report: Collaborative provision', HEQC Quality Assurance Group, London
Humphreys, J, and Ham, R (1994) 'An application of open learning for the UK physiotherapy profession', *Open Learning*, **9** (3) pp 3–8
Powell, A (1997) 'A framework for continuing professional development: A feasibility study: Final report', CSP, London
Quinn, F M, Phillips, M, Humphreys, J, and Hull, C (1997) 'Professional development for nurses: A national open learning partnership', *Open Learning*, **12** (1) pp 45–51

Race, P (13 November 1998) 'Give students the big picture', *The Times Higher Education Supplement*, pp 30–31

Thomson, V, and Hall, D (1994) 'Case study: A credit scheme for nurses and midwives', in *Health Care Education: The challenge of the market*, eds J Humphreys and F Quinn, pp 32–45, Chapman & Hall, London

Universities Council for the Education of Teachers (1994) 'What is Master's level?: Workshop report', UCET, London

Walker, A, and Humphreys, J (1994) 'Case study: Physiotherapy access to Continuing Education', in *Health Care Education: The challenge of the market*, eds J Humphreys and F Quinn, pp 46–76, Chapman & Hall, London

Walker, A (1996) 'Accredited practice development: A discussion paper', CSP, London

Winter, R (1993) 'The problem of educational levels (part I): Conceptualizing a framework for credit accumulation and transfer', *Journal of Further and Higher Education*, **17** (3) pp 90–104

Winter, R (1994) 'The problem of educational levels (part II): A new framework for credit accumulation and transfer', *Journal of Further and Higher Education*, **18** (1) pp 92–106

Woodman, D, and Redley, M (1996) 'The wretched document: An analysis of the talk and perceptions of academic staff on the process and procedure of validation and review, course planning and teaching preparation' in *Improving Student Learning: Using research to improve student learning*, ed G Gibbs, pp 264–95, Oxford Centre for Staff Development, Oxford Brookes University, Oxford

12

# Benchmarking, Assessment and the Multidisciplinary Curriculum

*Rebecca Johnson*

> Sir, I have found you an argument; but I am not obliged to find you an understanding.
>
> (Dr Johnson to the tedious interrogator Boswell, 1784)

This chapter joins some of the dots between day-to-day learning and academic provision and generally accepted levels of attainment within a unitized multidisciplinary context. It draws on extensive research into staff and student experience of unitization carried out by the Assessment and the *Expanded* Text project. A three-year consortium project funded by the higher education Fund for the Development of Teaching and Learning, it has two main aims. First, to identify gaps between staff and student understanding of the purposes and desired outcomes of assessment (at unit and 'graduate' level) and, second, to produce materials that bridge those gaps. In the joint process of researching and creating materials, the project has amassed a considerable amount of information that casts light on some of the consistently voiced problems associated with the 'graduate standards' debate, including assessment, reduced time for teaching, increased student numbers, insistence on end of unit assessment product rather than the process of learning, and 'graduateness'. In what follows I analyse existing assessment criteria for evidence of some of the benchmarks already in operation and suggest ways in which assessment criteria can be fed back into the curriculum to improve student understanding of their own 'graduate' status.

In the course of collating and evaluating current general assessment criteria relating to the work of students completing English honours degree programmes, there has been one recurring nightmare scenario – the student who has been given documentation in line with the recent recommendations made by the History Benchmarking Group to the QAA:

> documentation for each individual course ... an outline of the course structure, information about the nature and amount of assessment, ... a bibliography ... details of the degree scheme, criteria for all levels of classification and all forms of assessment in use ... (etc.).
>
> (History at Universities Defence Group, 1998b)

In many arts and humanities' lecturers' eyes such material is all the ammunition a student with the temper of Samuel Johnson will need to complain about a mark: 'Look, here's my argument where does it say in the documentation that I have to demonstrate understanding, huh?' A related concern is that any more detailed tabulating of learning outcomes or objectives for specific courses or programmes could lead students into a simplistic attitude to learning. The draft of the report cited above included staff fears that students:

> could be led to believe that, rather than having to engage in difficult intellectual exercises, they are ticking off achievement of particular attributes or skills which a matrix of skills presents to them
>
> (History at Universities Defence Group, draft report of the working party, 1998)

Perhaps reflecting these concerns, the fieldwork for both the seventh Graduate Standards Programme Report and the Assessment and *Expanded* Text consortium indicates that, to date:

> guidance and criteria relating to outcomes and levels are often phrased at a very general level and do not appear to be much used at the point of assessment.
>
> (HEQC, 1997b)

Also, consortium-wide research indicates that, although included in student handbooks, students do not understand the language that characterizes current general criteria. For example, a common criteria used to distinguish between levels of work in arts and humanities is 'knowledge of the subject'. Interviews with first-year students show that, for many of them, this means 'doing as much reading as possible'. Yet, what is clear from interviewing staff is that 'knowledge of the subject' does not mean the sum of what has been written, but, rather, the demonstration of understanding.

So why bother with general assessment criteria and how can such criteria become a more effective part of the teaching learning and assessment processes that characterize the diverse 'English' curriculum? After all, as many working in the discipline have pointed out, English is not about learning or knowing an object in the conventional sense. It is more about mastering discourses; having available appropriate responses.

In the process of answering this question I want to demonstrate how useful a benchmarking exercise in English might be for mapping out and maintaining the diversity of multidisciplinary programme designs. In particular, by making assessment an essential part of a teaching and learning strategy, we may be able to achieve an important shift away from single-subject discourse dominance 'to ensure equivalent intellectual intensity in breadth rather than depth' (Michael Scott, 8 December 1998).

The Assessment and the *Expanded* Text project has given each consortium site the opportunity to reassess aspects of its curriculum provision through the lens of assessment. The main aim of each site is to ensure that assessment is not merely an add-on, but is predicated on demonstrating the extent to which specified learning outcomes have been achieved; explicitly linking assessment with unit and programme content by thinking in terms of what students should be able to do and know after studying a particular unit and/or series of units. More particularly, the project aims to identify and close evident gaps between staff and student interpretation of what students should be able to do and know. The challenge is to produce materials that neither encourage students to produce carbon copies of model answers (which many staff fear will happen) nor mean that assessment continues to be the enigma it is for many students. As one first-year student said stoically in the course of an interview carried out for the Assessment and the *Expanded* Text project:

> you tend to struggle on [with an essay] on your own, and just try to make some sense of it. You think, well, I only have to get 40 per cent to pass at this stage, so you do your best and struggle on, thinking, well, if I get enough in they can see I've done the work, it should be enough to pass.

In the project's view, assessment criteria are crucial to the successful operation of a unitized educational programme and essential to effective learning within that programme. As the Graduate Standards Programme Report (HEQC, 1997b) pointed out:

> in a decentralized system, mark schemes convey information about the relative importance of different skills and content that is not made explicit elsewhere; and the process of developing a mark scheme (and challenging it) requires assessors to address more clearly what outcomes they want students to achieve.

The opening up of 'English' so that it now includes film texts, linguistics, cultural theory, creative writing and so on has had far-reaching effects on students' experiences of the curriculum. To grasp the content of their programmes, students are expected to acquire not only mental flexibility to embrace the different types of study, but the capacity to assimilate and generalize effectively from extensive, disparate readings. As their sense of the varieties of texts and textual approaches grows, so they have to grapple with distinctive forms of analysis, including historical, theoretical, visual and so on. Many students find this daunting, as did this first-year student:

> at first I hated 'Progress and Modernism' so much, I thought, what on earth is the point of doing this? If I'd wanted to do a history degree I'd have done one!

More worryingly, they find it difficult to follow the learning outcomes of non-literary units into their assessment. A preliminary evaluation of English students' approaches to literary and film units that were both assessed by essay suggested that, faced with new types of text, students prioritized the learning outcomes they associated with essay writing about literary texts and wrote their film essays accordingly. Their lack of familiarity with the art of writing about film was further highlighted by the fact that only 14 out of 63 thought of watching film as essential essay preparation. This was despite the fact that these same students felt that film was a subject that had its own agenda, values and distinct theoretical issues.

Following up these provisional research findings, one of the consortium sites is working on a unit in popular writing, which includes television, film, literary texts and soap operas and also asks students to familiarize themselves with analytical models taken from film, literary and cultural studies. As such, the unit is a unique opportunity for students to come to terms with the multidisciplinary nature of their programmes of study. The aim of this arm of the project is to identify models of good pedagogical practice that enables multidisciplinary dialogue prior to the students' selection of a particular area of study for an extended essay. Furthermore, an ongoing reflective dossier has been adapted from film studies to promote student self-assessment and evaluation of the 'different' patterns of learning this subject matter promotes.

The fieldwork for the Graduate Standards' Programme was explicitly searching for common understandings of criteria used for the same types of degree. What it found was that 'a common language was already in use on the process of assessment, but its meaning varied according to institutional, professional and subject contexts' (HEQC, 1997). Before national 'graduate' standards could be thought about, these meanings had to be clarified and further elaborated within these specific settings, hence the setting up of the benchmarking groups and a unique opportunity to 'encounter literature's implication in institutional structures, its deep functional utility' (Greenblatt, 1997). The data above from the Assessment and the *Expanded* Text project suggests that any attempt to make judgements about academic standards in English will need to take into consideration, as history did, 'that there are many different and suitable ways of constructing and making available the great richness and diversity of the subject' (History at Universities Defence Group, 1998b). The value of a common language is that it offers a standard against which individual departments can measure their diversity.

Building on the preliminary information relating to assessment made available in the Council for College and University English's report to the QAA (1997) and the documentation available across the consortium, the Assessment and the *Expanded* Text project has begun to identify the common language and consensus of understanding of terms that appear in the general assessment criteria employed across the subject. The compilation is made from its four consortium sites, which are the Universities of East Anglia, Northumbria, Sheffield Hallam and Staffordshire. There are strong parallels between the English degree programmes offered by these four universities, parallels that have been reinforced by strong external examining links. The project takes the general assessment criteria (including creative writing, which has its own criteria) currently made publicly available at each of these sites and looks for common understandings of key competences, such as the ability to argue. I then report on the implications of this information for questions of graduate standards.

What is striking about the project's preliminary comparison of general assessment criteria is that although:

> when we devise and teach English courses, we may have all sorts of educational outcomes in view – increased knowledge of a cultural heritage, enhanced sensitivity in reading, greater self-confidence in the presentation and discussion of ideas, social and cultural empowerment, personal maturity
>
> (Womack, 27 February 1993)

the only outcome we explicitly and publicly evaluate is writing, and one particular type of writing at that – the essay. Take, for example, two sets of assessment criteria for the lower second degree category (both presented as general assessment criteria in student handbooks):

> Site A. Work must display application, intelligence and the ability to form an essay within standard scholarly conventions. It will, however, lack the argumentative coherence or conceptual sophistication of work graded in the upper second class degree.

> Site B. An answer which is competent but which shows some limitations in the knowledge expressed. The candidate tends to stick closely to what has been taught, or shows dependence on secondary literature, or sticks to what s/he thinks the examiner expects to read, or be limited to one

> aspect of the question. There may be weaknesses in expression (choice of word, punctuation, spelling, syntax) and presentation.

A key question then becomes do we really want the 'essay'/exam answer to be the distinguishing mark by which a unitized English degree is publicly judged and estimated? Moreover, do we want our students' abilities to master the essential ingredients of the academic essay (subject knowledge, argument, synthesis of secondary literature, adherence to scholarly convention, analysis, a high level of literacy) to be the benchmarks determining the highs and lows of English 'graduateness'? The History Benchmarking Group addressed these issues directly. The benchmarking consultation document, for example, states that 'the essay remains a central component' in a diverse unitized history curriculum and an 'essential element of all History assessment' of final-level degree work 'because of the integrative high-order skills which they develop'. However, it also recommends that:

> all departments should give students the opportunity to be assessed by essays of various types and to have their critical and communication skills assessed in other forms. (History at Universities Defence Group, 1998b)

In addition, 'published criteria should be available for all forms of assessment'.

The assessment criteria that the Assessment and the *Expanded* Text project has gathered so far shows that criteria for oral assessment and so on are not generally included in student handbooks. This suggests that while assessment criteria for essays and exams are decided at departmental level, criteria for other types of assessment are left to individual lecturers to devise. A further aim of the Assessment and the *Expanded* Text project is to fill this void by collating and analysing documentation relating to the objectives, methods and grade-related criteria used in oral assessment across the consortium. A guide will be written that describes existing patterns and activities, draws up models of good practice and identifies a common language concerning the use of oral assessment within an 'English' honours degree programme.

As noted earlier, unitization has meant that 'English' degree students can take a multiplicity of subjects, each with their own epistemological reference points, distinguishing marks and favoured pedagogical and assessment practices. Like history, English comprises interlocking areas of interest – a continuum rather than a set of discrete subdisciplines. However, in the light of the History Benchmarking Group's recommendation that there be published 'assessment criteria' for all types of assessment, it is interesting that one of those areas interlocking with English has already devised its own assessment criteria. At many sites, creative writing units have their own assessment criteria. Analysing these criteria, it is clear that this is because there is a clear need to flag up the particular skills that a student taking creative writing will need to master. The assessment criteria for the lower second-level creative writing student at site A, for example, reads:

> Site A. The work shows a certain application and care for detail and development, but there are obvious weaknesses on show. The plot of a story or play isn't fully developed or realized, the structure of the poetry doesn't work and doesn't quite come off. Characters might be stereotyped or only partially, vaguely presented. Dialogue is sloppier and more hackneyed than it could be. There is a certain clumsiness in the layering of the various elements that make up the piece. Symbols and images are not sensually and distinctly rendered, so the piece reads as if the writer isn't quite in control; perhaps a marked tendency to tell us rather than show us what the writer's intentions are.

The criteria make clear the relationship between the mastery of certain skills and the validity of the assessed work. In comparison, the general assessment criteria cited earlier are more impressionistic. It is much harder to envisage the relationship between 'knowledge' and the validity of the assessed work than the representation of a character. What the comparison underlines, however, is the mental agility that an 'English' curriculum can demand of its students. As we have seen, a word such as 'knowledge' demands a whole host of teaching, learning and assessment materials that provide students with guidelines about what is and is not 'appropriate' knowledge within the paradigms of the subject. Creative writing, on the other hand, with its emphasis on 'showing' and the position of assessor as reader, demands more opportunities for writers to model their work, have it mulled over in public and read. Indeed, this is another gap between learning outcomes and assessment practice that students have identified and which another arm of the project is addressing. This point was made in an interview with a joint creative writing and English undergraduate student:

> The assessment was OK – it's university, what can you expect? But if reading is from the individual to the social, why can't a group assessment be taken into consideration alongside the tutor's?

In conclusion, there is a clear need to articulate more clearly subject-specific parameters, particularly the types of 'knowledge' that may or may not be included and considered appropriate within particular multidisciplinary degree programmes such as English and History. Preliminary attempts to do this have been made by groups representing certain disciplines. The Council for College and University English (CCUE), for example, responded to the QAA's consultation document 'Agenda for Quality' in the following way. Asked to comment on Part III – 'Developing a template for programme specification' – the CCUE stressed that the English subject community felt strongly that English must retain its own subject identity by means of a single benchmarking group. Explaining why the pairing of English and American studies as a benchmarking group was not a good idea, the CCUE explained:

> QAA needs to understand the disciplinary overlap between English and American studies is minimal. American studies, while it includes some study of literature, more often than not is based in disciplines which have little in common with literary study (e.g. politics, history, international relations, economics).
>
> (CCUE, 1997)

Equally, in the final version of the benchmarking consultation document issued by the History Universities Defence Group, it was clear that historians favour certain multidisciplinary continuums above others. Commenting on the mental flexibility that students are required to develop in order to grasp the content of their programmes, the Group's report concludes:

> As their sense of the varieties of history and historical approaches grows, so they have to grapple with the distinctive forms of analysis – e.g., statistical, sociological, economic – which may be particularly appropriate to them.
>
> (History at Universities Defence Group, 1998b)

Teasing out the various epistemological discourses that are strongly represented in different departments will make it easier to develop 'appropriate' subject-specific assessment criteria. The answer to the question 'How can assessment criteria become a more effective part of the teaching, learning and assessment outcomes that characterize the diverse "English" curriculum?' depends on several factors. Two of the most important are the particular blends of subject areas offered in specific programmes of study and the ways in which departments perceive, use and promote the assessment criteria. At present, as mentioned earlier, general assessment criteria have low usage, and profile. However, as the QAA's proposals for developing qualifications frameworks in the UK and developing benchmark information on subject threshold standards gather momentum, assessment criteria are likely to provide a key source of information for defining generic level descriptors and improving students' understanding of the learning outcomes of degree schemes.

## REFERENCES

History at Universities Defence Group (1998a) 'Draft report of a working party into benchmarking in History'

History at Universities Defence Group (1998b) 'Subject benchmarking consultation document for the Quality Assurance Agency'
HEQC (1997a) 'Assessment in Higher Education and the role of "graduateness"', HEQC, London
HEQC (1997b) 'Graduate Standards Programme Final Report Volume: The Report', HEQC, London
Greenblatt, S (1997) 'What is the history of literature?', *Critical Inquiry*, **23** (3) 460–80
Council for College and University English (1997) 'The English curriculum: Diversity and standards', a report to the Quality Assurance Agency
Scott, M (8 December 1998), Subject Association Conference, Quality Assurance Agency, University of Manchester
Womack, P (27 February 1993) 'What are essays for?', *English in Education*

For further details of the materials being produced to mind the gaps between learning outcomes and assessment practices, please contact the Assessment and the *Expanded* Text Project Officer on 0191 227 4993 or e-mail rebecca.johnson@unn.ac.uk.

Any versions of assessment criteria, criteria for oral assessment, dissertations and so on are very welcome. Please send to the Department of Historical and Critical Studies, University of Northumbria, Newcastle NE1 8ST

13

# Towards Multidisciplinary Benchmarking

*Stuart Billingham*

In late 1998, the QAA in the UK established an Advisory Group 'to consider the implications for benchmarking academic standards of modular and multidisciplinary programmes' (QAA, October 1998). There has been much debate, in this volume and elsewhere, within academe about the QAA's benchmarking projects in history, chemistry and law. In comparison, the QAA's focus on modular and multidisciplinary programmes has attracted little attention. This is surprising.

Modular programmes are very common across the whole of the higher education sector in the UK. Multidisciplinary degrees, whether modularized or not, are not only common but also very popular. The number of students on this type of degree course massively outstrips the total for those on single-subject programmes (HESA, 1998). In fact, they are by far the most popular type of undergraduate programme, measured in terms of applications and admissions (UCAS, 1996). Given this, it is surprising that there has been so little public academic interest in what the QAA intends when it refers to 'the implications for benchmarking academic standards' of these programmes.

At first glance, this phrasing might be taken to mean *only* that standards set for individual subjects should take account of the fact that they are not only taught on single-subject degrees. On its own, this task would pose sufficient problems for the Advisory Group. However, elsewhere in the Bulletin the QAA states that the Group 'will advise the Agency on how best to approach the task of standards benchmarking *in* such programmes' (emphasis added, QAA, 1998). Is the QAA considering separate standards for subjects when taught on these programmes? If so, a complicated brief is further complicated by the reference to 'modularity'.

The QAA directed the Advisory Group to explore benchmarking in relation to 'modular *and* multidisciplinary programmes'. This implies that the Group will examine all types of modular degree and all multidisciplinary degrees, whether modular or not. This is confused and confusing. Any degree might be modular. Currently, we have in the UK modular and non-modular single honours, multidisciplinary and interdisciplinary programmes. It might be possible to establish a benchmark standard for a particular type of modular programme, but surely not for all modular degrees? To attempt this would mean benchmarking 'modularity', which is absurd.

The key focus for the Advisory Group should be the modular multidisciplinary programme, and not only because it is very common and very popular. These programmes raise crucial questions about the relationships between individual subjects, the interface between subjects and courses, and different types of degree programme. Such matters are central to subject benchmarking. What, however, is a multidisciplinary programme?

It is tempting to define a multidisciplinary or combined degree programme quite simply as one in which two or more subjects are studied simultaneously. This might seem straightforward enough. However, within modular schemes, even so-called 'single honours' programmes often include modules from outside the subject (for example, to broaden the curriculum by means of options/elective schemes, and/or to provide 'key/transferable' skills). The simple answer to this is to define combined degrees as those that include two or more subjects in the award title.

So, the 'classical' tripos (with a pedigree stretching back to the mid nineteenth century), its modern modular counterpart the three-subject (sometimes known as the 'triple-minor') degree and the very common joint and 'major minor' awards are all multidisciplinary degrees. However, even with this definition, there are problems about whether or not we are comparing like with like.

Some multidisciplinary degrees involve only cognate subjects while others allow (or even encourage) students to combine subjects from very different academic traditions. The Advisory Group will have to carefully consider whether or not benchmark standards for a subject on a multidisciplinary programme need to vary in respect of the other subjects with which it can be combined. This question highlights not only the relationship between subjects offered on a programme but also that between the subjects and the programme as a whole.

In the early days of modularization, it was not uncommon to find combined degrees that were composed of subjects 'bolted together' with each having little knowledge of what the others were doing. Some are still like this. To compound matters, the subjects were themselves often composed of modules that were also 'bolted together' without any very clear overarching subject rationale. This buttressed the sense of a fragmented curriculum. Where there was a rationale, it often seemed to be no more than a watered-down version of the subject as traditionally taught on single-subject degrees. This reinforced the view of some that combined degrees were an inferior type of degree.

This is an approach to combined degrees that sees them primarily as a 'delivery vehicle' for individual subjects. In some cases, they have been a much-needed way of increasing the number of students studying a subject when single-subject programmes are struggling to recruit. This has been the case in some science subjects in some universities. In other cases, such a programme can be a useful way of introducing new subjects into the curriculum. The subject can be viable with relatively small student numbers as it is part of a much larger programme. In these and other ways, such programmes have been in the vanguard of widening access, improving student choice and promoting innovative curriculum development. Sometimes, however, the complexity of such programmes undermines their ability to fully deliver these benefits. Constraints on staff and other resources and, frequently, timetabling mean that student choice and flexible delivery is restricted.

These programmes are not 'courses' in the traditional and widely accepted sense. Subjects largely 'do their own thing'. Some staff may work with, and have expectations of, students as if they are only studying their subject. Common approaches to teaching, learning and/or assessment strategies are absent. There is unlikely to be any attempt to examine the distribution of student workload or the balance of types of assessment and learning experience between the different subject combinations. A significant consequence of the interplay between these features is that students frequently face conflicting, even contradictory, expectations and demands from their combined subjects. Additionally, and importantly for benchmarking, there may not be any agreement (either explicit or implicit) on the type of graduate the programme is trying to produce. In what follows, the term 'programme' is reserved for this type of curriculum strategy. There are, however, modular multidisciplinary degrees trying to be 'courses' in the more traditional sense.

The key point about combined degrees in this category is that they have an overarching philosophy and rationale to which contributing subjects and departments 'sign-up'. Aims and objectives most often refer to core skills, such as critical analysis, information search and retrieval, clear communication and the ability to work both independently and collaboratively, which can be delivered by each subject whatever its academic traditions. There may be a statement about 'graduateness' and the philosophy may emphasize the course's commitment to widening participation and curriculum innovation. There may even be some general principles regarding teaching, learning and assessment strategies.

The level of generality with which these principles, philosophy and rationale are stated will be affected by the range of subjects available. Where subjects form cognate groupings, the course philosophy and objectives may be quite specific to a tradition and even refer to particular types of knowledge, not just skills. Where subjects from very different traditions may be combined, then the statements will tend to be highly generalized and refer only to those skills that cut across subject specialisms. In either case, it is not uncommon to afford component subjects considerable autonomy. To this extent, the problem for students of conflicting, even contradictory, demands made by different subjects is not altogether eliminated. Indeed, it may even be compounded by another layer of expectations found in compulsory course modules. Despite these difficulties, there is in this strategy some basis for the establishment of benchmark standards.

The diversity of multidisciplinary programmes and courses, and the varying ways in which modularity is interpreted, raise key questions for benchmarking. Will the standards relate to the programme or course, to the component subjects or to both? If the benchmarks refer to subjects, are the standards to be the same as those set for a single honours degree in that subject? If standards will apply at the programme or course level, is it possible to identify a generic template for all modular combined degrees? If benchmarking will relate simultaneously to both subjects and programmes/courses, how will their articulation be defined? Even if the QAA only intends to examine benchmarking of subjects on modular multidisciplinary degrees, it will find a complicated set of questions waiting to be answered.

The QAA specifically refers the Advisory Group to 'programmes embodying the term "studies" in their title' (QAA, 1998). The Group cannot, therefore, avoid debates about the definition of 'disciplines', the delineation of boundaries between them and how, if at all, they differ from 'subjects'. The QAA is, of course, familiar with some of these matters, having published a list of 42 'Standard Subject Units'. Some of these refer to what many academics would recognize as 'disciplines'. Some are aggregations of cognate disciplines. Others reflect attempts to move beyond the idea of disciplines altogether.

One of the central features of multidisciplinary programmes and courses is that they bring together teachers who have differing views about the sanctity of their respective academic traditions. In this context, disputes about discipline boundaries or whether or not particular constellations of academic concern are best described as a 'subject' or 'field' of study, and what all this means for curriculum design and practice, become sharply focused. Debates that might once have been confined to the staff-room or the pages of specialist or educational journals now directly and significantly affect what is taught and, ultimately, students' learning experiences and outcomes.

Some within academe are comfortable with the idea that they teach within a subject area, defined by various subspecialisms and some common debates, the boundaries of which are shifting and contested. Being less than certain about 'disciplinarity', they have no problem using only the traditional name of their discipline to describe both its multidisciplinary and single subject versions. Caveats are unnecessary.

Others are concerned to preserve the distinctiveness of their 'discipline', of 'the canon' as they have received it and known it. If something other than this is to be taught, then some way must be found to signal that it is different from the 'authentic and complete' version found on the traditional single subject programme. This view of 'disciplinarity' is also strong outside academe and often imposed by professional bodies that attempt to restrict the use of certain titles. The adjunct 'Studies' has been used to signal different curricula in this context.

This, however, is largely a negative use of the term. For others, 'studies' reflects a positive decision to move beyond the confines of traditionally defined disciplines. It denotes a consciously multidisciplinary approach, as, for example, in education studies, cultural studies, women's studies, ethnic studies or media studies.

So, we have not only multidisciplinary programmes and courses, but also multidisciplinary subjects. Some of these are taught in multidisciplinary programmes and also as single subject degrees. Some subjects in multidisciplinary degrees are not multidisciplinary. Indeed, they may follow very closely the curriculum of the single honours degree in that subject or depart extensively from it. Equally, they may be combined with other subjects with similar or very different views about disciplinarity.

To date, there is no common framework for multidisciplinary degrees. There is not only the distinction between programmes and courses, outlined above, to contend with, but also a very wide range of views about the nature of subjects in such degrees. Benchmarking of subjects in these programmes/courses could be beneficial to both students and teachers if it starts the process of establishing common, general, criteria for the design of such degrees.

To achieve this, subject benchmarking must first of all clearly establish whether or not when two or more subjects are studied simultaneously (and appear in the award title) there must be some qualitative shift not only in what is taught but also how it is delivered, assessed and quality assured compared to the single subject degree. Those involved with combined degree programmes and courses know well the problems created when component subjects are evaluated as if they are being taught and studied on their own. That is, when the academic 'gold standard' is the single subject degree. This, however, is a more complicated issue than it might appear.

On the one hand, it seems obvious that a student studying two or more subjects should not be expected to study each to the same depth nor with the same breadth as the single subject specialist. On the other hand, if a student has the subject named in their award, what can a prospective employer, or postgraduate admissions tutor, legitimately expect them to know and to have studied?

At the same time, if some of the modules being studied in a subject in a combined degree are the same as those in a single subject degree at the same institution (and this is common with modularization), to what extent is it legitimate to vary our expectations of students between the two programmes? Is it not the case that a module is a module is a module? Such matters are raised regularly by external examiners, especially when examining modules shared by different courses/programmes. They are at the heart of quality assurance generally, and benchmarking specifically, of modular multidisciplinary degrees. This is where subject benchmarking can play a very positive role in relation to multidisciplinary programmes.

The QAA intends that benchmarking should focus on 'the intellectual attributes associated with successful study of a discipline to degree level' (QAA, 1998). If this can be successfully unpacked, then benchmarking need not interfere unduly with academic freedom to determine the subject know- ledge content of the curriculum. To this extent, it should be possible to delineate discipline or subject-specific skills that should be achieved irrespective of the type of programme in which the subject is being studied. In other words, these are minimum standards to be achieved by all in that subject. What is important is to recognize that, on some courses, students may acquire additional skills and develop other qualities in relation to the subject. The establishment of minimum standards for subjects would thereby not undermine the single subject degree. It would, however, remove it as the academic 'gold standard' against which all other courses are judged.

## CONCLUSION

Multidisciplinary degrees come in many shapes and sizes. Approaches to subjects in these degrees vary widely. Even within a multidisciplinary programme or course, there can be wide variations between subjects in relation to their expectations of students. The picture is even more complicated when comparing programmes at different institutions. In this situation, is it possible to establish benchmarks for subjects on these types of courses and programmes? If it is, the key will be found in the students' experiences.

In attempting to benchmark subjects in multidisciplinary programmes and courses, the Advisory Group will need to place the students' experiences at the centre of its strategy. Whether subjects operate very largely or only partly independently of one another, whether they are using the single subject degree as their 'gold standard', whether modules are shared with other courses, are not simply technical curriculum design issues that make benchmarking more difficult. They impact directly on the students' experiences and distinguish these from those occurring on single subject courses. To be of any real benefit, benchmarks for subjects in multidisciplinary degrees must clarify the expected relationship between subjects, between the programme/course and component subjects, and between both subject and course and the students' experiences. If they do not, they may work for the single subject degree, but they will fail the student doing the multidisciplinary one.

## REFERENCES

HESA (1998) 'Students in Higher Education Institutions (1996–97)', Higher Education Statistical Agency, London

QAA (October 1998) 'The Way Ahead', *Higher Quality*, **1** (4), QAA, Gloucester

UCAS (1996) 'Annual Report (1995)', UCAS, Cheltenham

# Part IV

# International Perspectives in the Development and Use of Benchmarks and Threshold Standards

# 14

# International Benchmarking – Fact or Fantasy?

*Helen Smith*

> The question is no longer, 'Do we need to change?' but rather, 'In what direction and how fast?' The argument about whether change is necessary is over.
>
> (Robert Zemsky, Director, Institute for Research on Higher Education, University of Pennsylvania)

The background and development of the UK's higher education approach to benchmarking has been fully described earlier in this book. Here, and in other chapters in Part IV, we see how benchmarking in higher education is also developing extensively in institutions worldwide. This chapter explores some of the cross and international perspectives on benchmarking where it already exists, and traces the higher education developments of recent years that may be influential in the emergence of such standards in other parts of the world.

## THE UNITED STATES

It is widely believed that the concept of benchmarking in the US originated in the early 1980s at the Xerox Corporation, due to increasing competition within the market. While the worlds of business and education retain clear distinctions, the application of benchmarking to higher education became an almost inevitable consequence of changing trends in higher education worldwide, which bore similarities to the market forces impacting on business. The last two decades have seen moves to dramatically widen access to higher education. Initially, funding for higher education was broadly based on student numbers – greater numbers equaling higher funding. It was not long before it was realized that quantity did not equate to quality, and that widening access to higher education offered the potential for an erosion of quality, probably not as far as to the 'lowest common denominator' but, nonetheless for the deterioration in standards of achievement to be measurable.

Perceptions of the need to improve quality and accountability were linked to almost universally worldwide decreases in government funding for higher education and the rising costs of other public services. At the same time, there were some widely aired perceptions in Europe as well as in the US that higher education provided benefits to individuals, but not necessarily to the wider society in which they live and so, as in Europe, the allocation of funding to US higher education moved from a system of being based on student numbers to one based on results (Harman, October 1998).

How, then, is it possible to begin to measure the intangible *quality* of education and learning with any degree of confidence? In the last decade, external funders in Europe and the US required performance indicators (PIs) as measurement tools in their search for an evaluation of the effectiveness of the funding. PIs were frequently based on numerical factors that, while measurable and objective, did not necessarily provide evidence of quality, as discussed in this volume in Chapters 3 by Appleby and 8 by Yarrow. In the past, the US has relied, even more so than the UK, on the peer review of colleagues from other higher education institutions assessing the quality of provision. Despite the sensitivity of some institutions to comparisons, many academics in the US were comfortable with the process. The system was, however, under increasing criticism because of its perceived potential for bias and the lack of positive critical appraisal of quality due to the reliance on numerical PIs. Increasingly now, individual states are requiring their universities to be measured on a national rating of outcomes of student learning, with the potential for increased funding as the incentive. Parallels with UK benchmarking initiatives, if not in terms of the motives, are not difficult to see, as detailed in Chapter 15 by Dary Erwin.

## AUSTRALIA

By the early 1990s, Australia was only slightly behind the US in its business benchmarking practices, and in the past eight years there has been an increased emphasis on quality assurance and accountability in higher education. There has always been competition among Australian universities for students, funding and status, but in the late 1980s, federal government policy overtly took account of market forces such as privatization, competition and tuition fees for students. The 1988 White Paper on Higher Education policy was the catalyst for the Unified National System, whereby the distinction between universities and colleges was removed and, consequently, some institutions merged, resulting in a smaller number of larger institutions, all of which are now known as universities. The White Paper stated, among other things, that future funding would be 'based upon agreed priorities for institutional activity and performance against those priorities' (in Meek and Wood, 1997).

At a time of national political changes additionally impacting on the already changing world of higher education, the financial opportunities afforded by increased numbers of overseas students became apparent, creating even greater competition among institutions. Against this background, in 1995, 80,000 foreign students were studying in Australia, contributing 1.9 billion Australian dollars to the national economy (Juddery, 15–21 May 1996). Quality assurance became a more prominent issue in the early 1990s, and there were specific recommendations from the Higher Education Council in 1992 for institutional profiles and funding based on achievements. As a result, the Committee for Quality Assurance in Higher Education was formed, offering voluntary involvement in quality reviews for universities. The fact that all universities chose to participate may have been due in no small measure to the financial incentives that were linked to higher rankings. The fundamental difference in quality assurance practice between higher education in Australia and in many other countries was that Australia then took into account both outcomes and the standard of internal quality assurance procedures. There is now increasing pressure to focus on measurement of outcomes. It is known that the government intends to introduce 'quantitative PIs and benchmarks' (Higher Education Budget Statement, 1996). Fears in the academic community of standardization, leading to loss of diversification, are as widespread as in other parts of the world.

## NEW ZEALAND

In New Zealand, the concept of benchmarking has existed for some time, although the term itself is not yet in common use in higher education. Two distinct approaches to educational standards in New Zealand are evident: one espousing the need for nationally agreed levels or standards is based on vocational requirements, while the other promotes the advantages of national examinations and league tables. Both agree on the benefits of identifying and rewarding high standards, and therefore accept the necessity for nationally agreed benchmarking, although their ideas of the type of benchmark may be very different. The focus in the New Zealand polytechnic sector, therefore, is to educate for the world of employment, the 'fit for purpose and practice' ethos of the UK. Chapter 17 by Zepke, *et al.*, provides more information on this approach and Chapter 16 by Woodhouse provides an overview of the issues as they impact the university sector.

## THE PEOPLE'S REPUBLIC OF CHINA

In the People's Republic of China (PRC), many aspects of higher education have undergone marked change as a result of new political attitudes and influences. In recent decades, there was 'central control and allocation' of graduates into the workplace (Williams, *et al.*, 1997). Graduates from the majority of State universities were assured of lifelong employment, but did not have free choice of their professional route. However, in recent years, economic growth and increased Western influences have altered attitudes. There is a growing acceptance of the rights of individuals to personal choice and achievement, and of the value to society of professional and individual autonomy. Higher education reforms in 1986, 1988 and 1995 have inevitably impacted funding. Prior to the reforms, financial subsidies and awards were offered to students as encouragement to enter higher education. Since 1988, this system has undergone gradual change, and the academic year 1995/96 was the first in which all students were expected to pay tuition fees.

In the PRC, it is still widely accepted that the benefits of higher education are not confined to the individual, but are disseminated into society – higher education itself being seen as 'the pursuit of knowledge and the cultivation of the citizenry' (Williams, *et al.*, 1997). There seems little doubt that changes in the economic markets and self-funding by students will soon produce conditions similar to those in higher education in the West. And so, while the terminology of benchmarking and standards that is current in other parts of the world may not yet be in common use in the PRC, conditions appear to be right for their emergence in the near future.

## HONG KONG

In Hong Kong, in the ten-year period from the mid 1980s to 1990s, the percentage of the age group eligible for undergraduate study rose from 2 to 18 per cent. This planned increase came about largely as a result of the review of education chaired by Sir John Llewellyn (Hong Kong Planning Committee, 1982), out of which came the recommendation for the setting up of a second polytechnic to provide additional higher education opportunities. At the same time, other colleges were successful in gaining funding from Hong Kong's University and Polytechnic Grants Committee and in being granted Ordinances in order to be able to award degrees. By 1990, universities and polytechnics were encouraged to increase the numbers of both undergraduate and postgraduate students, and, by 1994, the legislation had been enacted for polytechnics to become universities (Cannon, October 1997).

The cultural, demographic, economic and political causes of the expansion of higher education in Hong Kong over this period have been complicated. Setting aside political influences, it is clear that Hong Kong is experiencing conditions and developments in higher education similar to those in other parts of the world, which could lead to the development of benchmarking as a quality measure. The extent to which that happens, and in what timescale, is likely to be influenced by ongoing higher education developments in the PRC (as outlined above), as well as by economic change. The degree of such influence is speculative, but there exists in Hong Kong a potential for innovative international quality developments.

## JAPAN

At the end of the Second World War, the Japanese education system as a whole underwent reorganization, bringing it into closer alignment with that in the US. One obvious difference between higher education in Japan and in the West is its funding source. In Japan, there are between two and three times as many privately funded higher education institutions as there are national (those primarily funded and overseen by government) and local ones (financed and overseen by provincial or city government) (Teichler, September 1997), with private institutions accounting for approximately a quarter of university student numbers. Any developments in quality assurance must therefore inevitably be influenced by, and gain the cooperation of, the funding providers.

There remains in Japan a widely held perception of university hierarchy, and the sense that graduation from the more prestigious universities will lead to enhanced career opportunities. This results in strong competition for places that originates during school years. In addition, the Japanese determined in 1983 that by the year 2000 the numbers of foreign students studying in Japan should increase from 20,000 to 100,000. While this increase in numbers began and continued on target, the majority (80 per cent) came from neighbouring Asian countries, and when Japanese economic and employment opportunities decreased in 1992, the number of overseas students similarly declined (Teichler, September 1997). International opportunities for students inside and outside Japan do exist, although input and output are not evenly balanced. There has been government encouragement for the development of one-year programmes, taught in English, in the hope of attracting students from the US and other countries. However, despite government scholarships and subsidized tuition, there are fewer overseas students choosing to study in Japan than there are Japanese students studying abroad.

It may be timely, then, for Japan also to consider the benefits of benchmarking. While some Western students' perceptions of cultural and language differences and difficulties will not disappear overnight, the benefits of internationally accepted standards may tempt others into international study opportunities, with the potential for broad social and financial advantages to the host countries.

## SOUTH AFRICA

In South Africa, increased democracy since 1994 has resulted in notable changes to the education system. Review and redefinition of aims and processes have resulted in improvements in resources, access and opportunities. The South African Qualifications Authority (SAQA), appointed in 1996, was charged with an examination of benchmarking issues similar to that of the UK's QAA, and the development of a National Qualifications Framework (NQF), which has similarities to that in New Zealand, to embrace notions of the continuation of education – the 'lifelong learning' concept in the UK. The NQF is likely to work on a basis of integral programmes or qualifications rather than small units of learning, as the latter have been perceived as having potential to fragment the overall picture and not produce a coherent assessment of achievement. Chapter 18 by Digby Warren offers valuable insights into the detail of the South African context.

## OVERVIEW

It is clear that oceanic divisions are, in this context, no more than geographical notions. Higher education in many parts of the world is facing similar issues. Terms such as quality, accountability, institutional autonomy and lifelong learning are mirrored around the world, as is the interrelated issue of funding. Anxieties and concerns, too, are shared. There are widespread fears that threshold standards will lead to standardization and prescription with consequent negative impacts on the current diversity of higher education provision. Benchmarking is viewed as more than simply a set of standards: it is seen as a means of comparing the performance of higher education institutions, as well as being a means of identifying and adapting good practice.

Is there, then, a fundamental difference between benchmarking in the UK and the USA? In the UK, is it more likely to be imposed – with subsequent effects on motivation and compliance – whereas in the USA it may be adopted as a method of choice by individual universities, thereby posing much less of a threat to institutional autonomy and potential diversity of provision? If this ethos of choice were to prevail in the UK, then the potential benefits of adapting (but not adopting *per se*) the good practice of other institutions would seem to have much merit in the continuing quest for widely acceptable benchmarks and the enhancement of quality.

The outstanding theme of benchmarking in the USA, both in industry and in higher education, is that it is outcome-driven – it is the search for better practice in order, ultimately, to improve performance. The following are therefore key questions to ask in this context.

- How good are we?
- How good can we be?
- How do we get better?

(See www.innovet.com/ben1.htm on the Internet for more on these questions.)

Real improvement involves long-term change in institutional ethos and practice – potentially of measurable benefit to the institution, its staff and students, but only when those concerned are involved in the process and are committed to it and its anticipated positive outcomes.

## INTERNATIONAL BENCHMARKING ISSUES

If benchmarking is to have potential for international application, how then may its benefits be realized and in what form? Should nationally agreed subject benchmarks be greeted only with relief that we have come this far or could some international educational agreements result from the wealth of existing and emerging debate and experience? The benefits of threshold standards to quality issues such as international collaborative provision and student exchanges are clear. There may also be tangible financial incentives to continue to support benchmarking initiatives. In the last ten years, the number of US students studying abroad has almost doubled, the majority choosing to come to the UK. At the same time, numbers of foreign students choosing to study in the US rose by more than 5 per cent. There is increased evidence of global competition for students, with notable numbers of US students travelling in recent years to Australia, Canada, Costa Rica and Mexico as well as the UK and other countries (Marcus, 18 December 1998). Incentives therefore exist to support the further development of international subject benchmarks. It is an unfortunate fact of life in the increasingly pressured world of higher education that, unless such issues are deemed to be either nationally imposed or immediately financially compelling, they will not have a high priority.

## CONCLUSION

As the cost of higher education is increasingly being borne by students, their families or employers, universities are all too aware of the need for accountability and the provision by them of accurate, up-to-date evidence of the quality of educational experience they offer. If benchmarking is to become the durable currency of comparability that is needed, then it must be clear, credible, transferable and current. It will only have value if it is widely accepted within – and possibly across – subjects. This notion may be little more than an item on a 'wish list', but anything less can offer few advantages over the current system. Perhaps we have already come full circle. The challenge, then, to international higher education is to ensure that we do not simply retrace old paths. Could benchmarking be a step in the right direction towards standard setting but not standardization?

## REFERENCES

Alstete, J (1995) 'Benchmarking in Higher Education: Adapting best practices to improve quality', ASHE–ERIC Higher Education Report No. 5, The George Washington University, Washington

Australian Government Publishing Service (1996) 'Higher Education Budget Statement', Australian Government Publishing Service, Canberra

Australian Government Publishing Service (1988) 'Higher Education: A policy statement', White Paper, Australian Government Publishing Service, Canberra

Bourke, A (October 1997) 'The internationalization of Higher Education: The case of Medical Education', *Higher Education Quarterly*, **51** (4), pp 325–46

Burn, B (1971) *Higher Education in Nine Countries,* McGraw-Hill, Maidenhead

Cannon, I (October 1997) 'Higher education in Hong Kong', *Higher Education Quarterly*, **51** (4), pp 308–24

Cave, M, Hanney, S, and Kogan, M (1991) *The Use of Performance Indicators in Higher Education*, 2nd edn, Jessica Kingsley, London

Gellert, C (ed) (1993) *Higher Education in Europe*, Jessica Kingsley, London

Department for Education (1993) *Study in Europe*, Jessica Kingsley, London

Working Party of the Committee of Scottish University Principals (1992) 'Teaching and learning in an expanding Higher Education system', Scottish Centrally Funded Colleges

Harman, G (October 1998) 'The management of quality assurance: a review of international practice', *Higher Education Quarterly*, **52** (4), pp 345–64

Hong Kong Planning Committee (1982) 'The first report of the planning committee for the second polytechnic', Hong Kong

Innovation Network: www.innovet.com/ben1.htm

Juddery, B (15–21 May 1996) 'International students earn $1.8 billion for universities', *Campus Review*, **6** (3)

Marcus, J (18 December1998) *TheTimes Higher Education Supplement*, **1** (363), p 10

Meek, V, and Wood, F (1997) 'The market as a new steering strategy for Australian Higher Education', *Higher Education Policy*, **10** (3/4), pp 253–74

Teichler, U (September 1997) 'Higher Education in Japan: A view from outside', *Higher Education*, **34** (2), pp 275–98

Turmeau, W, and Maclennan, M (1990) 'Towards 1992: Higher Education in Scotland and the European Community: A discussion paper', Single Market Committee of the Scottish Economic Council, Glasgow
Umakoshi, T (1997) 'Internationalization of Japanese Higher Education in the 1980s and early 1990s', *Higher Education*, **34**, pp 255–73
Williams, G, Liu, S, and Shi, Qiuheng (1997) 'Marketization of Higher Education in the People's Republic of China', *Higher Education Policy*, **10** (2), pp 151–57

# 15

# The United States' Perspective on, and Experiences of, Performance Indicators and Threshold Standards – How is Quality Determined?

*T Dary Erwin*

Just like in the UK and Europe, the emergence of performance indicators by various states in the US reveals the desire by our stakeholders to know more about educational institutions and how well they function. A credible response is crucial in order to maintain existing institutional autonomy, funding levels, teaching methods and the validity of evaluation measures. This chapter describes the nature and meaning of performance indicators, their current role in the educational process and suggestions for standard-setting or benchmarking with learning outcomes.

Traditional budgetary practices of public US colleges and universities distribute monies according to student enrolment and maintenance of current costs. In ways similar to those in the UK and Europe, the emergence of performance budgeting – that is, allocating monies based on institutional results, not just headcounts – is gaining in popularity in the US. The old system of basing appropriations on enrollment growth gave 'little reason to strive for better performance' (Osborne and Gaebler, 1993). The notion that quality matters are essentially a foregone conclusion (Burke and Serban, 1998) as applied to public funding of higher education has vanished. External constituents are now grappling with what types of performance measures to select, as well as how to use them.

## WHAT IS MEASURED IS FUNDED AND WHAT IS FUNDED IS VALUED

According to Krueger and Jones (1996), what is measured by institutions is often funded by government, and what is funded is valued in educational institutions. Often, data already available within the institution are inserted into governmental reports or institutional reviews because of numerical simplicity, lower cost or availability due to some other purpose. As is illustrated later in this chapter, these available measures, usually called performance indicators, are often indirect or misleading measures about learning. Educational institutions reinforce the use of performance indicators as surrogates when we refuse to supply programmatic learning outcomes because of their complexity or cost of collection. Governmental funding agencies, and even managers within academe, seize these indirect measures, inflate them to an undeserved status as overall educational indicators and then allocate funds by their amounts. Funding, in turn, reinforces the value of these overapplied indirect measures.

Krueger and Jones also claim the reverse is true – that what is valued is funded and what is funded is measured. As is well known, access – the opening of US higher education to the masses – has received much emphasis over the past few decades. Thus, having a greater number of students was a criterion that was valued, and funding formulas were developed that were largely based on headcounts. As long as enrolments rose, everybody was happy. But, in time, as in other settings, overly emphasizing the number of students served meant a lessening of attention to quality in some institutions. While US graduate education is praised, undergraduate education has been criticized for lacking quality since the early 1980s. A number of reports proclaimed the decline of quality and accountability in US higher education, including 'Integrity in the college curriculum: a report to the academic community' (Association of American Colleges, 1985), 'Involvement in learning' (National Institute of Education's Study Group on the Conditions of Excellence in American Higher Education, 1984), 'To reclaim a legacy: A report on the humanities in higher education' (National Endowment of the Humanities, 1984) and 'An American imperative: Higher expectation for higher education' (Wingspread Group on Higher Education, 1993).

## A NEED FOR MEASURES OF QUALITY

The backdrop for greater accountability requirements relates to government officials' need for greater understanding of higher education and a change in higher education's funding priority. On the one hand, government officials are trying to understand better the nature and value of educational services. Brick and mortar projects are easily seen, but the fruits of the educated mind are less tangible. On the other hand, other government funding priorities, such as elementary and secondary education (K-12) healthcare, penal system needs and mental health reform, have lessened the proportion of US state money allocated to higher education (Ruppert, 1997). Higher education came to be viewed as primarily benefiting individuals not society (Nettles, Cole and Sharp, 1997). When universities increased student fees by about 58 per cent (Alderman, 1994), state demands for accountability increased even more. Levine (1997) has outlined the consequences related to finance and governance in this new climate. Originally, evaluation systems of institutions were mandated for improvement purposes. Many US institutions responded weakly and policymakers are now considering upping the ante to more institutional comparisons (Gaither, Nedwek and Neal, 1994) and moving beyond improvement to more accountability.

A shift has been occurring in the monitoring of social service agencies in general. Traditionally, monies were awarded to agencies up front, with little follow-up about effectiveness. Structures were put in place to maintain control and tight management. While these practices will no doubt continue, Neave (1988) identifies a shift towards the 'evaluative state'. That is, consumers and funders of social service organizations are demanding systematic profiles of quality received at the end of the service. Higher education in the Western world is grappling with this new accountability and its responses to it.

US policymakers essentially prescribed the reporting of performance indicators:

- because of the need to demonstrate quality and worth to constituents;
- because of the need to gauge an institution's progress towards state or government goals;
- as a guide for planning and budget decisions;
- as a guide for identifying areas for improvement (Ruppert, 1997).

## DEFINITIONS AND MEANINGS OF PERFORMANCE INDICATORS

Over the past decade or so, a number of common terms have emerged, but what are generally called performance indicators are used as quality metrics by external constituents on funding. As defined by the Organization for Economic Cooperation and Development (OECD, 1989), performance indicators are 'numerical values which provide a measurement for assessing the quantitative or qualitative performance of a system'. Cave, Hanney, Kogan, and Trevett (1988) provide a similar definition: 'an authoritative measure –

usually in a quantitative form – of an attribute of the activity of a higher education institution'. The application of performance indicators range from economic measures to efficiency measures to effectiveness measures (Sizer, Spec and Bormans, 24 February 1992). Performance indicators are truly international in scope (Dochy, Segers and Wijien, 1990) and may serve as signals for making 'international comparisons in educational quality, effectiveness and efficiency' (Gaither, Nedwek and Neal, 1994).

The selection of performance indicators and levels of standards for performance can befuddle educators. Actually, the term 'performance measure' is a more direct term related to student learning than is performance indicator. As is illustrated later, most performance indicators have comprised available measures of resources or inputs into the learning process.

Lately, the reporting of traditional performance indicators has become considered insufficient for judging quality. The level of performance, sometimes referred to as standards, benchmarks, threshold or competency levels, is the added dimension beyond just simple reporting of performance indicators. Statistics, of course, summarize the frequency and amount of these performance indicators. However, the interpretation of any statistic is usually limited unless it is compared to something else. Essentially, any kind of statistical measure can be compared in three ways – using norms or percentiles, criterion referencing or self-reference.

Norms are simply percentile ranks or the relative location and frequency of the measure within a numerical distribution. For instance, the graduates' average score on some test may place that institution at the 57th percentile (or whatever percentile), meaning that the average student at that institution scored at or below 57 per cent of the total for the students in the norm group. In the second way to compare or benchmark, criterion-referenced interpretation relates to the mastery or competence in the knowledge, skill or personal characteristic of interest at a given level or standard. Criterion-referenced interpretations typically have a designated score or rating scale level, above which is mastery or success, below which is failing or inadequate performance. Norms or percentiles are ranks that have little meaning related to learning while criterion-referenced interpretations relate directly to learning. The third way of comparing is self-reference. As the term implies, intracomparisons are only made, and compare change over time, within an institution. The disadvantage of self-referencing is the limited generalizability of the data to performance at other institutions or with knowledge domains.

## DETERMINING QUALITY IN PROGRAM EVALUATION

Essentially, there are three main information-based approaches to formal, programme evaluation of higher education institutions in the United States.

These overlapping approaches are performance indicators, programme reviews and learning outcomes, often collected from State-mandated testing programmes. The status and role of these three areas are discussed below.

In the US, the lists of performance indicators that were formulated early on were heavily weighted towards management and business practices, much as was the case in the UK and Europe. Outputs such as graduation and retention rates then received attention, but, most recently, learning outcomes have been finding their way on many States' indicator lists. Typical performance indicators include the following:

- total number of degrees awarded by the institution and programme and the time taken to gain a degree;
- enrolment/retention/graduation data by gender, ethnicity and programme;
- external or sponsored research funds;
- admission standards and measures of first-year class against standards;
- numbers and percentages of accredited and eligible programmes;
- total student credit hours produced, by institution and discipline;
- remediation activities and indicators or remedial effectiveness;
- transfer rates to and from two- and four-year colleges;
- pass rates for professional licensure exams;
- placement data for graduates;
- results of follow-up satisfaction studies (alumni, students, parents and employers);
- faculty workload/productivity data (Ruppert, 1997).

One of the more well known national projects utilizing performance indicators involved the National Association of College and University Business Officers (NACUBO) in collaboration with the accounting firm Coopers & Lybrand. A total of 38 functional areas, such as accounts payable and parking, were outlined, with commonly defined resource and participation measures within each of these areas. Outputs and learning outcomes were generally not included, but benchmarks were developed with comparable universities and even businesses and industries. Participation was voluntary, and only 120 institutions supplied data for 1992–93. In the future, activity measures such as teaching loads and cost ratios will be collected by academic discipline, but the future of the project is uncertain because of institutions' sensitivity to comparison (Gaither, Nedwek, and Neal, 1994).

Programme review – another of the main evaluation approaches – utilizes the time-honoured academic system of peer review. Comfortable for teaching staff, peer review usually involves colleagues from other universities coming in to offer opinions on quality and resources. In the US, peer review rankings are most visible in consumer magazines such as *U.S. News and World Report* or *Money Magazine*, which are largely based on opinions of admission directors and presidents and on measures of resources.

Historically, peer review has been attacked in the US as being biased and ill focused. In the early 1980s, the then US Secretary of Education William Bennett criticized accrediting associations where peer review is central. While the UK has in the past employed government inspectors (HMIs) and more recently has used peer reviewers working through the QAA subject review process, using a structured scheme leading to a graded profile, and quality creditors to review curriculum or used more formal rating schemes, the US relies more on teaching staff to periodically review their colleagues' practices. The effectiveness of peer review must be considered because US accrediting bodies sanction qualification for federal financial student aid at the institutional level and entry into individual professions at the discipline level.

In ways that compare with the UK's characterization of the 'scratch my back and I'll scratch yours' syndrome or Elsworth's (27 February 1994) 'connoisseur' review, peer review lacks sufficient credibility among US government officials and external decision makers. Bennett's criticisms focused on the lack of measures of quality in accreditation reviews, which in the 1980s overly emphasized inputs such as entering admission tests of ability or resource measures such as the number of library books or classroom space utilization instead of quality outcomes. These inputs or resource measures are, at best, indirect measures of quality and not measures of what students learn or how they develop.

According to Ewell (1998), the pressures to ensure greater quality in student learning are still mounting with US accreditors. First, US institutions are moving from a teaching to a learning paradigm. US schools focused more on the delivery and resources associated with instruction than what or how well students learned. Second, over half of US college students attended more than one institution. Final graduating institutions have done little to ensure final learning or the validity of learning at other institutions, and accreditation has allowed this practice to flourish. Third and last, stakeholders such as employers have been left out of the accreditation process and so the credibility of university self-review suffers.

In addition to performance indicators and programme reviews, learning outcomes collected by means of student testing programmes have been, and continue to be, popular evaluative systems. Currently, eight states use common tests of student learning (Nettles, Cole and Sharp, 1997). Legislators in some states call for 'an annual report card' comparing all universities within a state. For instance, the State of Tennessee has required the use of the

American College Testing Program's College Outcome Measure Project (ACT-COMP) test for over a decade. ACT-COMP scores and other institutional effectiveness data can add 5.45 per cent to the institution's instructional budget. Other US states, such as Arkansas, require other tests, such as the ACT's Collegiate Assessment of Academic Proficiency (CAAP) to measure student learning in general education.

Statewide testing programmes satisfy government officials' desire to compare educational institutions on the basis of a common metric. In the 1980s, the selected tests were initially measures of basic skills, but then general education tests became popular instruments for State policy mandates. Tests of elementary and secondary education students are particularly popular now.

Selection of particular tests also reinforces certain constructs that constituents deem important. (For a review of tests designed to measure critical thinking, problem-solving and writing – the three most popular general education goals in the US – consult the National Postsecondary Education Cooperative web site: http://nces.ed.gov/npec/evaltests/ Case studies of US institutions that successfully use proprietary tests to improve student learning may also be found at this same web site.)

Statewide tests are criticized for their test format, which is generally that of multiple choice, for its lack of content validity as applied to particular institutions and for its expense. In spite of these criticisms coming largely from within higher education, external groups favour their continued and, indeed, even more widespread use. Often, universities have not been present at the policy table (either voluntarily or involuntarily) when test selections were made.

One of the more controversial aspects of statewide testing is the setting of a particular cut-off score or rating scale level to designate an adequate standard of learning. Selecting a single threshold of performance seems like a simple act, yet setting a cut-off is a complicated and controversial process (later in this chapter this matter is discussed further).

## PERFORMANCE BUDGETING AND FUNDING

Burke and Serban (1998) distinguish between performance budgeting and performance funding. Performance budgeting, they say, 'occurs when State governments or coordinating boards use indirectly reports of institutional achievements on performance indicators as a general context in shaping the total budgets for public colleges or universities'. Additional funding depends on the 'judgement of State governments or coordinating boards', and politics can assume an even greater role.

Performance funding attempts to remove some of the political aspects of funding by making it formula-driven. Performance funding is defined as 'special State funding tied directly to the achievements of public colleges and universities on specific performance indicators' (Burke and Serban, 1998). For instance, in Tennessee, institutions may earn up to 5.45 per cent of their operating budget each year from these indicators and intended outcomes:

- performance of graduates on an approved standardized test of general education;
- performance of graduates on approved examinations in a major field study;
- satisfaction of alumni and enrolled students, programme accreditation;
- quality of non-accreditable undergraduate programmes as determined by external review;
- quality of Master's degree programmes as determined by external review;
- level of minority enrolment and enrolment *vis-à-vis* mission-related goals;
- graduation and retention rates;
- institutional success in the strategic planning process and improvement actions.

In a more extreme case, South Carolina moved to 100 per cent performance funding in 1996 based on the following performance indicators and outcomes:

- expenditure of funds to achieve institutional mission;
- curricula offered to achieve mission;
- approval of a mission statement;
- adoption of a strategic plan to support the mission statement;
- attainment of goals of the strategic plan and academic and other credentials of faculty;
- performance review system for faculty to include student and peer evaluations;
- post-tenure review for tenured faculty; compensation of faculty;
- availability of faculty to students outside classrooms;
- community and public service activities of faculty for which no extra compensation is paid;
- class sizes and student–teacher ratios;
- number of credit hours taught by faculty;
- ratio of full-time faculty to other full-time employees;
- accreditation of degree-granting programmes;

- institutional emphasis on quality teacher education and reform;
- sharing and use of technology, programmes, equipment, supplies and source matter experts within the institution, with other institutions and with the business community;
- cooperation with private industry and percentage of administrative costs compared to academic costs;
- use of best management practices;
- elimination of unjustified duplication;
- amount of general overhead costs;
- SAT and ACT scores of students;
- high school class standing, grade point averages and activities of students;
- postsecondary non-academic achievements of students;
- priority on enrolling in-State residents;
- graduation rates;
- employment rates;
- employers' feedback on graduates;
- scores of graduates in employment-related exams;
- number of graduates who continue their education;
- credit hours earned by graduates and transferability of credits to and from institutions;
- continuing education;
- accessibility for all citizens of the State;
- financial support for reform in teaching education;
- amount of public- and private-sector grants (Nettles, Cole, and Sharp, 1997).

In the US, 21 states report performance budgeting practices, while 13 states report performance funding policies. These states are listed in Tables 15.1 and 15.2.

**Table 15.1** *States using performance budgeting practices*

| *Year* | *Number (Percentage)* | *States* |
|---|---|---|
| 1998 | 21 states (42%) | Colorado, Florida, Georgia, Hawaii, Idaho, Illinois, Indiana, Iowa, Kansas, Mississippi, Nebraska, Oregon, Oklahoma, North Carolina, Rhode Island, Texas, Maine, West Virginia, Louisiana, South Dakota, Washington |

**Table 15.2** *States using performance funding practices*

| *Year* | *Number (Percentage)* | *States* |
|---|---|---|
| 1998 | 13 states (26%) | Colorado, Connecticut, Florida, Illinois, Indiana, Louisiana, Missouri, Ohio, Oklahoma, South Carolina, South Dakota, Tennessee, Washington. |

*Source:* Burke and Serban, 1998

## METHODS FOR DETERMINING CUT-OFF SCORES

Faculty and administrators often face the dilemma of how to establish standards or thresholds for an assessment method. An assessment or evaluation method can be administered in an effort to see what students have learned from a programme, but, in the end, a cut-off score or level on a rating scale determines how many students benefited from the programme. Setting a cut-off score or level is rather simple to conceptualize if the programme is teaching specific skills and the final assessment is attempting to measure whether or not the individual has obtained the skills that were taught. This becomes more difficult if the programme involves individual learning and development that are more continuous and difficult to measure (Shepard, 1980).

When determining a cut-off score or level, there will almost invariably be a student who will score below that level who actually knows the material. On the other hand, there will be a student who does not know the material sufficiently but will pass nevertheless due to a low cut-off score or level. As a result, setting a cut-off score is a process that requires continual revision, and the expectations of the test administrators must be kept in check to ensure that neither too much nor too little is being expected of the students. Concepts such as the standard error of measurement should also be considered in setting standards (a book by Crocker and Algina, 1986 is a good source of further information on such methods).

Setting cut-off scores for selective response format assessment methods is discussed below because of particular difficulties involved with this format. Setting standards on rating scales or checklists for constructed response formats is inherently less difficult if behavioural anchors are used. Admittedly, there is no perfect method for setting a level of mastery for assessment instruments.

Generally, three broad classes of setting standards for selected response formats, such as multiple-choice tests, are used:

- judgments based on holistic impressions;
- judgments based on review of test items or content;
- judgments based on students' test results (Crocker and Algina, 1986; Shepard, 1980).

All three methods are used to determine the percentage of test items a student with a minimum level of competence should answer correctly. It is important to remember that minimum competence is not a level attained by the average student, but a level that all graduates in the major or basic studies must obtain.

The first method – that is, judgements based on holistic impressions – requires several qualified judges to set a level of competence for a particular assessment measure. The cut-off score is determined by simply averaging the level of competence score provided by each judge. Judges are typically experts in the area being assessed and it is advisable to select additional judges who are from the same discipline to serve as consultants. Standards will achieve higher credibility if several of the judges are from other institutions. For example, professionals in the field, accreditation officials and government officials would be examples of additional judges to poll (Erwin, 1991). The problem with this method of setting a cut-off score is that judges from different disciplines will emphasize different areas of competence that may result in fluctuating standards.

Another way to approach setting standards is by using judgements made about the content of assessment methods. This method also uses a team of judges, but, instead of looking at the test as a whole, each judge reviews each test item separately and rates its importance. There are several procedures for reviewing test content (see Angoff, 1971; Ebel, 1979; Jaeger, 1978;

Martenza, 1977; and Nedelsky, 1954). According to Angoff's procedure, each judge reviews each test item and assigns a probability that a minimally competent student will answer it correctly. To assist the judges in making probability judgements, it can be suggested that they imagine a group of 100 borderline test-takers and predict how many of them would answer the question correctly. Adding together the judges' probability estimates for each test item results in the total score students are expected achieve. A cut-off score can be determined by finding the mean of all the expected total scores.

A study by Impara and Plake (1997) examined teachers' abilities to estimate the actual proportion of correct responses that would be achieved by two groups of students. Looking at the difference between the actual students' performances for the items and the teachers' estimates, Impara and Plake found that the teachers' estimations were not very accurate, despite their familiarity with the students. In a follow-up study, Impara and Plake proposed a yes/no method of setting standards that is described by Angoff (1971). This method asks the teacher to imagine a single real person who is typical of the target group and respond by saying whether or not that individual would answer the item correctly. Like the traditional Angoff method, the summation of the teacher's yes/no responses are expected to give an accurate estimate of the proportion of correct responses there will be for all of the students combined (Impara and Plake, 1997). The traditional Angoff method and the yes/no method produced very similar results when the actual performance and the estimates were analysed. Although the results of the two methods are similar, teachers found the yes/no method to be much simpler, because imagining the performance of an actual student was easier than imagining the proportion of an entire group that would get an item right.

Martenza's method builds on Angoff's traditional method by having each judge rate each item on a scale of one to ten points, with ten points being 'extremely important' and one point 'of little importance'. For example:

| *Test item number* | *Importance* |
|---|---|
| 1 | 10 |
| 2 | 5 |
| 3 | 1 |
| 4 | 8 |
| 5 | 6 |
| | Total 30 |

After totalling the importance ratings, the figure is divided by the total number of test items. In this case, it would be 30 divided by 5. Multiplying the resulting figure by ten provides the percentage score that a student would need to obtain in order to reach minimum competence on this test. For this example, a single student would need to get at least 60 per cent correct in order to reach minimum competence on this test (Martenza, 1977). The primary disadvantages of judging test content are that judges tend to disagree and to omit item ratings if the item is outside their area of expertise. Using this method, it also has to be remembered that the judges' reviews are hypothetical and may result in unrealistic expectations.

The third method of setting standards – judgements based on analysis of group results – is sometimes preferred because students' responses are taken into account whereas the prior two methods do not utilize learning data. In this approach, students who took the test are separately rated as masters or non-masters of the discipline. Masters are students who are deemed competent (because they have mastered the material) or who have the desired traits. Non-masters are students who are not competent or do not possess the desired traits. Separating the students in this way allows the judges to set a cut-off score that discriminates between the two groups. The chief advantage of this procedure is its reliance on how students actually perform rather than on what judges believe will happen (Shepard, 1980).

## CONCLUSIONS

The role and status of performance indicators and measures in the US have been presented in this chapter. While some educators still debate the existence and role of accountability in higher education, the use of performance indicators and measures to provide partial funding of universities continues unabated in the Western world. In fact, our reluctance to participate fully in programme accountability discussions has contributed to the selection of some invalid measures to assess institutional quality and, particularly, student learning. Performance indicators, sometimes chosen by non-educators, often have no relationship with measuring what is the primary mission of most universities – student learning and development. It is to higher education's advantage to refocus some performance indicators more towards learning outcomes and away from efficiency measures that do not reflect our work with students.

Another step in the process of using information about quality for funding and governance is the setting of standards or benchmarks with performance indicators and measures. In the US, a long history exists setting standards in elementary and secondary education. Having specific educational objectives or tests of learning in place has not been enough; levels of competence or standards are called for in determining advancement to higher grade levels, regardless of teachers' marks or course grades.

Nettles, Cole and Sharp (1997) surveyed the US state boards and conducted focus groups regarding current and future assessment policies. Their summary of responses from state oversight boards of higher education are very telling with regard to the near future:

- about two-thirds of the US state boards see the need for development of common assessment methods;
- requests for additional funds for their state institutions must include links with assessment activities;
- legislative and public pressures were calling for greater accountability, not necessarily institutional improvement;
- institutions are anxious about being compared and evaluated.

Many politicians and, in fact, many university heads and government officials do not support the rational approach of performance indicators and measures in resource allocations. This rationality distracts from 'the pork barrel appeal' (Lasher and Greene, 1993) or resource allocations linked to political whim. Yet the reasons for reporting performance indicators and measures are the same now as over a decade ago – 'increased fiscal constraints, call for relevancy to the workplace, and a growing concern for return on the public's investment' (Gaither, Nedwek and Neal, 1994). Turning up our noses at the process does little to address the underlying issues. Educators need to do a better job of explaining what can be learned, how best it can be learned and what the value of learning is.

## REFERENCES

Alderman, (1994) 'Avoid these hidden money traps', *Money Guide: Best College Buys* pp 6–12

Angoff, W H (1971) 'Scales, norms, and equivalent scores' in *Educational Measurement*, ed R L Thorndike, American Council on Education, Washington, DC

Association of American Colleges (1985) 'Integrity in the college curriculum: A report to the academic community', Association of American Colleges, Washington, DC

Burke, J C, and Serban, A M (1998) 'Current states and future prospects of performance funding and performance budgeting for public Higher Education: The second survey', Nelson A Rockefeller Institute of Government, Albany, New York

Cave, M, Hannay, S, Kogan, M, and Trevett, G (1988) *The Use of Performance Indicators in Higher Education: A critical analysis of developing practice*, Jessica Kingsley, London

Crocker, L, and Algina, J (1986) *Introduction to Classical and Modern Test Theory*, Holt, Rinehart, and Winston, New York

Dochy, F J R C, Segers, M J C, and Wijnen, W H F W (1990) *Management Information and Performance Indicators in Higher Education*, Van Gorcum, Assen/Maastricht

Ebel, R L (1979) *Essentials of Educational Measurement*, 3rd edn, Prentice Hall, Englewood Cliffs, New Jersey

Elsworth, G (27 February 1994) 'Confronting the bases in connoisseur review and performance indicators in Higher Education: A structural modelling approach', *Journal of Higher Education*, pp 163–90

Erwin, T (1991) *Assessing Student Learning and Development*, Jossey-Bass, San Francisco

Ewell, P T (1998) 'Examining a brave new world: How accreditation might be different', paper presented at the second annual meeting of the Council for Higher Education Accreditation, Washington, DC

Gaither, G, Nedwek, B P, and Neal, J E (1994) 'Measuring up: The promises and pitfalls of performance indicators', Clearinghouse on Higher Education, The George Washington University, Washington, DC

Impara, J and Plake, B (1997). 'Standard setting: An alternative approach', *Journal of Educational Measurement*, **4**, pp 353–66

Jaeger, R M (1978) 'A proposal for setting a standard on the North Carolina high school competency test', paper presented at the spring meeting of the North Carolina Association of Research in Education, Chapel Hill, North Carolina

Krueger, D, and Jones, D (1996) personal communication

Lasher, W F, and Greene, D L (1993) 'College and university budgeting: What do we know? What do we need to know?' in *Higher Education: Handbook of theory and research*, ed J C Smart, Agathon Press, New York

Levine, A (1997) 'How the academic profession is changing', *Daedalus*, **126**, pp 1–20

Martenza, V R (1977) *Applying Norm-referenced and Criterion-referenced Measurement in Education*, Allyn & Bacon, Newton, Massachusetts

National Endowment of the Humanities (1984) 'To reclaim a legacy: A report on the Humanities in Higher Education', National Endowment for the Humanities, Washington, DC

Neave, G (1988) 'On the cultivation of quality, efficiency, and enterprise: An overview of recent trends in higher education in Western Europe: 1986–1988', *European Journal of Education*, **21** pp 7–22

Nedelsky, L (1954) 'Absolute grading standards for objective tests', *Educational and Psychological Measurement*, **14**, pp 3–19

Nettles, M, Cole, J J K and Sharp, S (1997) 'Benchmarking assessment: Assessment of teaching and learning in Higher Education for improvement and public accountability: State Governing, Coordinating Board and Regional Accreditation Association Policies and Practices', Ann Arbor, MI: Center for the Study of Higher and Post-secondary Education, University of Michigan, Ann Arbor, MI

Organization for Economic Development (OECD) (1989) 'Performance indicators in Higher Education', *Innovation in Education*, **52**, p 1

Osborne, D, and Gaebler, T (1993) *Reinventing government: How the entrepreneurial spirit is transforming the public sector*, Penguin Books, Plume Books, New York

Ruppert, S (1997) 'Root and realities of state-level performance indicator systems' in *Public Policy and Higher Education*, eds L Goodchild, C Lovell, E Hines and J Gill, Simon & Schuster, Needham Heights

Shepard, L A (1980) 'Standard setting issues and methods', *Applied Psychological Measurement*, **4**, pp 447–65

Sizer, J, Spee, A, and Bormans, R (24 February 1992) 'The role of performance indicators in Higher Education', *Journal of Higher Education*, pp 133–55

Study Group on the Conditions of Excellence in American Higher Education (1984) 'Involvement in learning: Realizing the potential of American Higher Education', National Institute of Education, Washington, DC

Wingspread Group on Higher Education. (1993) 'An American imperative: Higher expectation for Higher Education', An American Foundation, Racine, Wisconsin

16

# Assuring Standards in New Zealand's Universities

*David Woodhouse*

## BACKGROUND

When the UK's Academic Audit Unit (AAU) was established in 1990, one of its terms of reference was 'to consider and review the universities' mechanisms for monitoring and promoting the academic standards which are necessary for achieving their stated aims and objectives' (Williams, 1992). When the HEQC succeeded the AAU, the phrase 'academic standards' became 'academic quality and standards' (HEQC, 1993). When New Zealand's AAU was established in 1993, several of the UK's terms of reference were copied, including the phrase 'quality and standards'. In April 1994, the then UK Secretary of State for Education invited the higher education sector to give greater attention to the comparability of academic standards. This statement resulted in the HEQC's paying explicit attention to standards, and carrying out the Graduate Standards Programme (HEQC, 1997), which led to the QAA's current work on benchmarking threshold standards (QAA, March 1998).

As noted, in conceptualizing New Zealand's AAU, New Zealand's universities had drawn heavily on features of the UK's AAU/HEQC. Therefore, it would not have been surprising if the HEQC's actions on standards had provoked similar attention in New Zealand. In fact, neither New Zealand's universities nor New Zealand's AAU (nor New Zealand's government) found it necessary to follow the HEQC's lead in mounting such a major investigation into standards. This is due to several factors that are relevant to the assurance of standards in New Zealand's university system. These include:

- the origin of most of the existing universities in a single University of New Zealand;
- the fact that no polytechnics have yet become universities;

- the small size of New Zealand's university system;
- continuing cooperation between the universities;
- some particular emphases of New Zealand's AAU;
- national accountability requirements;
- international links.

## QUALITY AND STANDARDS

Before considering the above factors in turn, there are some relevant observations on quality and its relation to standards.

A question commonly heard in heated discussions about quality a few years ago was 'Your quality may be high, but what about your standards?' It is rather obvious that the answer requires a precise definition of both words. The following are the definitions used by New Zealand's AAU.

Quality means meeting or fulfilling requirements, often referred to as fitness for purpose, where the purpose is set out in the objectives of the higher education institution.

The word 'standard' denotes a level or grade, such as an explicit level of academic attainment. In addition to standards in academic disciplines, standards of student support, academic management and so on can be set out. One function of standards therefore is that of being a means of measuring whether or not the higher education institution has achieved its specified objectives – that is, measuring its quality.

However, the concept of quality incorporates the concept of standards if the objectives include explicit specification of levels of attainment. This means that, rather than being clearly and totally distinct, quality and standards can be brought arbitrarily close. It also means that close and detailed attention to quality can result in firm control of standards. New Zealand's university system benefits from this situation.

## THE UNIVERSITY OF NEW ZEALAND

There are at present seven universities in New Zealand. Six were in existence before 1961, when they were part of (or associated with) the unitary University of New Zealand (UNZ), while the seventh, founded in 1961, was briefly associated with the UNZ before the latter split into its component parts. The habits of collaboration established over nearly a century continued to affect the system and are still visible to this day. However, they are increasingly difficult to sustain under the stringent application of the paradigm of the competitive free market by New Zealand's government over the last 14 years.

One instance of the continuing effects of collaboration is in the area of student transfer. Even if the facility were not often used, it was accepted that students should be able to transfer between the colleges of the UNZ. In 1961, therefore, rules existed for this, and they have been augmented over the years. This caused some problems for the University of Waikato (the university founded in 1961) as it wished to develop new and different structures, and felt hindered by this requirement for comparability. None the less, the system persisted and its existence means that, in theory, transfer between New Zealand's universities should be a simple matter (although the rules are now so extensive and complicated that difficulties do occur in practice). However, their existence does exert some slight pressure towards the maintenance of common standards.

## THE BINARY LINE

In the UK (as also in Australia), early in this decade, many institutions that were not formerly universities were suddenly rebranded. Aside from any questions of 'better' or 'worse', the university sectors were quite evidently far more diverse after the rebranding than before it, and so the question of what can be said about 'universities' generically becomes very pertinent here.

In 1990, New Zealand's higher education sector consisted of 7 universities, 25 polytechnics and 6 colleges of education, and only the universities were permitted to offer degrees. This meant that the university sector was not only small but distinctive, and its characteristics were relatively easily identified. Since then, non-degree institutions have been permitted to award degrees (under approval by the NZQA). Some of the larger polytechnics now offer many degree courses, and the diversity of institutions within the polytechnic sector is now extreme. The intention is that all degrees, whatever their origin, have certain core characteristics (that are set out in law), but it is a matter of discussion as to whether or not they do and how this is achieved as the institutions are (intentionally) different in nature and operate under different external quality regimes. Thus, questions are being asked about what can be said generically about 'degrees'.

Some polytechnics are now moving to seek university status. If they are successful, the questions currently being asked about 'degrees' will come to be asked about 'universities'.

## SYSTEM SIZE

As noted, there are only seven universities in New Zealand's education system. This means that corresponding staff from all universities can meet to discuss common issues, and the group is small enough that each can actually interact with all of the others – all vice-chancellors, international officers, heads of geography departments and so on. Although there can now be tensions in such meetings (for example, of the marketing managers or the PR officers), the small number of institutions in the system is conducive to the instances of cooperation described later in this chapter. With such small groups, ideas are shared to the mutual benefit of quality and standards, even when the spectre of competition puts some restraints on explicit attention being given to disseminating good practice. (Such dissemination is actively undertaken by the AAU.)

## CONTINUING COOPERATION

Following the dissection of the UNZ, coordinating structures were set up, such as the Universities Grants Committee (UGC). The UGC, which was responsible for sector planning and advising the government, had a Curriculum Subcommittee. All new university courses had to be approved by the Subcommittee, which covered not only aspects related to academic quality, but also whether or not the new course would be unnecessarily duplicative of other offerings already available at other universities.

In 1990, the UGC was abolished. At that time, the government set up the New Zealand Qualifications Authority (NZQA) and charged it with establishing a consistent approach to the recognition of academic and vocational qualifications in post-compulsory education (New Zealand Government, 1990).

In the same Act, the New Zealand Vice-chancellors' Committee (NZVCC) was constituted as a legal entity with the jurisdiction to approve university degree qualifications and accredit university institutions to offer those qualifications. Functions of the NZVCC include:

- setting up inter-university course approval and moderation procedures;
- exercising in relation to universities the powers of the NZQA to approve courses and accredit institutions to provide them;
- making recommendations to the NZQA on criteria for entrance to universities.

### Committee on University Academic Programmes (CUAP)

Through the NZVCC, the universities agreed to continue the collaboration represented by the UGC's Curriculum Subcommittee, and so proposals for major new courses and qualifications are still subject not only to local consultation and internal approval processes, but also to interinstitutional approval. The latter scrutiny is now carried out by the NZVCC's Committee on University Academic Programmes (CUAP), which comprises one representative from each university and one from each of the polytechnics, colleges of education and the New Zealand University Students Association. (NZVCC, 1997)

Following the application of its own internal procedures to programme design or amendment, a university must submit for CUAP's approval any proposals relating to the introduction of a new academic qualification, programme or course, or to major changes in any existing ones. The proposal must:

- include the purpose of the course, and its relationship to the institution's strategic planning goals;
- indicate content, teaching methods, assessment procedures and resources;
- give evidence of consultation with relevant professional bodies or other groups;
- set out the plans for monitoring the programme's quality;
- outline the intended graduate profile of those who complete the qualification.

The CUAP circulates each proposal to all of the universities for comment before it makes its decision. The inclusiveness of this circulation, as of CUAP's membership, is only possible in a small system and is a major factor in its success.

The NZVCC and the NZQA jointly drew up the following criteria to be applied to any proposal:

- the acceptability of the proposed course to the relevant academic, industrial, professional and other communities, in terms of the stated objectives, nomenclature, content and structure;
- the adequacy and appropriateness of the regulations that specify requirements for admission, recognition of prior learning, credit for previous study, course structure, assessment procedures and the normal progression;
- the availability of appropriate academic staffing, teaching and research facilities, and support services;
- the adequacy of the means of ensuring that assessment procedures are both fair and appropriate in terms of the stated objectives;
- the adequacy of the provisions for monitoring course quality, reviewing course regulations and content, and determining whether or not courses shall continue to be offered.

Each of the five criteria is the subject of attention from the proposing university, from the other universities when the proposal is circulated and from the CUAP itself (although each party may concentrate its attention on different aspects). The whole process is also the subject of attention from the AAU (see below).

In practice, the CUAP's attention to any particular proposal may focus on any part of any one of the criteria, depending on what has been noticed by some member of the CUAP or other person consulted. However, the CUAP's actions most often relate to the academic part of the first of the criteria listed above (by circulation around the universities), while discussions within the CUAP often relate to the second criterion (concerning regulations) and the resources aspect of the third criterion (NZUAAU, 1997a).

In time, the AAU's auditing of the universities' processes relating to programme development, implementation and monitoring should assist with the third, fourth and fifth criteria, leaving the CUAP more free to concentrate on the first and second ones (Hall and Woodhouse, 1999)

As the totality of quality assurance processes applied to each programme include both those at the respective university and the CUAP ones, the AAU audits the CUAP as well as each university (see below). It was as a consequence of a recommendation in the AAU's first audit of the CUAP (NZUAAU, 1997a) that the CUAP has begun to require the specification of the intended graduate profile on successful completion of a qualification. Following another recommendation, the CUAP now also requires a detailed report from each university as the first cohort of students completes a new course. The report must show to what extent the original intent of the course has been achieved, including the projected graduate profile.

## National subject meetings

Within New Zealand's university system, the NZVCC provides some funds to assist the academic staff in each discipline to meet at intervals of three years or more. The primary purpose of these meetings is to discuss academic and administrative issues, such as curricular developments, course structures, teaching approaches, the relationship of research and teaching, examining and assessing, transfer of credits and relations with other educational institutions (NZVCC, 1997). These meetings provide an opportunity to share examples of good practice, compare assessment practices and standards, and refer to international comparisons.

A report must be provided to the CUAP that covers at least:

- development of the subject in New Zealand's universities, referring to other institutions in New Zealand, making international comparisons and major new developments;

- collaboration among the universities and other institutions and the further exchange of good practice;
- library and other resources and special facilities.

Consideration is being given to ways in which the meetings might more specifically address matters of quality assurance.

### External examiners

In the UNZ, moderation of assessments took place across the system to maintain parity, and this tradition has continued. Departments at two universities may have a 'mutual exchange' agreement, where each acts as a corporate external examiner for the other. After a few years, partners are changed.

More formal external examiner appointments take place at the higher levels of courses. New Zealand's bachelor degrees have the same pattern as Australian and Scottish degrees, namely three years to an ordinary degree, with a fourth-year honours course. External examiners, sometimes called external assessors, are appointed for most honours and masters courses, and some universities are beginning to use external examiners at third-year level. The appointment and reporting process varies between universities, and the AAU (see below) has made some recommendations about tightening control of it in several universities. The Victoria University of Wellington has recently begun to collect and analyse examiners' reports for general patterns and problems to permit improvements.

Within each university, some analysis of pass rates and so on takes place, but this analysis is not universally shared. (See also under International benchmarking, Universitas 21, later in this chapter.)

## THE ACADEMIC AUDIT

### Establishment, role and effect

Having set in place the CUAP as a quality mechanism at discipline level, the NZVCC reviewed quality assurance processes in other countries, as well as the plans of the NZQA for the non-university sector in New Zealand, and decided that some institution-level mechanism was also needed. It therefore decided to establish the Academic Audit Unit (AAU), with the following terms of reference (Woodhouse, 1998):

- to consider and review the universities' mechanisms for monitoring and enhancing the academic quality and standards that are necessary for achieving their stated aims and objectives;

- to comment on the extent to which procedures in place in individual universities are applied effectively;
- to comment on the extent to which procedures in place in individual universities reflect good practice in maintaining quality;
- to identify and commend to universities good practice with regard to the maintenance and enhancement of academic standards at national level;
- to assist the university sector to improve its educational quality;
- to advise the NZVCC on quality assurance matters;
- to interact with other national and international agencies and organizations in relation to matters of quality assurance in education;
- to carry out such contract work as is compatible with its audit role.

In fulfilling these terms of reference, the AAU focuses on mechanisms for:

- quality assurance in the design, monitoring and evaluation of courses and programmes of study for degrees and other qualifications;
- quality assurance in teaching, learning and assessment;
- quality assurance in relation to the appointment and performance of academic staff;
- taking account of the views in respect of academic matters of students, external examiners, professional bodies and employers;
- quality assurance in research, especially in the context of its relationship with university teaching.

The AAU is funded jointly by the universities, but is otherwise independent of both the universities individually and the NZVCC itself. It is governed by a Board appointed by the NZVCC but contains very few academic members.

Between them, the five foci are comprehensive, so the AAU is responsible for the whole range of academic and related activities. However, in any cycle of audits, the AAU may concentrate on one or more areas in order to investigate them in more depth. The AAU has developed procedures for investigating the existence and effectiveness of various aspects of each university's quality assurance processes. The procedures stress the need for the university to carry out a self-audit first, and provide the AAU with a report on its quality assurance processes that incorporates the conclusions of this self-audit. The AAU's visiting panels include academics from NZ and overseas, and members of the business community.

The AAU's accountability is to the public, and its audit reports are widely distributed public documents, which ensures that there is pressure on the universities to take very seriously any flaws that are identified in their mechanisms. The audits are thoroughgoing and universities are introducing or enhancing quality assurance processes where the audit (or the prior self-audit) detects gaps or shortcomings.

In 1997, the AAU commissioned an independent review of its operation. The review found that 'the audit process has been effective in bringing about a culture shift in the universities with respect to quality matters. ... The procedures developed by the AAU ... have been a stimulus for reform in the universities' (NZUAAU, 1997b).

## External reviews

Quality assurance agencies generally review the institutions under their aegis at either institutional level or at programme/discipline level. Examples of the former are the US's regional accreditors, the Swedish Hogskoleverket and the UK's former HEQC. Examples of the latter are the Dutch VSNU, the UK's HEFCE and all professional or specialized accreditors, such as the Engineering Council. Some agencies review at both levels, such as the New York State Board of Regents, the UK's QAA and, to some extent, the French CNE. It seems that review at both levels is appropriate: reviewing at only programme level can leave institution-wide systemic problems undiscovered, while reviewing at institution-level only can be non-specific (it is, after all, the academic departments that do the work of the institution). However, when both levels are reviewed by an external agency or agencies, unless the work is well coordinated, it places a heavy burden on the institutions.

In order to obtain the benefit of two-level review, but without this duplicative burden, the AAU expects its universities to carry out regular systematic reviews of their departments and/or programmes. The review procedures and timetable should be clearly set out in each university's procedures manual, and should include mechanisms for appointing, training and supporting review panels, obtaining input to the panel from a wide range of sources, and acting on the panel's report. The review panels should include members from outside the university, and preferably outside New Zealand.

When the AAU audits a university, it audits the university's review procedures, reads review reports and investigates the university's actions on the review recommendations, including the effects of these actions. This covers the institution's reviews of other component parts, such as the library or student services, not merely programmes and departments.

This approach ensures that the dual level of review occurs, and also goes a long way towards ensuring that the programme/department-level process is effective, while leaving as much autonomy as possible with the institution and minimizing the external intervention. As the universities' terms of reference for these reviews usually include standards of research and teaching, currency of the curriculum, acceptability of the graduates and so on, the audited review process is a powerful mechanism for achieving high standards of national and international comparability.

Another form of external review at programme level is that carried out by professional and statutory bodies for the purpose of accreditation. The AAU also investigates the actions of the universities in response to these reports

## ACCOUNTABILITY

### Mission statements and charters

The basic characteristics of each of the four categories of State higher education institutions are spelt out in the Education Amendment Act (New Zealand Government, 1990). For universities, it says:

> universities have all the following characteristics:
>
> - they are primarily concerned with more advanced learning, the principal aim being to develop intellectual independence;
> - their research and teaching are closely interdependent and most of their teaching is done by people who are active in advancing knowledge;
> - they meet international standards of research and teaching;
> - they are a repository of knowledge and expertise;
> - they accept a role as critic and conscience of society;
> - and are characterized by a wide diversity of teaching and research, especially at a higher level, that maintains, advances, disseminates, and assists the application of knowledge, develops intellectual independence, and promotes community learning.

Such a characterization is useful (perhaps essential) in an environment in which evaluation has become a widespread phenomenon as it provides some core parameters against which to evaluate an institution. The AAU audits universities against the characteristics listed here, as well as against each university's more specific objectives.

Every State higher education institution is required to produce a charter, setting out the institution's mission (purpose), values (philosophy) and broad goals. The charter is then submitted to the Ministry of Education for approval by the Minister of Education, although there is no clear-cut specification of the grounds on which approval could be withheld. Relevant considerations that are indicated or implied by the Education Amendment Act include that:

- the charter must contain goals and purposes appropriate for the type of institution (s. 184);
- before submitting a charter for approval, the council of the institution shall consult with staff and students and community groups and individuals (s. 185), so a charter should reflect the views that have been expressed;
- the charter should refer to standards of teaching and learning to be achieved (s. 190);
- codes of conduct to be observed in the management of the institution (s. 190).

Over the last five years or so, the following minimum content for charters has emerged (Woodhouse and Hall, 1997):

- the mission statement and guiding principles;
- the distinctive character of the institution;
- the aims and goals of the institution;
- the constitution of the council of the institution;
- a section on entrepreneurial activities, which establishes safeguards for students and staff to protect those involved in commercial activities from exploitation, and which also explicitly states that government-funded programmes will take priority over other activities, as well as a statement recording that an institution will ensure that the financial or other risks associated with entrepreneurial activities are adequately taken into account;
- an account of the consultation process followed in the development of the charter.

In considering a proposed charter, the Minister must also take account of the institutional autonomy and academic freedom guaranteed in the Act (ss 160, 161). Ultimately, the Minister can, within the confines of the Act, dictate the terms of a charter, but, in practice, will approve it unless satisfied on reasonable grounds that there is reason to withhold approval. Although the extent of vetting of a higher education institution's charter in New Zealand may seem quite low, it is more extensive than in many other places. The charter is to be valid for at least five years.

## Statements of objectives

Every year, each of New Zealand's higher education institutions must develop a triennial statement of operational objectives, the achievement of which would fulfil, or make progress towards fulfilling, the goals set out in the charter (New Zealand Government, 1990, s. 199). The statement of objectives must be approved by the Minister of Education as being adequate for this purpose. It must also specify the set of outputs the higher education institution can deliver. The institution then becomes responsible for delivering those outputs agreed with the Minister of Education. The statement of objectives must also include performance measures or indicators that will allow the achievement of the objectives to be verified. The institutions are not required to set objectives in relation to equal employment opportunities or equal educational opportunities, but are required to report annually on their actions in these matters and, therefore, in practice, usually set out the planned actions in advance as objectives. An analysis of these statements in terms of whether or not the objectives were specific, measurable, achievable, relevant and time-bound was carried out in 1998 (Lamont, 1998).

## Statement of service performance

New Zealand's higher education institutions are required to produce prompt and informative annual reports that include both financial information and a statement of service performance that reports in terms of the performance indicators agreed with the Minister of Education. The Ministry of Education monitors statements of service performance for the purpose of ascertaining whether or not the outputs achieved by institutions match the outputs for which they have been funded in both quantitative and qualitative terms. However, formal approval of the annual reports is the responsibility of the financial auditors who operate under a different arm of government (the Office of the Auditor-general OAG), which may have different interpretations of the reporting requirements pertaining to tertiary education. The AAU is liaising with the OAG and the Ministry of Education to remove overlap and achieve consistency in the external auditing processes.

A longitudinal study of higher education institutions' annual reports has evaluated them by means of an index. The index is based on 26 disclosure items that capture the essence of reporting quality from a public accountability perspective, weighted on a three-point scale according to perceived importance. For each item, criteria define the quality of disclosure on a five-point scale. These calculations, as well as informal inspection, show that, since the State reforms introduced the requirement for greater public accountability, higher education institutions' annual reports have been transformed from terse financial statements to comprehensive, well-presented, informative documents comparable with the best produced in the business sector, and better than those compiled by their counterparts in Australia, Canada, the UK and the USA (Tower, *et al.*, 1995; Coy and Dixon, 1996).

## INTERNATIONAL BENCHMARKING

New Zealand's universities have long been involved in the traditional form of national and international academic 'benchmarking' by virtue of joint research work, peer review of research proposals and journal articles, study leave, external examiners and so on. More recently, they have begun to undertake formal benchmarking activities that are more systematic, involving explicit and planned exchanges of information on various practices, and leading to the adaptation of observed practices for use in the home institution. The University of Otago has an in-house guide to benchmarking (Meade, 1994), and several projects have been completed, with more under way.

### Commonwealth Benchmarking Club on University Management

This Club was set up in 1995 to help its members to compare their core management processes with those of other institutions, identify areas of strength and weakness within their own university and provide a mechanism for capturing best management practices as they develop worldwide. It is based on process, rather than statistical, benchmarking, as this can be more easily carried out across boundaries of geography, sector or size (CHEMS, February 1997). The Victoria University of Wellington was involved in the process in 1997. While it found the activity valuable on this occasion, it has not continued in the Club, preferring to be free to choose benchmarking partners and topics.

### Universitas 21

Universitas 21 is a network of about a dozen broadly based research universities, in Australia, Canada, New Zealand (The University of Auckland), the UK and USA. It was established to facilitate international collaboration and benchmarking (University of Melbourne, July 1997). Initial projects include the development of quality indices for benchmarking, secondment of staff and exchange of students, with possibilities of coordinated curriculum development and management of information systems in the longer term.

An interesting possibility is that such a network may be a more natural constituency for an external quality assurance agency, rather than such agencies' scope being defined geographically (the Global Alliance for Transnational Education (GATE, 1997) is already moving in this direction).

Other international networks are being established with which NZ's universities are forming links, such as the group of 'innovative universities'.

### Course experience questionnaire

The course experience questionnaire (CEQ) was developed in Australia and is now distributed annually to tens of thousands of graduates there to ascertain their experience of their university courses, particularly in the light of their post-university experience (Johnson, *et al.*, 1996). In New Zealand, the University of Otago has used the CEQ for several years (along with other systematic surveys, such as those of employers), and five other universities are just gearing up to do so too. The results will be shared across the university sector (and perhaps with any polytechnics that use the CEQ). Because of the way the results differ between disciplines, it is useful for a small sector to be able to compare its results with a larger similar one (in this case Australia). Other similar surveys are being developed and used, permitting measurement and comparison of outcomes in relation to existing students, alumni of research degrees and so on.

### External examiners

New Zealand's twin difficulties with external examiners are that it is too small a system for national external examiners to be adequately 'distant' from the programme they are examining, but its geographical distance from international external examiners means high costs and/or significant time factors are incurred if they are employed. International examiners are, of course, used for doctorates and often for other degrees too.

A current proposal is that greater coordination (perhaps via the national subject meetings described earlier), could establish an interinstitutional 'external examiner team' for the subject, comprising local staff with one overseas examiner. In this way, the cost of the overseas examiner could be shared across the system.

The AAU reviews the procedures for appointing external examiners and handling their reports when it audits the universities. It also reads a selection of reports. In this way, it forms an opinion on the rigour of the system, and commends or recommends accordingly (see also earlier, the text on external examiners).

## CONCLUSION

In summary, New Zealand's universities have a network of measures in place to assure standards within each university (with the external support of the AAU), across universities (with the external support of the Committee on University Academic Programmes), and internationally (by using benchmarking, international surveys and so on).

## REFERENCES

Commonwealth Higher Education Management Service (February 1997), Commonwealth University Management Benchmarking Club for 1997: Members' Handbook, CHEMS, London

Coy, D, and Dixon, K (November 1996) 'Annual reporting continues improvement', *Chartered Accountants Journal*, pp 38–9

Global Alliance for Transnational Education (1997), *Certification Manual*, GATE, Washington

Hall, C, and Woodhouse, D (1999), 'Accreditation and approval in New Zealand: Major surgery for the National Qualifications Framework?' in *Programme Assessment and Accreditation in the South African Higher Education System: National and international perspectives*, eds A H Strydom, L Lategan, L Muller and J Stetar, Bloemfontein, (to appear)

HEQC (1993), *Auditors' Manual*, HEQC, London

HEQC (1997), 'Graduate Standards Programme Final report Volume 1: The Report', HEQC, London

Johnson, T, *et al.* (1996) 'The 1995 Course Experience Questionnaire', Graduate Careers Council of Australia, Melbourne

Lamont, G (1998), 'Summary Report on Analysis of Statements of Objectives 1998–2000', Ministry of Education, Wellington

Meade, P (1994), 'A Guide to Benchmarking', Griffith University, Brisbane

New Zealand Government (1990), 'Education Amendment Act', Wellington

NZUAAU (1997a), 'Committee on University Academic Programmes: Audit report', NZUAAU, Wellington

NZUAAU (1997b), 'Report of a Review of New Zealand Universities Academic Audit Unit', NZUAAU, Wellington

NZVCC (1997), 'Committee on University Academic Programmes: Functions and procedures 1998', NZVCC, Wellington

QAA (March 1998), 'Developing benchmark information on subject threshold standards', *Higher Quality*, **1** (3), QAA, Gloucester

Tower, G, Coy, D and Dixon, K (1995) 'The Annual Reports of New Zealand's Tertiary Institutions 1985–1994: A review', Accountancy Department Discussion Paper Series, No. 160, Massey University, Palnerston North

University of Melbourne (July 1997), 'Universitas 21', *University of Melbourne Gazette*

Williams, P (1992) 'The UK Academic Audit Unit', in *Quality Assurance in Higher Education*, ed. A Z Craft, The Falmer Press, London

Woodhouse, D (1997) 'Qualifications and quality in New Zealand', in *Standards and Quality in Higher Education*, eds J Brennan, P de Vries and R Williams, Higher Education Policy Series 37, pp 61–77, Jessica Kingsley, London

Woodhouse, D, and Hall, C (1997) 'Evaluation issues in Higher Education in New Zealand' in *Enhancing Institutional Self-evaluation and Quality in South African Higher Education: National and international perspectives*, eds A H Strydom, L Lategan and A Muller, pp 376–411, Bloemfontein, South Africa

Woodhouse, D (1998), *Audit Manual: Handbook for institutions and members of audit panels*, 3rd edn, NZUAAU, Wellington

17

# Benchmarks and Threshold Standards – A New Zealand Polytechnic's Perspective on the Approach

*Nick Zepke, Guyon Neutze, Linda Leach*

Benchmarks and threshold standards affect every part of our lives. New parents assume their children will walk, talk and balk at certain stages and worry if they don't. In schools, teachers ensure that standards, sometimes unstated, are met in such things as clothing, equipment and behaviour. What children learn and what they are to achieve are also benchmarked by society at large, by institutions, by parents and even by students. In further and higher education in New Zealand as elsewhere (see descriptions in other chapters in Part IV) a mixture of stated and unstated benchmarks and threshold standards have always applied.

In this chapter we first describe a wide variety of developments in benchmarking and setting threshold standards in New Zealand's educational setting outside the university sector. Second, we offer a critique of national benchmarking and threshold standards.

## BENCHMARKING IN NEW ZEALAND

To date, benchmarking is a term used infrequently in New Zealand's education sector. We began this project with a variety of possible definitions in mind. These definitions were fed by a survey we conducted with academic leaders and policymakers in further and higher education (Zepke, 1998b). They confirmed the existence of a range of concepts relating to benchmarking. Examples include:

> The setting of standards by a select group that purport to be those that everyone else should strive to achieve.

A national standard against which students are measured.

Comparing one's performance against that of a selected market leader.

Comparing outcomes with other similar organizations.

An assumption that it is possible to develop national comparisons of achievement.

These concepts uncovered two key themes:

- benchmarking to compare organizations, qualifications and people;
- benchmarking to measure according to pre-set standards.

These two versions accompanied us as we explored New Zealand's educational landscape. Both feature in a general movement towards more explicit, national and institutional standards.

## An historical perspective

Benchmarking processes and threshold standards existed in New Zealand's training and education before the railways. National examinations, such as matriculation, trade certificates and drivers' licence tests, set threshold standards for entry to higher education, employment and adult life. School Certificate exams were scaled. English was used as the benchmark subject in a quest for intersubject relativities. University degrees were used both to benchmark achievement and to serve as thresholds for entry into certain professions. Other national benchmarks included grades for primary and secondary school teachers and national school certificates for 15-year-olds.

The word 'benchmark' originated in industries such as construction and surveying where it referred to the establishment of levels on a vertical plane. It existed in trade education at least as early as the 1960s (Ashby, 1998). Respondents to our survey reported encountering the term in further and higher education in the late 1980s. By the early 1990s the New Zealand Qualifications Authority (NZQA) – a government agency charged with developing a uniform National Qualifications Framework – was using it in publications on moderation of assessments. (NZQA, 1992).

Yet the word 'benchmarking' was never widely used in education and training. Even the NZQA, though engaged in defining levels on a vertical plane in the form of the National Qualifications Framework (NQF), which is pre-eminent in post-compulsory education in New Zealand outside the university sector, and developing unit standards for the Framework, did not use the term to describe those developments. A government report on assessment policy, 'Assessment for Better Learning' (Department of Education, 1989) made wide use of benchmarking concepts but little use of the term itself. By the mid 1990s, the word was still rarely used. Beneath the surface, however, benchmarking was active.

## The current situation

Whether labelled or not, benchmarking issues inspire hot debate. Two voices currently vie for educational dominance in New Zealand. Both advocate national standards, but from different perspectives. Each voice represents a variety of interest groups, forming a loose coalition around this issue. The first coalition includes industry, Maori and emerging health professionals, who traditionally have had little influence on education and training issues (Zepke, 1998a). This voice calls for the abolition of national examinations and norm-referenced assessment. It advocates the establishment of standards, based on nationally defined levels of knowledge, skills and attitudes and protected by a complicated system of moderation. The other interest group comprises traditional holders of power, such as universities, prestigious secondary schools and influential business leaders. All want to reward excellence; schools and business leaders also want to retain national examinations and publish nationwide league tables of schools (*The Dominion*, 27 October 1998).

What is emerging from these debates is an educational landscape occupied by two opposing loose coalitions. The first, formed around benchmarks in the NQF, is absent in the primary school sector. The second, which espouses excellence by means of national assessment, is gaining a foothold. In the secondary school sector, the first coalition is strongly entrenched in vocational areas; the second is gaining ground in traditional academic schools. The further and higher education sector comprises a number of fluid realms. There are 7 universities, 25 polytechnics, 4 remaining colleges of education, and literally hundreds of Private Training Enterprises (PTEs). The larger urban polytechnics and most of the colleges of education are seeking university status and offer mainly degree programmes; smaller regional polytechnics and PTEs concentrate on skills-based training for traditional blue- and white-collar occupations. The first coalition dominates in the regional polytechnic and PTE realm; the second has a significant foothold in the university and degree-awarding polytechnics.

Both the emergent and the traditional coalitions are driven by the wish to produce people for the marketplace. This notion is endorsed by the objectives of politicians. The then Minister of Education Lockwood Smith (1991) observed that the world is a competitive place and 'we do our young people a grave disservice if we shield them from that reality and the curriculum ignores it'. In 1992 he said, 'We need to build a qualifications system that is practical, and relevant to the needs of industry' (Smith, 1992). These political pronouncements serve the interests of both coalitions. The NQF of the first coalition serves the needs of industry by preparing competent workers for the marketplace. The benchmarking efforts of the second prestigious coalition attempt to graduate people to leadership in the marketplace. Both coalitions see national benchmarks as essential.

The NQF is the instrument of benchmarking for the first coalition. It is constructed in 8 vertical levels, each with 16 criteria. For example, each level describes the degree of psycho-motor skills. At level 1, 'basic practical skills only are learned'; at level 2, 'practical skills are well-developed'; at level 5, 'advanced technical skills' are included. Interestingly, levels 6 to 8 do not include descriptors for psychomotor skills. Cognitive skills at level 1 are described as 'limited and basic knowledge'; level 2, 'basic theoretical knowledge and understanding of process'; level 5, 'advanced technical, theoretical and applied knowledge and understanding'; levels 7 and 8, 'high degree of theoretical and applied knowledge, with additional specialist body of knowledge' (NZQA, 1993).

These levels define achievement benchmarks and entry thresholds for different qualifications. For example, at level 2, learning leads 'to further education and training at higher levels and to certificated qualifications for semi-skilled occupations'. At level 4, learning, in addition to further education and training, leads to 'certificated qualifications for skilled crafts and trades'. Level 5 is designated for 'craft or technical occupations', level 6 for 'senior technical, para-professional and technological occupations', level 7 is the first degree benchmark and level 8 is the benchmark for postgraduate qualifications for 'higher academic, professional and managerial occupations' (NZQA, 1993).

National qualifications are benchmarked to these levels: certificates to levels 4 and 5; diplomas to level 5 and 6; first degrees to level 7; and postgraduate degrees to level 8. There are, at present, no national degrees, all such qualifications being owned by providers such as universities and polytechnics. Polytechnic degrees are appraised against these levels. Although not all qualifications are tied to the NQF, even provider-designed qualifications are often written to the NZQA's levels. Our own institution, for example, teaches a number of non-Framework programmes that are, nevertheless, described in terms of the NZQA's levels.

The NQF is largely made up of what are termed 'unit standards'. These curriculum-descriptive documents include purpose statements, elements (learning outcomes), performance criteria and a number of contextual notes such as range notes, entry information, moderation options and special instructions. As an example, a level 4 unit standard in core health is 'apply knowledge of individuals, groups and communities in a health and wellness context'. One element reads: 'describe normal human behaviour'. A performance criterion reads 'assumptions about normal human behaviour are described from a variety of perspectives'. The range is 'cultural, spiritual, mainstream and complementary health sciences' (NZQA, 1998). Unit standards are pegged to NQF levels and benchmark learning rather than qualifications.

NQF unit standards are combined by institutions to create subjects. These, as components of qualifications, are also benchmarked to NQF levels. For example, the unit standards 'describe normal human structure and function in individuals of all ages' (level 3) and 'describe abnormal structure and function in individuals of all ages' (level 3) have often been combined in subjects labelled 'Introduction to Physiology'. This subject becomes a level 3 subject and is benchmarked with all other level 3 subjects. Another dimension of the NQF's benchmarking is the use of credits to describe the amount of learning achieved in a unit standard/subject. 'Introduction to Physiology' has 10 credits – a benchmark to alert people to the size of the subject. Degree-level learning in the NQF is treated similarly and even university degrees, not currently in the NQF, benchmark subjects using levels and credits:

> Level and credit are important mechanisms for achieving this consistency. ... The NQF ... offers a set of conventions for level and credit to which providers' systems can be related, thereby making qualifications easier to compare.
>
> (Ministry of Education, 1997b)

Other functions of the NZQA are to accredit institutions to teach NZQA-controlled qualifications and to approve provider-proposed degrees. Approval and accreditation processes are based on criterion statements that serve as benchmarks for institutions. There are, among others, standards statements about educational objectives, the financial capacity of the institution, the qualifications of the staff, quality systems, consultation, assessment, moderation, student support, and delivery processes. Applicants are evaluated against these benchmarks and advised how to reach the standard if they do not in the first instance.

National benchmarking across providers is ensured by a complicated system of national and regional moderation. The NZQA describes 12 moderation methods from which Industry Training Organizations (ITOs) select preferred options and develop moderation action plans for providers within their own domain (NZQA, 1992). This system operates across all sectors offering unit standards from the NQF, and it is industry that dominates. A moderation meeting may include representatives from secondary schools, private training providers, polytechnics and universities. The NZQA (1992, 1996) suggests that exemplars may be used as benchmarks in moderation processes: samples of:

> candidates' work that have been assessed can be used as benchmarks. They can be used to illustrate, in a range of settings, the level of performance that is required for meeting standards.
>
> (NZQA, 1992)

Independently of the NZQA's influence, a number of institutions are using 'competitive benchmarking' to monitor their achievements against those of other institutions (Illinios State University, 1998a). One medium-sized polytechnic, for example, has elected to compare its performance against that of two similar institutions. They compare annual report data, especially key ratios, such as student–teacher ratios (Zepke, 1998). Most providers use a form of 'internal benchmarking' (Illinios State University, 1998). Internal practices are analysed regularly in a self- and peer review process to ensure that the quality of programmes meets internal institutional standards.

Another, more traditional coalition also supports national standards, but in a different form. National testing in the school system is one manifestation of this. One recent Green Paper (Ministry of Education, 1998) advocated the reintroduction of reading, writing and maths tests 'at the key transition points of Standard 4/Form 1 and Form 2/Form 3', years 6 and 8 of school life, which starts at the age of 5. Currently, the national Education Review Office (ERO), a kind of national school inspectorate, is advocating external tests in years 2, 3 and 4. The earlier testing is justified in the following way:

> The risk is if you leave [it] too late ... the opportunity for remedial recovery begins to slip away. National assessment will provide nationally consistent standards against which teachers will be able to compare their own judgements. ... It will also provide information about individual pupils, giving parents an independent source of information.
>
> (*The Dominion*, 14 October 1998)

In the secondary sector, traditional national examinations such as the School Certificate (in year 10) and Bursary (in year 12), long under attack, have survived as norm-referenced benchmarks of success, because of support from the second coalition:

> qualifications in the senior secondary school should take into account that consistency across schools is best achieved through assessment on common tasks independently marked. This would suggest there is an important place for appropriate external assessment.
>
> (Smithers, 1997)

School rankings, based on external assessment results, have been published in newspapers. This has effectively used these qualifications to benchmark the success of schools too.

In the further and higher education sector, the second view of national benchmarking is not dominant. However, in the writings of various academics, (Elley, 17 November 1994; Hall, 1994, 1995) universities have aligned themselves with some of the second coalition's goals. While they have not advocated national examinations to replace NFQ development, they have strongly and consistently attacked benchmarks based on national competency standards. One focus of attacks has been a perceived absence of excellence in the concept of competence. Hall (1994), in summarizing the opinions of academics in a Victoria University survey, raises excellence as an alternative benchmark to competence. Excellence goes beyond competence in that it denotes outstanding achievement. Lecturers were asked to place competent performance on a four-point scale – 1 for excellent, 2 for very good, 3 for good and 4 for satisfactory:

> Approximately 73 per cent of the respondents identified 3 and/or 4 as their conception of competence ... 42 per cent identified performance well beyond the expected level of the class as an element of excellent work.
>
> (Hall, 1995)

This benchmark of excellence mirrors that of the second coalition. These contrasting views of benchmarking have sown the seeds of the future.

## Future developments

Crystal ball-gazing is notoriously imprecise. The future is invisible, especially in rapidly changing political, social and economic conditions. Our main premise is that benchmarking is here to stay. This part of the chapter addresses the question, 'Which of the competing forms will prevail in the further and higher education sector?'

Indications in two of New Zealand's Green Papers, published in 1997, suggest that the sector is to be gathered under one umbrella:

> The Government could establish a minimum quality requirement (a 'threshold') which is consistent for all tertiary qualifications, programmes and providers by using for example the National Qualifications Framework. ... Government subsidies could then depend on the qualifications, programmes and providers meeting the quality threshold.
>
> (Ministry of Education, 1997a)

The quality threshold is expected to ensure that qualifications are credible, portable, durable and educationally sound; that programmes are well-designed, delivered and assessed; and that educational institutions are accountable for the quality of their programmes. The Green Paper selects an 'external validation with light Government control' approach to achieve the quality threshold. This approach is given substance in the White Paper, which creates a three-tier benchmarking process. In the first tier will be the Quality Assurance Authority of New Zealand (QAANZ). It will be charged with assuring the quality systems of all publicly funded further and higher education. This means that universities, polytechnics and private providers will dance to the same quality tune. The QAANZ will not approve qualifications or accredit providers itself. Instead it will have the sole authority to grant recognition to the second tier of bodies to provide credible and rigorous validation processes within the tertiary sector. The second-tier validation agencies will be the present quality assurers, such as the NZQA (to be renamed the Quality Validation Services – QVS), the New Zealand Polytechnics Programme Committee (NZPPC) and the Committee on University Academic Programmes (CUAP), and any other agencies that may be recognized by the QAANZ. These agencies will approve, accredit, monitor and audit the internal quality assurance systems of the third tier, the providers within their sector, ensuring that the quality of their programmes exceeds the threshold. Decisions on whether or not a required standard is met will be based on professional judgements by such bodies. The system will be designed to 'ensure that standards, processes and decisions are fully transparent and publicly accessible' (Tertiary Education Review, 1998).

Given the political objective of preparing people for the global marketplace, it is not surprising to see this attempt to bring the benchmarks of the two coalitions together. Such attempts are likely to continue into the future. While both coalitions will accede to these attempts, they will try to strengthen their positions within the White Paper's proposed framework. The first will try to extend its domain into the higher education sector, the second will try to preserve its autonomy. The tension between the two opens up a number of potential futures for benchmarking.

In one future, benchmarking is the preserve of validation agencies such as the NZPPC, QVS and CUAP. While all qualifications articulate with the NQF, and benchmark statements are similar to one another, the QAANZ's audit function is enabling rather than directive, and validation agencies become independent and powerful. They develop and maintain their own interpretations of the benchmarks. In the university sector, for example, the CUAP uses its recently bestowed audit function to interpret benchmarks according to values traditionally held by universities, including notions about excellence, norm-referencing, autonomy and international standards. The NZPPC interprets the same benchmarks according to its values of competency, standards-based assessment and practical emphasis in learning. Industry Training Organizations (ITOs) establish their own validation agency and benchmark according to values such as application to the workplace, immediacy of use, fitness for purpose and efficiency. Maori Private Training Enterprises (MPTEs) also establish their own validation agency and benchmark using principles of Maori sovereignty, empowerment and cultural autonomy.

In a second future, the QAANZ is dominant and uses its audit of second-tier agencies to force a unified interpretation of, and compliance with, a remodelled and extended NQF. This is achieved by a range of government actions. Funding is pegged to the achievement of educational and financial benchmarks as signalled in the White Paper. Periodic public reports are published on failings to comply with quality standards in the sector. There is ever-increasing political demand for accountability in public spending. So, while the CUAP, NZPPC, QVS, ITOs and MPTE labour away with the third-tier institutions in their own sectors, standards are increasingly imposed centrally. However, given the political landscape in New Zealand, some variations are accommodated. For example, national standards of competence and a scale of nationally recognized excellence co-exist; a form of norm-referencing is retained; industry has an integral part in the auditing process; and the different practices of the Maori are acknowledged. However, in practice they are subsumed under universally imposed conditions, such as financial criteria, prescribed language, validation processes and quantitative systems of evaluation. This lip-service to difference encourages the coalitions to resist centralization, and government is frequently called on to act as referee in disputes. Its decisions consistently favour centralization of national benchmarking.

Our view is that the second future is unrealistic. Although the Education Review Office (ERO) has assumed a hegemonic position in the primary and secondary sectors, historical factors suggest that the ERO model is unlikely to prevail in the further and higher education sectors. The White Paper foreshadows a QAANZ that, unlike the ERO, will not have direct control of providers. It also permits the third tier to negotiate its own validation processes with international agencies. True, the university sector has been brought in to the national quality system, but its ability to use international validation processes allows it to circumvent the controlling functions of the QAANZ. While many Maori have been strong supporters of the NQF, their support is vanishing, and the current state of race relations in New Zealand suggests greater autonomy for the Maori rather than less. Political élites, such as coalitions of business leaders and traditional educators, while supporting national benchmarking by national examination, remain opposed to a controlling authority in the further and higher education sector. In fact, the political will to support a strong auditing agency seems weak and a variant of the first future is the most likely direction of the dance. This could take the form of strong control by increasingly independent second-tier validation agencies.

## UNPACKING BENCHMARKING

So far we have shown that benchmarks, in various guises, play a huge part in further and higher education. While we do not dismiss benchmarking, for example in social policy, we see grave risks in simply accepting it uncritically. Here, we question benchmarking – in terms of the current political context its philosophical foundations, the consequences of implementation and, finally, in its educational outcomes.

For 15 years now, New Zealand has been flushed with market fever. The individual purchaser in the educational marketplace, not government, is supposed to decide on key issues. Consequently, government has exited many areas it previously dominated, including education. The marketplace, however, has no respect for philosophies and works in unpredictable ways. People and organizations compete for dominance. Some win, some lose and some do not compete at all. The resulting chaos is a threat to the whole market vision. Government, an apostle of market theory, intervenes to support its vision. In this process, it has vigorously supported the most powerful economic groups and, in their interests, has moved to control and shape the autonomy of individuals and organizations. On the one hand, it enshrines their autonomy; on the other, it attempts to control it by imposing accountability measures. Benchmarking is part of the process. It is used as a political tool, both to create a leadership élite, and to train a competent, but docile and compliant workforce. This is embodied in the two coalitions – one in pursuit of excellence in the universities and traditional, prestigious secondary schools, and the other in the skills-based training of unit standards.

So, benchmarks are strongly associated with market-led education. They are the instruments by which rigidities are established and maintained by the two New Zealand educational coalitions. They lead to the creation of élites and compliant workers. We question marketplace fever and its intense focus on benchmarking people for the employment marketplace. We suggest other purposes of further and higher education – personal development, exploration, discovery and creativity; preparation for life in the wider human community; critique of the status quo; and initiation of change. An education process that espouses these aims will view it neither as a commodity, nor as a political tool, but as a right. In this alternative social and political vision, benchmarking is redundant.

The philosophical intent of benchmarking is the pursuit of certainty; incorporating the assumption that educational quality can be defined and measured objectively and reliably. For example, the NZQA and NZPPC approve, accredit, and evaluate programmes and institutions using the same benchmarking standards. Differing interpretations of these by separate panels have led to discrepancies in decisions. One of the respondents in our survey commented on the different interpretations of industry benchmarks:

'I'm aware of NZQA moderators who can't agree on standards for their industry'. The benchmark 'excellence' is particularly susceptible to criticism, as it seems to be undefinable. Hall (1995) admits that 'excellence is far easier to recognize after the event than to define it in advance'. League tables used to benchmark institutions, similarly, fall far short of certainty. Learner success in examinations is influenced by many uncontrolled variables. Among these we count socio-economic status, gender, ethnicity, undiscovered learning disabilities and culture.

Philosophically, the pursuit of certainty is based on the assumptions, first, that a world exists that can be described in terms of universally true statements and, second, that benchmarking enables judgements that are accurate and unaffected by personal values, feelings and perceptions. We question both assumptions. A number of writers have argued that knowledge is constructed by social groups (Young, 1971; Apple, 1990). For example, religions receive their own truths about the world; oral traditions, like those of New Zealand's Maori, construct unique worlds; feminist knowledge provides new constructs of society; capitalist and socialist philosophies provide entirely different constructs of the human condition; transcendental thinking acknowledges realities in which all forms of knowledge are transient and restrictive. Benchmarked education not only ignores this diversity, but affirms an objective knowledge tacitly agreed to in New Zealand by two dominant coalitions.

Even within the objective tradition, writers argue that there are different forms of knowledge. Habermas (1971) visualizes three kinds of human interest that generate different kinds of knowledge. There is 'technical knowledge', which services the world of work, 'practical knowledge', which informs communication, and 'emancipatory knowledge', which leads to empowerment. Neither practical knowledge nor emancipatory knowledge can be said to establish objective truth as both rely on personal experiences to construct meaning. Doubt has even been cast over the objectivity of technical knowledge. To writers such as Capra (1982), the objective world is itself a construct of the observer. In that case, its technical skills are disciplines defined by those constructs.

Given all this, it is difficult to assert that benchmarking is able to establish objective standards. Moreover, even when set, benchmarks will be interpreted subjectively as they are seen through changing filters such as values, beliefs, personal attraction or aversion, health or mood. We therefore question whether benchmarking can be objective in this sense.

We also question that benchmarking can be reliable. Reliability refers to the ability of people to use benchmarks consistently on different occasions, and for different people to make similar judgements against the same benchmark. Two examples of classroom-based assessments illustrate our concern about reliability in benchmarking. In the first, 15 markers assessed 15 scripts on a simple scale of fail, pass or credit. There was wide variation in the grades awarded, with more than half of the scripts being given all three possible grades. In no case did all the markers agree (Rowntree, 1987). In the second, of 300 essays marked by 53 assessors, 34 per cent received all 9 of the possible grades and no essay was given fewer than 5 different grades out of the 9 (Cowie, 1977). In our view, the kind of certainty claimed for benchmarking is dubious.

Our third critique of benchmarking concerns a consequence of it – the elimination of diversity and the enforcement of conformity to suit the purposes of dominant interests. The establishment of national benchmarks is designed to ensure conformity. This leads to a narrowing of educational focus, which confines learning to that which is quantifiable or prepares people for the marketplace. Subject matter is much more susceptible to national control and, most importantly, learning is confined to what is being tested. As a result, diversity is stifled in subject matter, learning, teaching, what learners aspire to, and how they express themselves.

Both the setting of national benchmarks, and their specific focus, are determined by the two dominant educational coalitions – first, industry and groups such as private training providers, Maori and healthworkers from non-traditional professions and, second, traditional holders of power, such as universities, prestigious secondary schools, and influential business leaders. For all their differences, they pursue a common goal. Both see the enterprise culture as a means to success in the global economy. These coalitions have assumed an hegemonic position in the debate about standards in New Zealand's education. According to Gramsci (1971), hegemony occurs when an already dominant social group establishes the authority of its ideas and processes with other groups and thereby gains their popular acceptance, even support. This is achieved by a predictable process (Lauder and Hughes 1990). First, existing practices are attacked, second, learned reports present the views of the hegemony as common sense, third, where necessary, a regulatory framework in established and, finally, the very language we use is shaped to support the hegemonic view. In this case, 'competition', 'national standards', 'quality', 'excellence', 'accountability', 'achievement' and 'competency' have been recruited to support the benchmarking culture, and in that form have re-entered everyday language. Groups opposing benchmarking, and supporting difference in education, are increasingly marginalized.

Our fourth critique is closely related to the third. Benchmarking seems to limit educational outcomes. It focuses learning on narrow, predetermined paths. For example, the skills development benchmarks of the NQF, demonstrate a reductionist approach that almost entirely ignores learning in the affective domain. Indeed one of us, acting as a writer of unit standards, was told to remove elements in the core health unit that dealt with values. The reductionist approach also confines learning to a set of rigidly defined competences. Unit standards in automotive studies, for example, focus on hundreds of very narrowly defined activities. Learning outcomes of unit standards are also unresponsive to change. In a unit on broadcasting, a standard for studio practice had been made obsolete by new technology even before it was published. Finally, the process of developing core health unit standards exemplifies the narrow political nature of benchmarking. Learning outcomes were decided according to the wishes of emerging health professionals, such as acupuncturists and massage therapists, because the established medical professions withdrew from the process.

Neither do the educational objectives of the second coalition escape criticism of narrowness. Excellence, in the main, also ignores the affective domain and seems focused largely on empirical evidence, deductive logic and well-established academic convention. In health education, for example, emerging professionals struggle for acceptance because they don't meet standards of excellence defined by narrowly conceived empirical and logical criteria. The establishment of particular constructs and conventions as benchmarks of excellence can lead to ridiculous situations. For example, essays on James Joyce's *Finnegan's Wake* on a literature course were assessed on criteria for logical structure and correct grammar! Accordingly, one intuitive and colourful essay, written in the spirit of Joyce's work, was failed. Undue emphasis on other 'basics' can also restrict learning. Without wishing to deny that competence in reading and mathematics are basic to learning, exclusive focus on such 'basics' is to the detriment of wider learning. It is the benchmarking test, not the learning, that then becomes the focus of attention.

## Rewrapping benchmarking

In this chapter, we have identified thriving benchmarking cultures in New Zealand's further and higher education sector. Like oil and water, these cultures have not mixed. They continue to struggle for dominance. The climate in New Zealand is favourable to the expansion of benchmarking, but we raise here some major questions about this state of affairs. We recognize that benchmarking is required in a humanitarian society and in successful enterprise. It can, however, also be an instrument for isolating and oppressing non-achievers and non-conformists. Its standards of performance in education can create obstacles to learning and divide society into those who lead and those who follow. On present evidence, it is the isolating, oppressing, obstructing and divisive version of benchmarking that is likely to prevail.

## REFERENCES

Apple, M (1990) *Ideology and the Curriculum*, Routledge, New York
Capra, F (1982) *The Turning Point: Science, society and the rising culture*, Flamingo, London

Cowie, C (1977) 'Using the Essay as an Assessment Technique', *S.E.T.,* **77** (1), New Zealand Council for Educational Research, Wellington

Department of Education. (1989) 'Assessment for Better Learning', Department of Education, Wellington

Elley, W (17 November 1994). 'Fundamental flaw at the heart of the new qualification plan', *The Press,* Christchurch

Gramsci, A (1971) *Selections from the Prison Notebooks*, Lawrence & Wishart, London

Habermas, J (1971) *Knowledge and Human Interests*, Beacon, Boston

Hall, C (1994) 'Obstacles to the Integration of University Qualifications and Courses into the National Qualifications Framework', Higher Education in New Zealand Occasional Paper No. 1, Syndicate of Educational Development Centres of New Zealand Universities, Wellington

Hall, C (1995) 'Why universities do not want unit standards', New Zealand Vice-chancellors' Newsletter, (35)

Lauder, H, and Hughes, D **25** (1), (1990) 'Social inequities and differences in school outcomes', *New Zealand Journal of Educational Studies,* **25** (1), pp 37–60

Ministry of Education (1997a) 'A Future Tertiary Education Policy for New Zealand', Tertiary Education Review, Ministry of Education, Wellington

Ministry of Education (1997b) 'A Future Qualifications Policy for New Zealand: A Plan for the National Qualifications Framework', Ministry of Education, Wellington

Ministry of Education (1998) 'Assessment for Success in Primary Schools', Ministry of Education, Wellington

NZQA (1992) 'Designing a Moderation System', NZQA, Wellington

NZQA (1993) 'Quality Assurance in Education and Training', NZQA, Wellington

NZQA (1996) 'Learning and Assessment', NZQA, Wellington

NZQA (1998) 'Unit Standards 6418 and 6413: The Framework Explorer', Public Catalogue Folio Infobase Disk, NZQA, Wellington

Rowntree, D (1987) *Assessing Students: How shall we know them?*, rev edn, Kogan Page, London

Smith, L (1991) Education policy: Investing in people, our greatest asset, Ministry of Education, Wellington

Smith, L (1992) welcome address at 'Qualifications for the 21st Century' international conference in 'Qualifications for the 21st Century Conference Papers', NZQA, Wellington

Smithers, A (1997) *The New Zealand Qualifications Framework*, The Education Forum, Auckland

Ministry of Education (1998) 'Tertiary Education in New Zealand: Policy directions for the 21st century', White Paper, Ministry of Education, Wellington

*The Dominion* (14 October 1998) Wellington Newspapers, Wellington

*The Dominion* (27 October 1998) Wellington Newspapers, Wellington

Young, M (ed) (1971) *Knowledge and Control*, Collier Macmillan, London

Zepke, N (1998a). 'The New Zealand Qualifications Framework and the politics of official knowledge', in *Research Making*, M Knight, WP Press, Wellington

Zepke, N (1998b) 'Benchmarking in New Zealand post school education: A survey of academic leaders', unpublished paper

18

# Approaches to Degree Standards and Quality Assurance in Post-apartheid South African Higher Education – Comparative Perspectives

*Digby Warren*

The educational mission of the longest-established university in South Africa is encapsulated in these words:

> We are determined to ensure that each degree programme ... produces the kind of graduates our continent requires to build stable democracies and growing economies in a rapidly changing, globally competitive environment.
>
> (Dr Mamphela Ramphele, Vice-chancellor of the University of Cape Town, April1998)

The statement is indicative of goals espoused by many other local institutions of higher education too. It evokes major transformative processes impinging on higher education in South Africa – the quest for more streamlined curricula that are more responsive to societal needs for informed citizens and capable graduates, allied to responses to pressures for greater public accountability and concern for quality and standards in education. Such developments are in line with international trends in higher education, typically 'an expanding system of higher education, offering enabling courses to a wider range of students ... [and] accountable both for the efficiency and quality of its activities' (Ball, 1989).

A key objective within this educational mission is to provide students with 'a foundation of skills, knowledge and versatility that will last a lifetime' (University of Cape Town's Mission Statement, UCT, 13 March 1996). It reflects the shift to a new paradigm of higher education, expressed in notions such as developing student 'capability' (Stephenson and Weil, 1992) or 'applied competence' – the term favoured by policymakers in South Africa (RSA, 1997; 28 March 1998). Underlying this paradigm, Barnett (1992) suggests, is the principle of 'operationalism' – the idea that education should enable students to apply their knowledge and abilities in varied and changing life circumstances. These new approaches to academic teaching epitomize attempts to engage with the challenges facing higher education in both the national and global context.

## TRANSFORMATION OF HIGHER EDUCATION IN SOUTH AFRICA

With the birth of a democratic South Africa in 1994, higher education, along with education in general, has been radically reviewed. Transformation has focused on three broad, interconnected areas:

- redressing past inequities;
- redefining the role of education;
- restructuring the system to make it more integrated, efficient and effective.

Under apartheid, a segregated and authoritarian system, with gross disparities in funding, facilities and quality of teaching, meant that white children were guaranteed a privileged education while millions of blacks received an inferior one, had little access to it or remained illiterate (Kallaway, 1984; RSA, 23 September 1994). In higher education in particular, where academic and professional education (universities) was separated from vocational training (technikons and colleges), similar patterns prevailed. During that time, institutions were racially based – whites enjoyed far greater chances of gaining admission and dominating places in the advantaged institutions. Consequently, the majority of graduates were white and most blacks with higher education qualifications obtained them from institutions with far fewer resources that were therefore perceived as setting lower standards. Gender imbalances were also evident in the under-representation of female students in the natural sciences and at the postgraduate level, as well as among staff (Bunting, 1994; NCHE, 1996). Severe inequalities in educational provision, attainment and skills perpetuated racial and gender hierarchies in employment, income and socio-economic power (RSA, 15 March 1995; NCHE, 1996).

To overcome the legacy of apartheid, a fresh vision for education was proposed by the new democratic government, building on policy advocated by the majority African National Congress party (ANC, January 1994, May

1994). The Department of Education's White Paper (RSA, 15 March 1995) argued for integration between 'education' and 'training' via the development of the National Qualifications Framework (NQF) as a 'prerequisite for successful human resource development' for 'the reconstruction of ... our society and economy' (RSA, 15 March 1995). By means of the NQF, the division between academic and applied knowledge, theory and practice – associated with the racist structure of economic opportunity in the past – could be bridged. Citizens could then be empowered to continue to learn and adapt to changing knowledge, technologies and occupations and the doors of learning could be opened to people whose academic or career paths had been blocked because their prior knowledge and experience had not been assessed or certified. Bold principles for the reform of education were enunciated. The system should promote:

- lifelong learning;
- open access for all – with an emphasis on redress for previously disadvantaged groups;
- allocate resources on the basis of equity – so there will be the 'same quality of learning opportunities for all citizens';
- strive to improve the quality of teaching and learning;
- operate by means of democratic governance;
- create a culture of accountability;
- increase its efficiency and productivity in terms of the personal learning and marketable skills that it develops (RSA, 15 March 1995).

This policy framework set parameters for an extensive investigation of the higher education sector, initiated by the appointment of the National Commission on Higher Education (NCHE) in February 1995 by President Mandela. Based on the Commission's recommendations and subsequent wider consultations, a final White Paper (RSA, 15 August 1997) delineated the functions of higher education and a vision, set of principles and goals for transforming higher education in South Africa. The role of higher education has been reconceived as a cluster of interrelated purposes, which are to:

- develop the abilities and talents of individuals so that they can benefit from opportunities offered by society;
- address the development needs of society and the labour market by preparing people for careers and professions;
- contribute to the socialization of enlightened and constructively critical citizens;

- add to the creation and sharing of knowledge in its pursuit of intellectual inquiry by means of teaching and research (NCHE, 1996; RSA, 15 August 1997).

Equivalent aims have been envisaged for higher education in Britain in the Dearing Report (NCIHE, 1997). Both conceptions of higher education point to new directions that, according to Scott (1995), characterize emerging mass higher education at our contemporary 'moment of affinity' between academe and societal change. This affinity is an increased interaction with the socio-economic arena and the shift from a closed intellectual system to an open one shaped by a growing partnership between knowledge producers and knowledge users.

The notion of a socially responsible higher education sector also permeates the rest of the 1997 White Paper. With the vision of a 'democratic, non-racial and non-sexist' system in mind, principles for transformation derived from the 1995 White Paper and the NCHE are endorsed:

- equity and redress to bring about 'equal opportunity for individuals and institutions';
- democratization of governance;
- development of conditions that would enable higher education to contribute to building knowledge and human capacity;
- quality achieved by 'evaluating services and products against set standards';
- effectiveness and efficiency in attaining desired objectives;
- academic freedom, protected by the South African constitution;
- institutional autonomy;
- autonomy balanced by accountability in terms of spending public funds and meeting national policy goals (NCHE, 1996; RSA, 15 August 1997).

At the system level, these goals include:

- establishing a single and coordinated system in place of the fragmentation among universities, technikons and colleges;
- providing a range of educational opportunities for an expanding and diverse student population;
- facilitating horizontal and vertical mobility by means of the NQF;
- promoting quality of teaching and learning and curricula responsive to the national context;
- advancing research and its application to technological and social development;

- building capacity to facilitate a more representative body of staff (NCHE, 1996; RSA, 15 August 1997).

## QUALITY ASSURANCE – THE NQF AND 'STANDARDS'

The drive for quality, effectiveness and accountability has entailed moves towards defining standards against which performance can be judged. This, in turn, has given rise to quality assurance bodies with remits that are challenging traditional practices and values in higher education. In the UK, the QAA, formed in 1997, has been charged with the development of a qualifications framework for higher education, subject threshold standards (minimum requirements for a degree pass) and a template for 'programme specification' of main degree subjects and intended exit-level outcomes (QAA, 1998). In South Africa, a national structure – the South African Qualifications Authority (SAQA) – was legislated in 1995 and appointed in May 1996, with the similar task of implementing an NQF and mechanisms for establishing standards and ensuring quality (RSA, 4 October 1995).

Proposals to introduce an NQF emanated in the early 1990s from an ANC-backed review of 'national training' involving representatives from labour, management, government and the education and training sector. It was prompted by dissatisfaction among employers and workers with rigid and outdated forms of training that failed to deliver the skills required to cope with rapid changes in technology and the workplace, and with a disarticulated system that imposed barriers to progression in learning and so excluded vast numbers of youths and adults (ANC, May 1994; SAQA, May/June 1997). A solution was seen in an NQF that would integrate training and education, widen access and facilitate mobility by means of flexible pathways of learning, portable credits, recognition of prior learning RPL and articulation among different components of the system (RSA, 4 October 1995 and 1996). The NQF is also designed to promote 'quality and relevance' in educational provision and 'assure stakeholders of the quality and value of programmes and qualifications' (RSA, 1996). These ends, policy-formulators contend, would be achieved by means of the development of a qualifications structure that reflects 'the achievement of specific learning outcomes, defined at different levels from beginner to postgraduate, in terms of national standards' (RSA, 1996).

The framework itself (ratified by the SAQA in August 1996) comprises eight levels divided into three bands, which are general compulsory education and adult basic education (level 1), further education (levels 2 to 4) and tertiary education (levels 5 to 8). It spans 12 general fields of knowledge (for example, business, commerce and management studies, human and social studies, health sciences and social services) rather than separate, discrete disciplines (SAQA, May/June 1997). Grounded in the principle of 'integration', these fields represent an endeavour to combine different areas of study in relation to key occupational clusters. Although the SAQA admits that knowledge can be organized in other ways, the NQF fields are now recognized by the Ministry of Education as the basis for developing curricula and standards (SAQA, May/June 1997; RSA, 15 April 1998).

It is the SAQA's responsibility to oversee the process of registering and monitoring standards and qualifications according to its guidelines. 'Standards' are defined, quite generally, by the relevant law as 'registered statements of desired education and training outcomes and their associated assessment criteria' (RSA, 4 October 1995). But what has been intended is that 'unit standards', or descriptions of specific outcomes for each of the modules or courses that comprise the building blocks of an entire programme or qualification, both the parts and the whole, will also develop 'generic' (crosscurricular) competences (RSA, 1996). Called 'critical outcomes' – so named because they are viewed by the SAQA as 'critical' to the capacity for lifelong learning – they embrace communication, teamwork, research, problem-solving and self-organization skills, 'technological literacy' and 'macrovision', or systemic thinking (SAQA, May/June 1997; RSA, 15 April 1998). Unit standards are meant to provide a guide for educators, learners and assessors, and to facilitate credit transfer. Apart from stating outcomes and assessment criteria, they should also indicate the unit's field, purpose, context, scope, level (of complexity and of study), credits and accreditation procedures (SAQA, May/June 1997; RSA, 28 March 1998). A 'qualification', the SAQA has determined, is a 'planned combination of learning outcomes' that, among other things, has a 'defined purpose', provides learners with 'applied competence' and enhances their employability and access to additional education. For registration purposes a qualification should specify exit outcomes and how 'integrated assessment' will be used to gauge these, the required credits at different levels, articulation possibilities with related qualifications and moderation options (SAQA, May/June 1997). In short, the NQF allows for standards to be set at both the micro (unit) and macro (qualification) level. Once approved by SAQA-authorized bodies, unit standards and qualifications are to be registered on the NQF and, thereafter, monitored by quality assurers accredited by the SAQA.

## HIGHER EDUCATION AND THE NQF

A prospective NQF and quality assurance system presented a virtual *fait accompli* that the NCHE and higher education sector has been obliged to deal with, sparking uneasy debate between institutions and government. Having affirmed the desirability of a unitary higher education system to redress the fragmented legacy of the past, an important task for the NCHE was to consider the alignment of higher education with the NQF. First, acknowledging that higher learning takes place in a multiplicity of institutions, the NCHE proposed moving from an institutional conception of higher education to a system defined in terms of higher education 'programmes' (NCHE, 1996). It therefore construed higher education as 'all learning programmes which lead to the award of a qualification' more advanced than level 4 on the NQF, and that 'research and scholarship' should be recognized as 'integral components' of higher education (NCHE, 1996). A 'programme' was defined as 'a coherent, planned and integrated sequence of learning activities' leading to a formal qualification (NCHE, 1996). Accepted by the Department of Education (see RSA, 15 August 1997), this seismic conceptual shift to a programme-based approach to higher education is having a major impact on curriculum practice in South Africa.

Second, the NCHE concurred that it was essential that 'programmes' be offered within a single qualifications framework incorporating flexible entry and exit points, in order to enhance mobility and progression (NCHE, 1996). Reservations about the NQF in the higher education community, however, also had to be addressed. Prescriptive standardization, it has been feared, would inhibit the diversity of higher education qualifications. Unit standards (a behaviourist methodology derived from industrial training schemes) would atomize and compartmentalize the learning process, contrary to the aim of integration. Another disincentive was the time, effort and cost that would be involved in registering a battery of thousands of unit standards. Certain higher education outcomes, such as understanding the knowledge-making rules of academic disciplines or the ability to critique, could not easily be measured in discrete units. Coherence and quality could be best ensured, it was believed, by means of the holistic assessment of the outcomes of an entire programme (NCHE, 1996; Kraak, 1994; CHET, 1998).

The NQF's actions have been less threatening to technikons than to universities as they already work with nationally agreed and standardized core curricula,. Transcending that divide, resistance to registering with an external agency such as the SAQA appears to be more marked among traditionally autonomous disciplines than among professional disciplines that are accustomed to being accountable to outside professional bodies and employers (CHET, Part II, 1998). Sensitive to the concerns about the NQF and the varied structures of knowledge in different 'subject fields', the NCHE recommended the option of registering 'whole qualifications' or an approach based on unit standards (NCHE, 1996). The NCHE also suggested (1996) that qualifications could be registered as 'national' programmes (applicable to technikons) or unique 'institutional' programmes (typical of universities), thereby seeking to accommodate the diversity of higher education offerings.

This hybrid model was finally acceded to by government, the 1997 White Paper declaring that all higher education programmes 'national or institutional, should be registered on the NQF, minimally at the exit level of whole qualifications' (RSA, 15 August 1997). Subsequently, the SAQA confirmed that whole programmes initially submitted to it (in 1998) could be registered for a five-year period, so long as they conformed with its specifications regarding 'qualifications' (CHET, 1998;SAQA, August 1998). The compromise over the NQF means that higher education institutions, particularly universities, in South Africa are able to establish threshold standards in the form of registered 'qualifications standards' rather than unit standards, subject to the benchmarks contained in national regulations and in their own institutional criteria for degree programmes.

The issue of standards of qualifications is likely to play an important role in the quality assurance system to be set up under national umbrella authority, the HEQC (RSA, 15 August 1997).

## BENCHMARKING AND PROGRAMME DESIGN – INSTITUTIONAL APPROACHES

The change to a programme-driven system of higher education has given impetus to a massive exercise in curriculum restructuring in South African universities. New curricula and modes of teaching and learning have become necessary in order both to accommodate a more diverse intake and to equip students with the knowledge and capacities that will enable them to succeed in their studies and future lives. Institutional approaches to programme development and benchmarking are illustrated here with reference to two eminent universities – the University of Cape Town (UCT) and the University of Natal (UN), which have been ranked among the top ten higher education institutions in South Africa in terms of undergraduate success rates, graduation rates and publication output (*The Sunday Times* survey, 18 October 1998).

In the midst of the national review of higher education (1996), the UCT adopted the Academic Planning Framework (APF), which initiated an internal, pre-emptive move towards programme-based education. The APF was presented as a proactive strategy to establish an academic basis for rationalization in a context of declining State funding. The idea was that the size, shape and organizational structures of the university should be determined by academic priorities. Central among these would be programmes suited to the changing demands on higher education, the changing student profile and the academic strengths of the UCT's staff (UCT, 13 March 1996). Evolving higher education policy and the UCT's new mission statement (1995) – to be 'an outstanding teaching and research university, educating for life and addressing the challenges facing our society' (UCT, 13 March 1996) – guided the formulation of the APF.

'Strong' programmes were posited by the APF as a means for accomplishing the goals of the university's mission. To qualify as such a programme, each degree would have to satisfy a number of criteria. Among other requirements, it should:

- be composed of a coherent combination of prescribed courses, with enough 'formative' prerequisites and electives to add variety and breadth;
- develop graduates with key skills in literacy, numeracy, computer use, oral and written communication, problem-solving and information-handling, and the potential for lifelong learning and meeting employer expectations;
- be flexible and supportive enough to cater for students from a variety of backgrounds;
- attract excellent teaching and research staff (in keeping with the ideal mentioned in the UCT's mission statement's of 'research-based teaching and learning');
- be compatible with the university's commitment to promoting scholarship and generating new knowledge;
- have recognized exit standards, measured by apposite forms of evaluation;
- be appropriate to the university's geographical location in Africa, and support national goals for development;
- in the case of undergraduate programmes, provide a strong 'taproot' for postgraduate study (UCT, 13 March 1996 and September 1997).

The APF implied a significant change in traditional curriculum practice. Importantly, it instituted a new emphasis on 'learner development', on providing a 'formative' education prior to specialization and promoting a range of 'generic' skills (UCT, 13 March 1996). In part, this was a response to the increasing diversity of students at the UCT, as at other historically 'white' higher education institutions. Between 1984 and 1994, for instance, the proportion of black students (African-speaking and those classified under apartheid as 'Coloured' or 'Indian') rose from 15 to 39 per cent, three-quarters of the African students in 1994 coming from disadvantaged schooling backgrounds (UCT, 1994). By 1997, black students totalled 47 per cent of the enrolment (UCT, April 1998). However, the explicit focus on student development also relates to the goal of fostering competent and employable graduates. It has encouraged new forms of educational intervention. Examples are 'foundation' programmes that combine 'bridging' courses or tutorial schemes (to redress gaps in prior learning) with the usual courses over an extended period of study; core transdisciplinary 'introductory' courses that strive to develop essential academic skills and lay a conceptual base for further study in a suite of programmes; and senior-level 'core' courses, which aim to rationalize, among cognate disciplines, the teaching of theory and research methods (see Warren, 1998).

A new approach to curriculum design was also required by the APF. Highly structured degrees, such as those offered in professional fields such as medicine and engineering, would, on the one hand, have to become more flexible – making room for 'breadth' and alternative routes for different students and more interdisciplinary courses – for better coherence. On the other hand, the mix-and-match, *laissez-faire* type of curriculum common in undergraduate degrees in the pure sciences, arts and humanities would have to become more coherently structured, while retaining a measure of choice to enable students to pursue particular interests (UCT, April 1998).

To facilitate programme planning and approval, a format for proposals was devised. The main elements of the guidelines were:

- contextual information about the academic and strategic rationale of the draft programme, its relationship to postgraduate opportunities and its connection with staff research;
- a 'graduate profile' indicating educational objectives with respect to the knowledge-base, types and level of skills, qualities and values;
- curriculum organization – 'foundation', compulsory and elective courses, and how these would contribute to coherence and flexibility, depth and breadth, skills development and addressing the varied needs of students;
- methods of assessing student performance and evaluating the effectiveness of programmes;
- available or desired resources (teaching, physical, technological) relative to estimated student demand (UCT, May 1996).

In the intensive bout of curriculum restructuring that ensued after the introduction of the APF at the UCT, a high-level committee – the Academic Programmes Working Group – scrutinized draft proposals against the criteria contained in the APF and, later, the Strategic Planning Framework (SPF), liaising with faculty-based programme committees (UCT, September 1997). Some draft programmes retained their traditional focus on a specific discipline or field – for example, architecture, accounting, chemistry, economics, fine art, music, national languages, nursing and psychology. However, there was also a notable shift towards new multidisciplinary programmes, such as cultural and literary studies, development and social transformation, environmental studies, gender and women's studies, historical studies, industrial and labour studies, law and humanities, and philosophy, politics and economics. As the process moves from planning to implementation (from 1999) of approved programmes, new structures will be needed for the evaluation and revision of programmes. It is expected that programme accreditation committees will be established in faculties for internal vetting of quality and compliance with institutional (APF and SPF) benchmarks of graduateness (academic literacy, information and computer literacy, effective numeracy, communication skills, 'Africa situatedness' and so on) for all programmes.

While the UCT was grappling with the shift to 'programmes' from 1996 on, the University of Natal (UN) embarked formally on this process in 1998. By then, the SAQA was already operational and higher education policy more finalized. Consequently, the UN was in a position to adopt an approach to curriculum development that blended the SAQA formulae with its own criteria for internal approval of programmes. The 'template' introduced for this purpose required details about:

- the types of qualifications (certificates, diplomas, degrees) awarded within the programme, and their NQF field, levels and number of credits;
- the purpose of the programme, its entry requirements (assumed learning, recognition of prior learning), its exit outcomes and how these would meet both UN graduateness benchmarks and the SAQA's 'critical outcomes';
- the specific modules that comprise the programme, rules of combination and articulation possibilities;
- educational development provisions to support students from diverse backgrounds;
- integrated assessment (of holistic learning) and quality assurance procedures;
- possibilities offered for further research and staff development provisions to improve the professionalism of teaching staff;
- the financial viability and practical feasibility of the programme (UN, March 1998).

Among its 'requirements for graduates', the UN seeks to prepare students for lifelong learning by equipping them with transferable skills – research, problem-solving, writing and presentation skills, numeracy and information literacy, and enterprise skills – as well as various dispositions, such as appreciation of the values, concerns and history of local communities and the ethics of chosen careers, and sensitivity to moral and environmental issues (UN, 1998). Proposed programmes have to conform with these benchmarks and various other UN criteria (UN, 1998) very similar to those for the 'strong' programmes elected for at the UCT.

The programme development processes at both universities, as their academic planning documents reveal, have much in common. Programmes should have clearly defined purposes that should be linked to research, enhancing lifelong learning, general academic and transferable skills, and contributing to the development of society (UCT, 13 March 1996; UN, March 1998). Teaching and learning aims (latent 'threshold standards' for qualifications) must be made explicit, comply with benchmarks for graduateness and relate to appropriate forms of assessment. Undergraduate curricula should allow for breadth as well as depth. Flexible learning pathways and other provisions should exist for addressing diverse student needs resulting from the widening of access. Procedures for evaluating effectiveness and promoting improvement should be in place. At the same time, programmes should be viable in terms of financial, staffing and technical resources.

As well as similarities, some differences are also apparent in the approaches to programme design at these two institutions. While the UN expects each programme to make provisions for staff development, this key matter is being addressed by the UCT at the wider institutional level. (Annual staff appraisals, for example, are being introduced at the UCT, for individual development reasons as well as salary increments (UCT, March 1997; September 1998); work on the design of courses, curricula or materials and educational publications are being included among the teaching and research activities reviewed for promotion (for example, UCT, 24 April 1997).) The UN's requirements, of course, reflect the influence of the SAQA's regulations. For instance, in the 'outcomes' discourse and the inclusion of 'integrated' assessment, the NQF goal of 'intermediate exit qualifications within multiyear qualifications' (RSA, 15 August 1997) and technicalities such as the NQF's levels and credits. All 'provider' qualifications submitted to the SAQA, however, will probably have to be 'NQFized' (CHET, 1998).

## CONCLUSION – CURRICULUM TRANSFORMATION IN PERSPECTIVE

As the UCT and UN's experiences illustrate, many of the official principles and goals for the reform of higher education in South Africa are being actualized at the institutional level. Universities and technikons have been opening up access. Indeed, enrolments doubled between 1986 and 1996, and growing numbers of black students were admitted, so that total white enrolments at such institutions fell from 67 to 34 per cent in the same period

(*The Sunday Times*, 18 October 1998). Curricula are being redesigned so as to accommodate diverse students and develop competent, versatile graduates with a capacity for ongoing learning who will add to the political, social and economic life of the nation. This is occurring within the new framework of a programme-based higher education system in which unit and/or qualifications 'standards' – including intended learning outcomes tied to benchmarks and congruent forms of assessment – are meant to promote and assure quality in educational provision.

The move towards regulation via the SAQA and the NQF (besides governance and funding mechanisms) has posed a challenge to institutional autonomy. Academic autonomy may be understood as 'the power of an institution to determine its own goals and programmes' and the means by which these are realized. It is an administrative issue distinguished from the constitutional matter of academic 'freedom', by which is meant rights such as freedom of belief and expression in the pursuit or teaching of chosen knowledge (Moja, Muller and Cloete, 1996). Autonomy has, nevertheless, 'always been conditional upon the political context' (Tapper and Salter, 1995). In South Africa, since 1994, the shift towards greater State 'intervention' – meaning regulation as means for redress and development rather than political control (Moja, Muller and Cloete, 1996) – has been partly moderated by an inspired approach of 'cooperative governance', in contrast to the adversarial relations of the apartheid era.

This policy assumes a cooperative relationship between higher education institutions and the State, with stakeholder participation in policy development (by means of the new Advisory Council on Higher Education, for instance) and legally guaranteed autonomy in self-government exercised in tandem with public accountability (NCHE, 1996; RSA, 15 August 1997). The situation is akin to the changing nature of academic autonomy in the UK, 'from the idea of development initiated from below ... to the idea that universities need to make choices within boundaries that discriminate against some decisions while encouraging others' (Tapper and Salter, 1995). Concessions such as permitting higher education programmes to be registered as 'whole qualifications' rather than unit standards, and higher education institutions to decide on their own language policies, subject to the constitution (RSA, 15 August 1997), indicate that cooperative relations and qualified autonomy are, so far, being upheld.

Another test case for institutional autonomy will be the new system of quality assurance to be established under the HEQC. Its main functions will be programme accreditation, institutional auditing and quality promotion. Procedures and criteria are supposed to be formulated in consultation with the higher education community. A developmentally oriented, rather than punitive, approach is preferred, involving a mix self-evaluation and external review (RSA, 15 August 1997). Currently, institutional audits are being conducted by the Quality Promotion Unit, which was founded in January 1995 by the university sector. The main purpose of the audit is to ascertain whether or not adequate mechanisms for assuring quality are in place. Considerable latitude is given to academic autonomy. Institutions themselves select the areas for the audit, and they are evaluated against their own mission statements and goals (Singh, 1998). Given the government's insistence on 'a fit between institutional plans and national policy and goals' (RSA, 15 August 1997), the balance may in future tilt more strongly towards external accountability.

A positive effect of the change to a programme-defined system has been to encourage a more conscious and critical awareness of the purposes of higher education, the value of academic knowledge and skills, the needs of learners and the effectiveness of teaching. Increasingly, curriculum practice is being interrogated in terms of how far it promotes greater equity, social justice and personal empowerment. These are signs that a gradual shift to 'critical praxis' (Grundy, 1987; Sirotnik, 1991) may be taking place.

A key ingredient in transforming curriculum practice is the professional enhancement of academics as educators. Certain possibilities for this presently exist in South Africa. Every university and technikon has a unit dedicated to varying aspects of higher education development; eight out of ten of these operations are involved in staff development (SAAAD, 1997), either directly (for example, in teaching methods units, staff workshops) or indirectly (as part and parcel of collaborative work on assessment, course or programme design). There are also active professional bodies – notably the South African Association for Academic Development and the South African Association for Research and Development in Higher Education – that mount regular national conferences and sponsor independent journals. Most of their members are higher education development practitioners rather than subject specialists. Curriculum restructuring, however, presents an opportunity for the two groups to work jointly in a major developmental area.

Implementing an outcomes-based approach in higher education, though, will be a complicated and contested undertaking. Preliminary local experience suggests that outcomes-based education is more compatible with procedural or professional disciplines such as pharmacy (Lowes, 1998) than with conceptual disciplines such as the social sciences (Jeevanantham, 1998). Clarifying outcomes has proved to be a useful tool in the planning stages of curriculum design, but the tendency in outcomes-based education towards linear and fragmented curricula has been resisted in favour of integrated modules, cumulative skills development and meta-level learning (Luckett, December 1997).

With regard to higher education policy, institutions are required to incorporate staff development in their three-year rolling plans submitted for State subsidy; earmarked funds may also be allocated to staff and educational development projects (RSA, 15 August 1997). Such measures may induce institutions to adopt more systematic approaches to enhancing professionalism, and extend greater recognition and reward for excellence in teaching. Certainly, innovations in staff development (such as teaching portfolios, induction programmes, postgraduate courses on tertiary education) feature prominently in local conference papers and higher education journals. Budgetary reductions, conversely, could constrain initiatives in this direction.

A consistent theme in educational policy in South Africa is overcoming the traditional divide between 'education' and 'training' – 'integration' has been the fundamental rationale for the NQF. Programme development may hinder or hasten the achievement of this goal. The compromise of allowing higher education institutions to register 'provider' qualifications could result in a very diverse collection of programmes that would complicate the task of creating NQF articulation between and among universities and technikons, despite the SAQA's moves to regularize 'qualifications standards'. Yet, judging by the UCT, UN and other cases (such as new degrees in law and pharmacy at Rhodes University – see Thami, December 1997), one trend in programme design is towards explicitly fostering the 'transferable' skills valued by employers. Academic education seems to be reacting to the job market. A related trend, discernible in press publicity, is the growth of multidisciplinary programmes that orient study in higher education towards a variety of career options. Programmes (including postgraduate qualifications) are being offered in journalism and media studies, development studies, translation and interpreting, public health, conflict studies, labour relations and human resources, and public and organizational management, as well as in more technical fields such as agriculture, horticulture, fuel technology and real estate economics (*Daily Mail* and *The Guardian*, 21–27 August 1998). In light of this trend, a system of threshold standards based on 'qualifications', rather than on 'subjects' or specific disciplines, appears to be more appropriate in the South African context. Higher education in South Africa, moreover, is evidently reaching to fulfil its ascribed role of meeting national development needs by achieving the production and application of knowledge and the building of human capacity.

## REFERENCES

ANC (January 1994) 'A Policy Framework for Education and Training', ANC Education Department

ANC (May 1994) 'Implementation Plan for Education and Training', ANC Education Department

Ball, C (1989) 'Introduction', in *Higher Education into the 1990s*, eds C Ball and H Eggins, SRHE and Open University Press, Buckingham

Barnett, R (1992) 'What effects? What outcomes?' in *Learning to Effect*, ed R Barnett, SRHE and Open University Press, Buckingham

Bunting, I (1994) *A Legacy of Inequality: Higher Education in South Africa*, University of Cape Town Press, Cape Town

CHET (1998) 'Higher Education Qualifications in Relation to the National Qualifications Framework', report on a workshop at the University of the Western Cape in July 1998

*Daily Mail* and *The Guardian* (21–27 August 1998) 'Getting Ahead', supplement to the *Daily Mail* and *The Guardian* Graduate Recruitment Fair, in **14** (33)

Grundy, S (1987) *Curriculum as Praxis*, The Falmer Press, London

Kallaway, P (1984) Apartheid and Education: The education of black South Africans, Raven Press, Johannesburg

Jeevanantham, L J (September 1998) 'Writing OBE materials for the social sciences: Complexities and considerations', paper presented at the SAARDHE conference, Bloemfontein

Kraak, R (1994) 'Towards a New Qualification Structure for University Education in South Africa', University of the Western Cape, Academic Planning Unit, Cape Town

Lowes, M M J (September 1998) 'Development of a Problem-based Pharmacy Curriculum Based on Unit Standards', paper presented at the SAARDHE conference, Bloemfontein

Luckett, K (December 1997) 'Implementing Outcomes-based Education in a South African University', paper presented at the SAAAD conference, Broederstroom

Moja, T, Muller, J, and Cloete, N (1996) 'Towards new forms of regulation in Higher Education: The case of South Africa', *Higher Education*, **32**, pp 129–55

National Commission on Higher Education, South Africa (1996) 'Report: A Framework for Transformation', Parow, South Africa, CTP Book Printers

National Committee of Inquiry into Higher Education, UK (1997) 'Summary Report' – see: l

QAAHE (UK) (1998) *Higher Quality* (Consultation Issue), **1** (3)

Republic of South Africa (RSA) (23 September 1994) 'The reconstruction and development of the education and training programme', *Government Gazette* (15974)

RSA (15 March 1995) 'White Paper on education and training', *Government Gazette* (16312)

RSA (4 October 1995) 'South African Qualifications Authority Act', *Government Gazette* (16725)

RSA (1996) 'Lifelong Learning Through a National Qualifications Framework', report of the Ministerial Committee for Development Work on the NQF, Department of Education, Pretoria

RSA (1997) 'Green Paper: Skills Development Strategy for Economic and Employment Growth in South Africa', Department of Labour, Pretoria

RSA (15 August 1997) 'Education White Paper 3: A programme for the transformation of Higher Education', *Government Gazette* (18207)

RSA (28 March 1998) 'Regulations under the South African Qualifications Authority Act 1995 (Act No. 58 of 1995)', *Government Gazette* (18787)

RSA (15 April 1998) 'Green Paper on Further Education and Training', Department of Education, Pretoria

South African Association for Academic Development (SAAAD) (1997) *IHEDSA Directory* (of Academic Development units in South Africa), SAAAD, Johannesburg

South African Qualifications Authority (SAQA) (May/June 1997) *SAQA Bulletin*, **1** (1)

SAQA (August 1998) 'A Draft Framework for Qualifications in the Higher Education and Training Band of the National Qualifications Framework', discussion paper, unpublished draft

Scott, P (1995) *The Meanings of Mass Higher Education*, SRHE and Open University Press, Buckingham

Singh, P (1998) 'Quality Assurance, SAUVCA's QPU and its Quality-related Activities', discussion paper prepared for the Council on Higher Education, South Africa

Sirotnik, K (1991) 'Critical inquiry: A paradigm for praxis', in *Forms of Curriculum Inquiry*, ed E Short, State University of New York Press, Albany, New York

Stephenson, J and Weil, S (eds) (1992) *Quality in Learning: A capability approach in Higher Education*, Kogan Page, London

*The Sunday Times* (18 October 1998) 'Best in Higher Education', survey, *The Sunday Times*

Tapper, E R, and Salter, B G (1995) 'The Changing Idea of University Autonomy', *Studies in Higher Education*, **20** (1) pp 59–71

Thami, T (December 1997) 'Curriculum Development in South African Universities: Is it a contested site or a confluence of voices?' paper presented at the SAAAD conference, Broederstroom, South Africa

UCT (1994) The Transformation of the University of Cape Town 1984–1994, UCT, Cape Town

UCT (13 March 1996) 'Academic Planning Framework', interim report by the Academic Planning Committee, UCT, Cape Town

UCT (May 1997) 'Format for Programme Proposals', issued by the Academic Programmes Working Group, UCT, Cape Town

UCT (September 1997) 'Strategic Planning Framework 1997–2000', Strategic Planning Unit, UCT, Cape Town

UCT (March 1997) 'Implementation of the Staff Development Policy Approved in November 1995', UCT, Cape Town

UCT (24 April 1997) 'Academic Staff Appraisals', Faculty of Social Science and Humanities (in Dean's Circular DC02/97), UCT, Cape Town

UCT (April 1998) 'Vice-chancellor's Report: 1997', UCT, Cape Town

UCT (September 1998) 'Proposals for a Merit System for Academic Salaries', discussion document, UCT, Cape Town

UN (March 1998) 'Programmes Handbook: Guidelines for Programme Design, Specification, Approval and Registration at the University of Natal', UN, Durban and Pietermaritzburg, Natal

Warren, D (1998) 'Educational intervention in higher education: From academic support to academic development', *South African Journal of Higher Education*, **12**

19

# How Can Benchmarking Work to Best Effect in Higher Education?

*Sally Brown*

This book has explored issues and practicalities associated with the practice of benchmarking, drawing on the experiences of business and industry to illuminate how this can and should be done in higher education and ruminating, not always uncritically, on the transferability of what was essentially a management-led process to the academic context. This final chapter is a review of how best benchmarking can be further refined in higher education, and some additional questions are posed that remain unanswered. In doing so, we draw on discussions held at a SEDA conference on benchmarking and threshold standards at which a largely UK audience reviewed the essential issues that need to be tackled if we are to be able to make benchmarking an exercise that genuinely enhances the quality of the student learning experience.

First, it remains to be asked whether or not benchmarking is a genuinely viable exercise. In the UK as well as in the other nations represented in this volume and at the conference, questions remain about the extent to which the process can really be made to work in a meaningful and cost-effective way. It is becoming clear that funding bodies, academic leaders and quality managers (though not always academics themselves) are keen to seek measures of comparability between academic programmes and institutions, while wishing to avoid crude measures, such as league tables, that provide incomplete and often misleading pictures. Strenuous and resource-intensive efforts are being put into developing means by which standards can be assured, but there is no consensus on where the burden of payment for the exercise should lie, nor on what precise form this should take.

Second, the pace at which benchmarking is being implemented in several countries is causing concern. Many fear that haste in implementation will lead to errors in strategy as well as in practice. Lessons from industry suggest that effective benchmarking is a lengthy, iterative process, relying on motivated and committed teams working collaboratively to define thresholds and modal standards, to assess what is actually being done and to improve areas of weak performance, remedy problems and fill gaps where these are identified. Without dragging our feet, we need to ensure that the process of benchmarking itself is quality assured, and doesn't rely on hasty and ill-considered decisions made by unrepresentative panels working under unreasonable time constraints.

Worries also remain about the extent to which we can genuinely compare the outputs of institutions that are differentially financed. This issue is brought into focus most strongly in Chapter 18 by Digby Warren on developments in South Africa, but the matter remains at the heart of much of the debate in the UK and elsewhere. For benchmarking to be acceptable, we need to be certain that there is genuinely a level playing field when comparing standards. Systems where the best-resourced institutions inevitably achieve highest scores against criteria that are claimed to be neutral are totally unacceptable.

The means by which benchmarks are achieved is also contentious. In the UK, the QAA's subject assessment is based on a model of peer review, with subject specialists from broad subject areas reviewing the achievements of others (actually, frequently in an academic marketplace, their competitors) against their own aims and objectives, rather than a set of 'gold standard' criteria, in an attempt to recognize the impossibility of the task to compare subject provision in widely differing institutions against a single standard. Yet the same body is expecting pilot groups from across the sector to establish, at breakneck speed, standards of achievement that can be applicable at institutions across the land.

There are also issues around trying to give benchmarking currency across and between subjects, particularly as many subject areas believe theirs (biomedical science, critical theory, economics, particle physics, business analysis or whatever) to be essentially a more difficult subject than others. There appears to be no agreement on whether or not there is any way that we can realistically compare achievement from subject to subject without reverting to a concentration on generic skills.

A number of the approaches in benchmarking standards in different subjects attempt to divorce subject content from the benchmarking of standards and to concentrate on core intellectual attributes associated with particular subject areas. This begs the question as to whether or not it is possible to have benchmarks that exclude subject content contextualization. Perhaps the best way forward is to focus on generic attributes and outcomes, looking for key or core skills that all graduates could be expected to have identified and developed during a degree programme. There seems to be fairly wide consensus on what at least some of these key skills might comprise – students' ability to communicate orally and in writing, be effective team members, use IT and relevant numeracy skills, manage their own learning and develop intellectual and problem-solving skills. It may be possible, we would argue, to identify thresholds for these kinds of skills at different levels relevant to each programme and use them as a framework alongside which to articulate subject-specific achievements in different disciplines. Not everyone is happy with this approach, however, seeing it as shifting the focus too far from scholarship of the discipline.

Benchmarking also throws up particular problems with regard to complicated and multi-element programmes of study, including cross- and multidisciplinary degrees, as Stuart Billingham suggests in Chapter 13. There is a danger that academics teaching atomized and modular programmes might, against logic, expect the same levels of achievement in each discrete area of study if students are studying on a joint or interdisciplinary course as they would on a single subject honours degree, which is patently unjust. This is probably the area in which most work remains to be done, at least in the context of the UK.

The level at which benchmarks should be fixed also remains to be decided – whether this should be a basic threshold of achievement or more qualitative, indicating a modal standard. Early developments in the area have concentrated on a borderline between what is and what is not work at the level that might be expected of any graduate in a discipline – that is, in the UK, at the margin between a third class degree and a fail. However, this has made many deeply uncomfortable, concentrating as it does on the lowest common denominator, rather than exploring the full range of achievement at graduate level. Excessively high levels of specification of achievement, however, brings to the surface worries about an imposition (by the back door) of a national curriculum for higher education, especially if content is also to be broadly specified, as seems the case in some of the efforts of UK pilot groups. Arguably, the role of learning outcomes and level descriptors is not sufficiently clearly understood in relation to benchmarking and a substantial staff development exercise in this area is likely to be required if the problem is to be remedied.

In addition, the application of benchmarks to postgraduate study remains to be deliberated – if, indeed, there is any consensus that there is any meaningful purpose in trying to do so. We have yet to resolve the issue of whether or not there is genuinely a shared concept of graduateness, let alone one of postgraduateness. At the time of writing, even more so than with undergraduate degrees, we tend to assume that masters degrees and doctorates have some kind of universal currency, yet we recognize tacitly that it is harder to get accepted to do a Ph.D. at some universities than others, for example, and so these doctorates tend to have more kudos and currency in the employment and research marketplace. However, universities are often less rigorous in the definition and application of assessment frameworks for higher degrees than they are at undergraduate level, being less explicit about standards of achievement across the board at this level than is the case with undergraduate programmes, in recognition of the extreme diversity that is inevitably inherent at that level. Can we meaningfully compare the standard of a doctorate in electrochemistry with one in education, other than to discuss issues such as originality, independent study and intellectual rigour? This said, there are still a number of unreconstructed die-hards who would argue to the finish that a Doctorate in a 'hard' science is inevitably more difficult than one in a 'soft' social science subject, or vice versa!

Do we (and should we) also expect different levels of achievement from a fully-funded postgraduate working full time under the tutelage of a well-respected researcher in an established research team and from a mature, self-funded, part-time student with heavy caring responsibilities who receives little support from a half-hearted and overstretched supervisor with only tangential interest in the topic of study? Should input standards be taken into account? (In some subjects, it is almost impossible to be accepted for postgraduate study without a first class honours degree, but in others much lower levels of achievement are acceptable at entry.) Is there (and should there be) a difference in esteem between a taught masters degree and one attained by independent study? And where would new modes of Ph.D.s fit into the picture, such as taught doctorates, those supported at a distance by on-line means and Ph.D.s by publication?

The debate also continues as to whether or not any kind of international benchmarks are feasible. It remains to be found if there are ways in which we can meaningfully articulate standards of achievement across nations when students' experiences are so profoundly different. In a country with as small an academic community as New Zealand, authors in this volume indicate that comparison between two types of institution within the higher education sector in one country is complicated and impossible, so what hope is there that we can genuinely match the standards achieved in universities and colleges across the world? Yet, multinational recruiters have means by which to do so when recruiting graduates and postgraduates to work in business and industry worldwide. Perhaps we should involve them extensively in our attempts to benchmark academic standards internationally.

A final question remains, which brings us back to a point raised much earlier in this volume concerning how far our efforts to benchmark students' achievements are focused on the potential benefits of improvement rather than just measurement. Benchmarking is a source of data that alone has little value unless the results are put to good use. There is no point in merely pandering to the vanity of those who already think they are the best and further demoralizing those who know they are struggling to bump along the bottom, unless the information obtained is used to provide the basis for an agenda for action. The next challenge will be to find ways in which, having gained information about levels of students' achievements, we can build on that foundation within a complicated and diverse sector to enhance learning and ensure that graduates and postgraduates develop the intellectual abilities and relevant skills they need for their future lives, careers and continued learning throughout life.

# INDEX